BEX
Discard

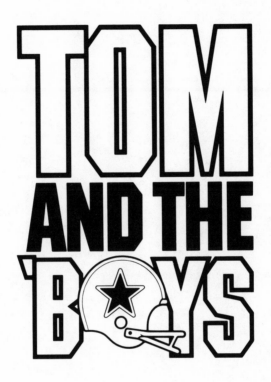

TOM AND THE 'BOYS

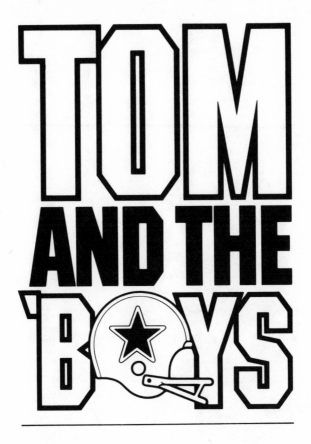

DAVE KLEIN

ZEBRA BOOKS
KENSINGTON PUBLISHING CORP.

ZEBRA BOOKS

are published by

Kensington Publishing Corp.
475 Park Avenue South
New York, NY 10016

First printing: October, 1990

Printed in the United States of America

This is for Steve Perkins, the best beat writer anywhere and the biggest Cowboy fan ever, whose talents were rare enough to make that combination acceptable. Not just next year's champion, he was every year's champion. I miss you, pal.

CONTENTS

ACKNOWLEDGMENTS

First of all, to Tom and the 'Boys, who were more helpful than they had to be and opened their homes and offices to a virtual stranger; to Michael Seidman, for handling so many different problems so well; to the concept of 323, always; and to Dallas, my second-favorite place to be.

Dave Klein
March 10, 1990

INTRODUCTION

Throughout all the interviews you will read in this book, you will find three words that were used by each of the players when asked to describe their feelings for Tom Landry, their coach: admiration; respect; fear.

But did they like Tom Landry when they played for him?

"Well," came the answers, "no, not really. He kept himself distant from the players. It was a very real distance, and most of the time it was cold. Like how? Well, like being afraid to say hello to him in the locker room, because you didn't want him to just walk past you . . . again. Like absolutely dreading Monday morning film sessions, because even if we had won the game he would publicly tear each of us up. Embarrass us. Humiliate us."

But how do you feel about Tom Landry now?

"Now? I love that man. He taught me more than football, much more. He taught me to be a man, to be brave, to stand up to anything and keep my poise. He's like a father figure. I talk to him now, much more than I ever did when I played for him. I would do anything in the world for Tom Landry."

And, finally, the first question in each interview: How did you feel when Tom Landry was fired?

"Man, it felt like somebody had just punched me in the stomach."

"If Jerry Jones was standing in front of me, I don't think I could have restrained myself."

"It was disgraceful. It was cruel. The man deserved a lot better from the Dallas Cowboys."

"How did I feel? Like my best friend had just died."

This, then, is about Tom Landry, who from 1960 through the 1988 National Football League season was the only head coach the Dallas Cowboy franchise ever had. Tom Landry, poker face and constant hat, arms folded across his chest, mind working, scheming, planning, plotting. Yes, even creating. Tom Landry, who came to symbolize the uniqueness of America's Team perhaps more than any of the superstar players he produced. Tom Landry, about whom swirled the magic and the mystique of the silver and blue, who for 29 years was the single constant factor in one of the finest professional football teams ever crafted.

And this, then, is about some of the men who played for him; who struggled, in the beginning; who exulted, much sooner than anyone could have predicted; who went through the peaks and the valleys and who helped to create the myth that sprouted almost full grown and polished, spurs jangling, personalities clashing, skills honed by a man who remained above it all, cool and detached and dispassionate.

And this is about Dallas, too, the early Cowboy years of the 1960s, when the black players were referred to, sneeringly, as "our super-niggers" . . . when a visiting newspaper reporter with two of his closest friends, Hall of Fame Giants Emlen Tunnell and Rosey Brown, was told by a cab driver that the best restaurant in town wasn't all that good if you had to eat alone, since his two companions, being black, would not be allowed entry . . . about a city that came to embrace this team and celebrate its victories and, yes, some of its dramatic, emotional defeats, too, for those games, as much as the winning, helped to mold and construct and shape the glamor and glitz and legend of the Cowboys.

America's Team was, indeed, created by Tom and the 'Boys.

This is about a team that put together 20 consecutive winning seasons, the fourth highest such figure in the history of all professional sports. It is about the finest players produced by the system that was developed and fine tuned by the genius of Tom Landry, and those few men around him who came in at the beginning and stayed through all the tears and all the laughter until they were all fired.

Dismissed. Impossibly, curtly told to leave.

As one of the players put it: "It was just horrible. Jerry Jones (who bought the franchise from H.R. "Bum" Bright on February 25, 1989) took everything we had built, every piece of Cowboy glory, every memory, put it all in one big pile and blew it up, man. There had to be another way to deal with Coach Landry. Why didn't he get the chance to announce his retirement? Why couldn't he have stayed with the team in some other capacity? I mean, to just fly down to Austin on a Saturday night and tell that old man he was fired? It was lousy. And to have him hear about it the day before, in a parking lot, from a newspaper guy? There just had to be another way. There had to be. I will never feel the same way about the Cowboys again. Not ever. I can't."

And many of these men celebrated the fact that in the first year of the Jerry Jones era, with his roommate and teammate from their days at the University of Arkansas, Jimmy Johnson, fresh from a successful career at the University of Miami as the new head coach, the Dallas Cowboys, the once proud and haughty team that almost never lost, won just one of its 16 regular-season games.

"That clown (Jones) was right," said one of the players. "Coach Landry could never have done what Jimmy Johnson did last season."

Never. Not in anyone's wildest dreams.

Perhaps it is a mark of how much the city meant to these players, too, that to assemble all the interviews found in Tom and the 'Boys the author had to leave town just once, to drive 120 miles south-southeast of Dallas to Graham, Texas.

Bob Lilly, arguably the finest defensive lineman of all time, lives there. But quarterback Roger Staubach, wide receivers Bob Hayes and Drew Pearson, middle linebacker Lee Roy Jordan, running back Tony Dorsett and defensive tackle Randy White all stayed in Dallas.

And they were, to a man, cooperative and pleasant and more than just hospitable to the visitor who entered their homes with tape recorders and questions and killed off large portions of a day or an evening.

Guys, it was my pleasure to watch you play, and even more of a pleasure to get to know you.

CHAPTER 1

BOB LILLY

THE ORIGINAL

To get to Graham from Dallas one must first find Texas Interstate 30 West, which will change later to I-20, except nobody thinks to tell you that.

You cruise, rather easily and unhurriedly, through the first leg, Arlington, which is the home of baseball's Rangers. This highway goes directly past their stadium, in fact.

Then you approach the bustling metropolis of Fort Worth, one half—in name, anyway—of the incredibly modern and surprisingly efficient Dallas–Fort Worth International Airport. Fort Worth, the sign says. Next Six Exits.

So far, so good.

Now you can hear the man on the telephone the night before, explaining the rest.

"You go about 20 miles past Fort Worth," Bob Lilly said, "and then get off at the Weatherford exit."

And right about when that happened, the author found himself in Texas.

Weatherford is a perfectly nice little town. It looks as though "The Last Picture Show" might have been filmed here. Or "Hud." Not enough sagebrush and scrub grass for "Red River Valley" or "Fort Apache," though.

Weatherbeaten Weatherford, in some places desperately crying out for demolition, a convenience store umbilically attached to a gasoline station on nearly every corner, begins, in its grays and

1

browns, to give the feeling of Texas. You know, the kind of Texas you used to see unfolding and unfurling in the old western genre films. Right, *that* Texas . . . barns and cattle, horses and boots, beef jerky and Pearl beer, most of the vehicles cleverly disguised as pickup trucks and tractors.

Weatherford (population 12,049, the signpost says) navigated, now the driver learns he is on two highways at once—county Road 180 and state Highway 80. Still, it's a one-lane highway with some hilly ground, but not much, and the hills aren't really all that high, just about as high as hills ever get in this part of the country. But when compared to the rest of the landscape, which is either flat with dirt or flat with grass growing on the dirt, these little hills somehow take on a larger appearance.

"Right about now," Lilly had said, "you should be on the road to Breckenridge. In fact, if you don't see a Breckenridge sign, you're probably lost."

Salvation arrives, in the form of a Breckenridge sign, but not before a road post announces the start (and, quickly, the finish) of a town called Cool, Texas. Population 238.

The next place to look for is Mineral Wells, and sure enough, there it is, right where it's supposed to be. Mineral Wells (population 14,348), somewhat more robust and vibrant than Weatherford, looms. "You should go through Mineral Wells (neither a difficult nor a time-consuming task)," Lilly had instructed, "and then start looking for a sign that says Graham, 36 miles. Oh, and it'll be on your right, and I think the highway turns into 337 right about there."

Son of a gun, there it is. The driver turns right, positioning himself, as advertised, on Route 337 North. That, in turn, changes to county Road 16 North which, wonder of wonders and after about another 40 minutes, turns into Elm Street, right here in Graham-by-God-Texas. Population 9,170.

One of the citizens proud to be in that number is Bob Lilly, the best all-around defensive lineman ever to play the game of football.

You can offer Deacon Jones and Doug Atkins (pass-rushing specialists), Alan Page and Merlin Olsen (close, but not quite),

Gino Marchetti and Andy Robustelli (different times, earlier times) and all of today's sorry candidates, notably Reggie White, and this voter will still go to the ballot box for Bob Lilly.

"When you get to Graham," Lilly had concluded his instructions the previous evening, "stop at the convenience store and call. You'll never find the house on your own."

OK, fair enough. But how could he have neglected to mention that prior to reaching Graham, about 25 miles south-southwest, one would see, on an otherwise innocent-looking road sign, what has to be the most intriguing name of any town in all of Texas.

An arrow pointing away from Graham (unfortunately) displayed the direction to Possom Kingdom Lake, which is not a lake at all but a place where people live.

(Where are you from, son? Oh, right, Possom Kingdom Lake. If yuppies discover it and move in, certainly the nation will get to know it as PKL.)

"Where are you?" inquires Ann Lilly, whose voice is a breath of reassurance for the insecure traveler, definitely a stranger in a strange land. "Oh, the Texaco convenience store? The one by the 'Welcome to Graham' bank sign, you mean? Right. Keep going straight, past the square in the center of town, watch for the cemetery (no, it wasn't called Boot Hill), and then make a left on Route 67. The second left after that, that's Fawn Trail. It goes up at a 45-degree angle. You can't miss the house. It's the one that looks back down the hill on town. We'll be waiting."

Ann Lilly was waiting when the rented New Yorker carrying the visiting New Jerseyan finally climbed Fawn Trail and the driver, clutching two tape recorders, a sheaf of notes, and a quiver of pens, approached the front door of a modest but solid ranch-style home.

"Welcome to Graham," Mrs. Lilly said. "Nice to meet you. (Firm handshake here.) Come on in, sit down. Would you like a drink? Something to eat? I'm makin' brownies. (Indeed; the tell-tale aroma was exquisite.) Bob called, he's on the way from town, he's running a few minutes late. Somebody must've recognized him and asked for an autograph, and he just loves to stop and talk, you know. Here (she proffered a photo album), pictures of his induction (into the Pro Football Hall of Fame, in 1980), and here he is with Coach Landry (the man he chose to be his presenter). I'll be right back. Should I turn off the stereo (classical music)? It might interfere with the tape recorder, right?''

You might be interested in knowing that all of this came out in one breath, a most impressive frenzy of friendliness. Ann Lilly went back to her brownies, and while the visitor was thumbing through the pictures of that Hall of Fame day (August 2, 1980) the doorway suddenly filled up with her husband.

Himself. The man who, when he played college football at Texas Christian University, was nicknamed "The Purple Cloud," purple, of course, being the uniform color the Horned Frogs wear. Besides, what other color of choice would be appropriate for people known as Horned Frogs, anyway?

"Hi," said Bob Lilly, his hand engulfing the visitor's. "Did you meet Ann? Do you need anything? Are you comfortable over there (in an oversized living room chair that would have been comfortable for Andre the Giant)? Yes? Okay, then let's get started. I know you made a long drive, and you didn't come all the way out here just to chat."

My first impulse was to ask him if he knows that he looks exactly like a younger (he's 51) and considerably larger Charlton Heston, but that would not have been professional. So he sat down, seeming to unhinge his 6-foot-5-inch body in sections, asked Ann for a glass of water, and noticed the visitor staring.

"Yep, I've lost a lot of weight," he said, eyes smiling, sandy-colored hair being visited these days with just a touch of gray falling down his forehead. "I played at 270, 275. But that wouldn't be smart now. I'm down to 235." Most former professional athletes, especially football players who have wisely chosen to lose weight later in life, seem to diminish, visually, to the point where a first-time visitor finds it hard to believe the size and the power that were once obviously present. But not in the case of Bob Lilly. This man would look big—rawboned, as they say in Texas—had his weight dropped even more. And lurking there just under the skin, somewhere behind the eyes, I think, certainly behind the smile and the friendliness, is that strain of toughness and determination that made him the great athlete he was. In all, a most impressive man.

It might be noted, merely as another small piece of information, that Graham-by-God-Texas is a dry town, and just before the interview got going, Bob Lilly asked Ann to call Jack and remind him to bring something back from Breckenridge. To the visitor's curious expression, he smiled and explained. "Graham is dry. Breckenridge isn't. Jack is one of our neighbors, and he works over in Breckenridge, about 30 miles away. When we need beer, Jack makes a beer run on his way home."

Now, to work.

The firing of Tom Landry?

"Well, of course, I don't know all the details, everything that went on behind the scenes," Lilly began, "but it sounded almost cruel, what happened to Coach Landry, being there as long as he was, being as successful as he was, being the kind of person he was. To find out he was fired through a newspaper or radio, whichever it was . . . through the media, anyway, it just seems like it could have been done a lot better. It seems to me he should have been made aware that there were serious negotiations going on and that if they did transpire he might be replaced.

"It certainly didn't sit well with me, and I'm sure it didn't sit well with any of my old buddies, either, although that's the way it happens when a player gets cut. But it shouldn't have been done that way to Coach Landry. It should have been handled diplomatically, more kindly."

And now the first reference to Jerry Jones, the Arkansas Traveler who bought the team. Not an angry, vengeful reference, but one with the clear and obvious information that he doesn't plan to exchange holiday cards or dinner invitations with the new owner, either.

"Listen, anybody who wants to spend that much money on the Cowboys certainly has the right to decide who he wants to (be his) coach, and for that reason I don't really fault Jerry Jones. I think he probably got a lot of the blame he really didn't deserve, because I read recently (Dallas Times Herald, March 4, 1990, columnist Frank Luksa) that he insisted that Coach Landry be notified before he held a press conference (to introduce the new coach, Jimmy Johnson).

"But it had already leaked out. In my opinion, now, it should have been handled differently from Bum Bright's standpoint, through Tex Schramm."

Bright, the man from whom Jones made the buy, had been embroiled in heavy negotiations for at least 30 days. At any time during those talks he could have contacted Landry privately, if only to inform him that the deal, should it go down, might include a new coach coming in as part of it.

Schramm, the team's president and general manager since the founding of the franchise in 1960, a man who had managed to survive previous sales, financial catastrophes and ugly personality clashes, put Jones and Bright together. Even so, at one point he was asked to remove himself from the negotiations. He would never return. To a man of such intuitiveness, that should have been warning enough to signal his imminent departure, and he, too, might have passed on a feeling of a similar fate to his longtime friend, Landry.

"Bright," wrote Luksa in the Times Herald, "claims Jones is unfairly blamed for the clumsy manner in which Landry was fired. Bright said had he realized Jones would be skewered, he'd have canned Landry, and wanted to as far back as 1987 but Schramm resisted. This much is true. Bright detested Landry. His reasons are obscure since by Bright's count, he spoke to Landry no more than two or three times . . .

"Bright recently reviewed events preceding the Saturday Night Massacre. Everyone comes off compassionate and concerned in his version. Great story—if half of it had been half-right. Bright places Schramm in his office on Friday morning (thirty-six hours before the firing) and has him calling Landry at Valley Ranch (the Cowboys' complex in suburban Irving) to tell the coach he's out. Never happened.

"Bright said Schramm told Landry to stay put because he, Bright and Jones were en route later with details. Never happened, but to continue Bright's fantasy: When they arrived, Landry, against orders, had disappeared.

"Therefore, Bright insists, 'Jerry was not rude to Tom. Particularly when given the fact that Tom was personally told the day before he was not (going to be) included in the new group.'

"A whopper, that. Landry wasn't told anything official on Friday. Schramm warned him of an ominous shift in the wind, based on a telephone conversation with Bright. Not even Schramm knew the deal was done on Friday. Bright had cut him out of huddles with Jones. Nor was Schramm summoned to Bright's office until Saturday morning, the 25th (of February).

"If what Bright claims is true, and it isn't, Landry knew he was fired on Friday. Think a bit. If Landry knew, there was no reason for Jones to fly to Austin on Saturday afternoon with Schramm and repeat the message in person. Yet they did because, obviously, Landry hadn't been told by powers now in control."

Lilly nodded his head. He had seen the Sunday column.

"I'm sure it was obvious to Bright that he was going to sell the team to Jones," Lilly said. "He's the one who should have handled it. All I know is I don't particularly blame Jerry Jones. He didn't know anybody coming in. I always thought Bum Bright should have been the one to do it, and he didn't. And so I guess it's his fault. You know, it was just unsavory, is all. That man should have had better treatment. I love that man. He was my idea of a coach, a leader, a father figure. We went through a lot together, Coach Landry and the guys, all the guys, on the early teams, because we started out weak and had to take all the hard knocks and losses before we finally started winning.

"Every once in a while, you know, Tom would let the frustration show, but not often. He always figured he had to be a role model, be strong and calm, for the players. I don't think there's anything I wouldn't do for that man. Maybe it was the frustration of all those early years that made us tough, but maybe it was just being with Coach Landry."

The early years of the Dallas Cowboys were marked by the acquisition of several key components, players who would meld and merge and become the guts of the burgeoning dynasty. It was this endeavor, in retrospect, that provided the first hint of the special, unique atmosphere that would come to pervade the front office, and yes, it was probably fair, at some point, to define it as arrogance. But even so, it was an arrogance born of success and confidence.

Between Schramm, Landry and a one-time baby photographer from Milwaukee turned personnel director and chief scout named Gil Brandt, the Cowboys found players where no other team had looked, took chances that the others wouldn't take, the others being hidebound, trapped in traditional do-this, don't-do-this dictums. "When you don't have anything," Brandt once said, "you'll take whatever you can find. We just got lucky enough to turn up some players who were diamonds in the rough." Much of the credit for the free agents and low-round draft choices and college basketball players must go to Brandt, who probably could have earned big money in France finding truffles.

Lilly points to those early years, to finding and signing those players and then infusing them with Landry's coaching and innovative theories such as the flex defense, as the spadework for the creation of the dynasty.

"We were putting together a lot of free agents and people who weren't supposed to be big enough like (middle linebacker) Lee Roy Jordan and people who weren't supposed to be able to hold the ball like (cornerback) Mel Renfro and basketball players like (cornerback) Cornell Green and track guys like (wide receiver) Bob Hayes and (safety) Mike Gaechter . . . and guys like (defensive end) George Andrie, whose college (Marquette, in Milwaukee) didn't play football in his senior year. Getting (offensive tackle) Ralph Neely through a series of breaks was very important. See, he had signed with Houston, which was then in the other league (the rival American Football League), but he really wanted to play for us and so he signed with Dallas, too. That went to court, and he was awarded to the Cowboys, but after the two leagues merged (1966), I think we gave the Oilers something in the draft the next year to make the deal official. Ralph became a very integral part of our team."

It should be noted that seldom had Dallas ever paid as much for a player, because that "something" the Cowboys gave the Oilers was their first-round, second-round and two fifth-round draft choices, all for the 1967 draft.

Lilly continues, shaking his head.

"Then we found Jethro Pugh (11th round, 1965, Elizabeth City State in North Carolina) and Rayfield Wright, who became a great offensive tackle but was a tight end at Fort Valley State College (seventh round, 1967). And you know, watching all this come about, I think it started to happen in 1962 when we had a lot of those players, and some older ones that other teams didn't want any more, and we all just started to think of ourselves as Dallas Cowboys, us against the world, and as if we had never played for any other team or any other coach. It was like a mission, a crusade, to get better and win something important for that old man."

One of the "born again" athletes was a linebacker from West Virginia named Chuck Howley, who had been drafted by the Chicago Bears in 1959, who had injured a knee and missed the entire 1960 season and was then traded—cheaply—to the Cowboys for 1961. Cheaply, because the price was a second- and ninth-round draft choice in 1963, and all Howley did was play for 13 seasons, appear in six Pro Bowls and earn the Most Valuable Player in Super Bowl V (a game the Cowboys lost).

Bob Lilly, of course, was the team's first draft choice in 1961, but in truth the early drafts weren't overly productive for the Cowboys. They found their gems on the free-agent market in those years, and by way of example only Lilly survived to start from the 1961 draft . . . only Andrie (sixth round) contributed from the 1962 draft . . . only Jordan "graduated" from the 1963 draft.

In 1964, however, Dallas came up with Renfro, Hayes and a quarterback who would not be available for another five years, something about a commitment to the United States Navy . . . some crew-cut kid named Staubach. Roger Staubach, that year's Heisman Trophy winner.

"Watching this all start to happen, watching how Coach Landry worked with us, I just got the feeling that something was going to happen," Lilly continued. "The first thing, the most important thing that he ever taught the defensive players was confidence. His flex defense was brand new, something he had designed from 16 years in the league as a player and assistant coach. He explained patiently, carefully . . . sometimes it seemed endlessly . . . that all his research showed that there were only a few basic plays that can be run, just a few plays, really, but you could disguise them before the ball is snapped. And each time a play is run, this has got to happen each time. You have keys, you see, that can be applied, various keys for various people (on offense), and that kind of makes the middle linebacker the rover, the guy who has to decide whether it's going to be a run or a pass, which direction, who's going to get the ball. Against Cleveland, for instance, Lee Roy Jordan would follow Jimmy Brown, and after a while we'd get to know when Brown was going to get the ball, which way he was leaning would tell us which direction he was going to run in, and being set in our flex formation helped us defeat blocks at the line of scrimmage."

Landry, in fact, went against one of the most basic of coaching tenets. He devised a system—in this case the flex defense—and insisted on using it even when he knew the people he had to play it weren't qualified. Those early Cowboy teams, then, had to pay the price for those who were still collegians, who would come to the team one day, absorb the concept of the flex and begin to make it work the way Landry always knew it would.

Ernie Stautner, a Hall of Fame defensive tackle with the Pittsburgh Steelers, joined the Cowboys as defensive line coach in 1966, and stayed until the Saturday Night Massacre in February of 1989. He emerged as perhaps the finest defensive line coach in the history of the game, developing those such as Lilly, Andrie, Pugh, Randy White, Ed "Too Tall" Jones, Harvey Martin, Larry Cole, John Dutton and Willie Townes.

"I had heard about the flex when I was still playing," Stautner recalled. "I played against the Cowboys a few times and saw it up close. But when I got to Dallas as a coach and Tom handed me the playbook, it was like a revelation. It was all there, the stuff I had spent years and years doing as a player, but not understanding it. The keys, the blocking schemes, the way to beat the offensive linemen. It was all there. I mean, it was a damned work of art, you know? But it was a tough bitch for the players to learn, because there's always something to see before you make a commitment, something you have to wait for before you can move and pursue. It kind of goes against a player's natural instinct, which tells him to chase the ball or the man carrying it. But once they learn, once they see it work, they're hooked."

But the defense needed time. It needed work and repetition and, most of all, it needed not only the same players coming back season after season but good ones, highly qualified athletes who fit the stringent parameters devised by Landry.

"In the beginning, we had a lot of trouble stopping the good teams," Lilly smiled, a bit ruefully. "We had a hard time with Cleveland and Jimmy Brown, Green Bay and Paul Hornung. The New York Giants always gave us trouble, and because Coach Landry had played and coached there, he always tried a little harder, walked around all week just a little more intense . . . and we paid a little more of a price if we lost to them. It was a slow, slow process, but eventually we learned what he wanted, and he got together the kind of players he needed. Suddenly, we had our defense and the people to play it."

In retrospect, it didn't take long. From a record of 0-11-1 in the charter season of 1960—the tie coming in Yankee Stadium, 31-31 against the Giants—the Cowboys quickly approached what for them, given their situation and experience, would be a notable achievement—a .500 record. They were 4-9-1 in 1961, followed by consecutive seasons of 5-8-1, 4-10, 5-8-1 and, finally, 7-7 in 1965.

It was 1966 when the Cowboys took off, an incendiary rocket from the Lone Star State. The first four games of that season told all that needed to be told—Dallas beat the Giants, Vikings, Falcons and Eagles by the combined score of 183-45. When it was all over, when the Cowboys had come in with a 10-3-1 record, the only teams to have beaten them were Cleveland, Philadelphia and Washington—by a total of 13 points.

This was a good year to become a great team, because the war between the NFL and the AFL had ended. Peace was at hand, and with it a so-called AFL-NFL World Championship game, pitting the winners against each other (the two leagues would continue to play separate schedules until 1970) as the highlight of the season, and every team wanted to be the first to thrash the up-starts.

You are probably more familiar with this annual game today as the Super Bowl.

So here were the Cowboys, the new kids on the block, if you will, and they emerged as the highest-scoring team in the league, three times surpassing 50 points in a game. At the same time, they showed off their finely tuned defense—yes, the flex—which held its opponents to a total of 239 points in 14 games, and in five of those games restricted the opposition to a single touchdown.

On the other side were the grizzled old veterans, the mighty Green Bay Packers, making their final run at glory under Vince Lombardi—an assistant coaching colleague of Landry's when both served under Jim Lee Howell on the Giants' staff. Lombardi was the offensive coordinator, Landry the defensive coordinator, and it is safe to say that no team had ever been in better hands from both sides of the line of scrimmage.

This was the Packer team of Paul Hornung and Jim Taylor, Jerry Kramer and Forrest Gregg, Willie Davis and Bart Starr, Ray Nitschke and Herb Adderley and Willie Wood and on and on and on, a veritable Who's Who of those enshrined in the Pro Football Hall of Fame.

They had won the Western Conference, these old Packers, and now they were coming down to the Cotton Bowl to see which team—the old or the new, the basic or the flashy—would repre-sent the establishment, the NFL, in the first of what would become the single most dramatic game of the football season, the yet-to-be-christened Super Bowl.

"Our offense did real well that day," Lilly said, somberly. "But we . . . the defense . . . damn, we just didn't play very good. And they won. It was close and we could have had it, but they won and we didn't and looking back, I guess they deserved it. That year . . . in that game . . . they were better than we were. Not by much, but better."

The game, played on New Year's Day of 1967, was one of the most exciting and dramatic of the decade. With less than a minute left and Green Bay holding a 34-27 lead, the Cowboys came roaring downfield and just missed.

"I mean, just missed," Lilly sighed. "We got to their 1-yard line, and then we had an offsides flag (the guilty offensive tackle was Jim Boeke) so we're back on their 6 and when Don (Meredith) went back to pass, the linebacker (Dave Robinson) broke through and was all over him as he threw the ball. There was some confusion. We always had a tight end come in on that play to block the linebacker, but both tight ends (Frank Clarke, Pettis Norman) were in, so it was left to Hayes to block Robinson, and he just wasn't big enough or strong enough. The pass went into the end zone . . . I can still see it wobble because of Robinson's hit . . . and instead of our guy (Hayes) catching it, it sailed high and the safety (Tom Brown) intercepted. That was it. Over. We came within one play of maybe going to the first Super Bowl."

And a year later, in the wake of a 9-5 season that still produced the Eastern Division championship in the National Conference, the Cowboys defeated Cleveland in the first year of division playoffs, 52-14, and found themselves in the NFL championship game for the second straight year.

It was against the Packers again, too, only this time it was up there, in the little ice cube of a town then populated by only about 60,000 hearty (or masochistic) souls.

"I mean, you will never be able to understand how cold it really was unless you were there," Lilly said. "Remember, we played in Texas. Most of us were used to Texas weather. And while it sometimes gets a little chilly, you know, maybe even every two or three years it gets to snow, we don't usually have to put up with that kind of horror."

It was December 31, 1966, and the game long since became immortalized as the Ice Bowl.

"You know, it wasn't that cold when we got there, not like that," Lilly remembered. "But early in the morning of the game, the temperature dropped to minus 16 degrees, and the wind chill factor was minus 48. Andrie was my roommate, and when we got up and saw what it looked like outside, all ice and snow and sliding cars, he walked calmly into the bathroom, got a glass of water, came back to the window and threw the water onto it. It turned to ice before it ran down to the bottom."

He paused, and a deep pain seemed to touch his face, momentarily.

"You know, that day I thought we had the better team, but nobody could play their game in that kind of weather. Our game was speed, getting the ball deep to our receivers, running everything wide and fast, and there was just no traction. And the cold sapped your strength. Sure, I know, it was just as cold for both teams. Coach Landry tried to tell us that. But the Packers were more accustomed to cold. We just couldn't believe how bad it was, how absolutely painful."

And yet it wasn't until the final 26 seconds, on Green Bay's field and in Green Bay weather, that it became Green Bay's game. It happened on a 1-yard dive by quarterback Bart Starr, who slipped in behind guard Jerry Kramer to barely make the end zone and create a 21-17 Packer lead.

"And I still hear people say that Kramer was offsides on the play," Lilly smiles. "Do I think he was? Well, let's say he anticipated by about this much (and he held his enormous hands up, palm facing palm, about a foot apart). Hey, they beat us, and it was fair and square, but those two games . . . you know, with the first two Super Bowls under our belts who knows how much more we could have accomplished. Those games really took an emotional drain on us, snuffed out what had been great seasons. It was just so damned frustrating to have come so close two years in a row."

Landry, in a rare emotional outburst the following summer, prior to the start of the 1968 season, rededicated himself to winning the league championship. "I am tired of sucking hind tit to the Green Bay Packers," he said, somewhat out of character.

There was still sorrow ahead for the Cowboys, even though 1968 turned into a 12-2 season, and even though 1969 was an almost as sparkling 11-2-1.

This time the sorrow had another name. Not Green Bay, but Cleveland.

"We couldn't even get out of our own conference," Lilly

snorted. "We'd win our division, then play the Browns for the conference championship and those two years in a row we just got our butts kicked. I mean, we weren't even close, not offensively, not defensively, and it was so damned frustrating that after the first one Meredith, who had been ripped mercilessly for years in the Dallas media, just up and retired. He announced his retirement in the locker room in Cleveland, just said, 'I quit, that's it,' and that was it. We had a chance in that game, but he threw a couple of interceptions and the Browns scored with them and, well, it was over. I don't think Don's Cowboy career (1960–1968) was exactly pleasant for him. Maybe it would have been better if he and Tom just weren't so all-fired different."

With Craig Morton at quarterback, the Cowboys won the Eastern Division again—and once again lost the conference championship game to Cleveland. It was a blowout, a 38-14 whipping, and, strangely, Lilly thinks that was finally the one that led to the long-awaited breakthrough.

"I mean, we had just got so damned tired of losing those games in the playoffs, of being the bridesmaids year after year, that it seemed different when we showed up for training camp the next summer. The guys who would normally fool around and such came in serious. Deadly serious. And there was a different kind of intensity, plain enough for everybody to feel it. I don't know, maybe we tried too hard, maybe we were pressing, because as strongly as I felt about that season, and as hard as the guys were working to make it right, we just couldn't seem to get untracked the first part of the schedule."

Dallas won three of its first five games, made it five of the first seven, which was exactly the halfway point of the 14-game season, and then crashed.

"We lost to the Giants the next week," Lilly remembered, "and in those years that was something we almost never did." (In fact, that 23-20 loss came during a 9-of-10 Dallas victory run against the Giants dating back to 1964.) "And the following week I thought we had gone right through the bottom of the world and dropped into hell."

It was a nationally televised Monday night game in the Cotton

Bowl (the last season the Cowboys would use that ancient edifice). They were playing St. Louis, and the Cardinals had already scored a 20-7 victory in the third game of the season.

"It was just flat-out embarrassing," Lilly said. "We couldn't do anything right. Nothing. We were awful, played like a bunch of high school kids, and I think it probably could have been worse except the Cardinals were so busy laughing they couldn't concentrate."

The score was 38-0. "Just an old-fashioned ass-kicking," he said. "No excuses, no explanations. We just didn't play. Coach Landry was sure a barrel of laughs the next morning, you know?"

But something had clicked, something had shifted. Perhaps the humiliation triggered a deeper pride, because the Cowboys wouldn't lose again from that November 16 game until the day they showed up in Super Bowl V in Miami.

"Yeah, I guess that was the best streak of football we played in my career," Lilly said. "We had it all going, the offense and the defense, the special teams, the emotion. It all came together. We just somehow knew we were going to win the games from then on, even when they were close and the other team was outstanding. We just felt it. I remember we had a couple of real blowouts (45-21 and 34-0 against Washington, for instance) and a few real tight ones, too (6-2 over the hated Browns in Cleveland), but it didn't matter. We knew we were going to win. It was a special kind of feeling. I don't think it happened before or since, and I know I can't explain it."

The final game of the regular season was a 52-10 embarrassment of cross-state rival Houston, one of the AFL teams being met for the first time, but the Cowboys needed just a small favor from Landry's old team, the Giants. "They had to lose," Lilly explained. "We had spent so much time fooling around earlier that we were tied with the Giants at 9-4 and if they won they would have gone to the playoffs. So we had to win, they had to lose."

The Giants cooperated. They scored first in a game at Yankee Stadium against the Los Angeles Rams (coached by George Allen, who would move to the Redskins and touch off the superheated

Dallas-Washington rivalry that burned its way across a decade), held a 3-0 lead, and then lost the game, 30-3.

The Cowboys were in the playoffs.

"Nothing was going to stop us this time," Lilly said. "We had played the best we had ever played, and we knew it. We were probably at the top of our game right there."

The first playoff opponent was Detroit, and the Lions didn't get a thing. "I remember we got a safety and the offense managed a field goal and that's all we needed," Lilly smiled. He was right. The score was 5-0.

Next came the NFC championship game in San Francisco, a last hurrah for the great old 49er quarterback, John Brodie. And even though Morton failed to complete a single pass that day, it was the defense and a strong running game by rookie Duane Thomas that put the Cowboys in their first Super Bowl by virtue of a 17-10 victory.

The Cowboys lost that Super Bowl, 16-13 to Baltimore, once an NFL team that had been the victim of the greatest upset in pro football two years earlier when they lost Super Bowl III to the New York Jets. "I know we were the better team," Lilly said. "There were a few bad breaks, a few calls, and suddenly we lost."

The key, probably, was a fumble by Thomas, the moody rookie halfback, early in the third quarter—on the Colts' 1-yard line. The ball was slapped out of his hands by Baltimore linebacker Mike Curtis, and a huge pile quickly assembled as players from both teams tried to find the elusive pigskin. Suddenly, referee Jack Fette, still trying to disassemble the mound of massed bodies, heard Baltimore defensive tackle Billy Ray Smith chirping: "We got it, we got it! Our ball, our ball!"

Billy Ray began pointing upfield, jumping up and down with gleeful abandon, and Fette took the path of least resistance.

"Colts' ball," he decided, taking away what would have probably been a Dallas touchdown—one to add to a lead of 13-6—or certainly a field goal at worst.

Who had the ball?

"Our center, Dave Manders," said Lilly, shaking his head. "The damned thing had bounced right into his hands and he just fell

down and cradled it. We had the ball. When the pile was un-
packed, Manders calmly handed the ball to Fette. The films
showed him recovering. The Colts were laughing, knowing what
Billy Ray had managed to do. But the decision stood. We lost the
ball on the 1-yard line after our own guy had recovered it."

And on the final play of the game, with six seconds remaining,
Jim O'Brien kicked a field goal to give Baltimore a 16-13 victory.

As the teams walked off the field, a Dallas helmet flew into the
air, traveled 40 yards and came to rest, ironically, almost exactly
on the 50-yard line. Photographs of it, sitting there, seemed to
symbolize the frustration of this franchise.

"It was my helmet," said Bob Lilly. "I just couldn't stand it
anymore. We gave it away in the fourth quarter, with two interceptions that should never have happened, and even after all that
other stuff, we still had the lead. It was just so damned frustrating."

Perhaps it was that mute testimony to five years of "infernal
frustration," as Lilly put it, but the following season was as right
and as sweet as the years before had been bitter. The Cowboys
played to an 11-3 record in 1971, winning the final seven games
of the regulation schedule, crushing first Minnesota and then San
Francisco in the playoffs and moving into Super Bowl VI un-
checked and unstoppable.

"We beat Miami big, by three touchdowns (24-3), and it seemed
like the Cowboys finally made it over that last hill. We were champions. Not next year's champions, not someday soon, but right
now. We had come out of the pack. Anyway, we had done it. I
had the Super Bowl ring, we had been proven right, that hard
work and sticking to a system nobody else agrees with can win
for you if you want it bad enough.

"I guess it was one of those hard lessons we learned from Coach
Landry. And it sure took a long time, but we learned it. And we
did what we set out to do. You know, I always thought we were
more grateful, and our victory was more satisfying, because of the
ordeal and the hardships we went through."

Lilly played three more seasons, all of them winning years but
none of them providing a return to the Super Bowl.

"That was all right," he says. "I had my Super Bowl, my satisfaction. And I was proud to watch, that first year I was retired, how easily Coach Landry and the other people in charge rebuilt the team almost immediately. You know, in 1975 they brought in a bunch of young boys, 12 of 'em, some of 'em Randy White and Bob Bruenig and Thomas Henderson, great defensive players, and we still had a lot of the old guys on there, like Lee Roy and Jethro and Mel and Rayfield, and that sort of helped the kids play better, maybe mature faster. I was really proud when we became the first wild card team to get to the Super Bowl, and getting so far with so many rookies made it almost OK when we lost that Super Bowl (21-17 to Pittsburgh). I knew the Cowboys were on the way again, it was like passing the torch to the next generation."

Could Lilly have played again? Did he retire too early? "Nope, I played 14 years, and maybe I could have held out for one more, but my neck was really painful. It hurt every day, I didn't hardly sleep that year, and I went through some of the worst pain I've ever known. I couldn't even play racquetball, which I did all during my career. I still can't, because when I hit the wall it goes into spasms. I just walk, exercise some, and I wish I could be more active. But that's probably the injury that gets the most older players to retire, the neck. I remember Cliff Harris (a Pro Bowl safety who played from 1970 through 1979 and was one of the Cowboys' most famous free agents, out of Ouachita [Ark.] Baptist) told me one time he had to think about retiring because he just couldn't hit any more, the neck hurt too much. Hey, somebody who makes his living tackling people can't play if he can't tackle."

The significance of the Cowboys' nearly three-decade run at excellence, Lilly feels, was their consistency. "Coach Landry never let us get too relaxed, too pleased with ourselves," he explained. "We didn't win the championship every year, and we certainly didn't go to the Super Bowl every year, but we won enough, consistently, made the playoffs every year for what, 18 straight? We just kind of knew we would do that, and it got people not only in the state of Texas but all over the country intrigued with us, with what we had been able to do for all those years.

"The Cowboys, basically, were synonymous with winning, and while we didn't win 'The Big One' (the Super Bowl) but twice in all those years, it seemed like we did a lot better than that because we were always in the playoffs. And we were in the Super Bowl five times (between years V and XIII). I think that's the reason we were highly favored in the state, why people all around became such great fans.

"Another thing. Coach Landry would keep the older players around . . . always just enough of them . . . to kind of stabilize the younger players, set a good example. We had a very good work ethic and a lot of good leadership. See, not hardly any of us were yes-men, and we had a lot of respect for Coach Landry and the other coaches, but I don't feel it's the same on the blackboard as on the field. Things happen a lot faster, you can't think about what you're going to do every minute, every play.

"So we changed stuff on the field. Now, he knew, of course. He gave us the playbook and the game plan and he knew that if we performed at the very utmost of our ability and concentration we'd win. If we did it all his way, we'd probably have been in the Super Bowl every year. But see, it's hard to concentrate that much on the field during a game . . . or if you're hurt a little, have some players out. But every year we'd get to a certain point, get together as a defense and decide that since we couldn't please everybody all the time, that included him, too, and so we'd decide what to do and how to play certain defenses and we sort of played his game plan but it was our own game, too.

"I mean, I'd been there a while. And some of the others, Lee Roy and Jethro and Mel . . . and we knew when those other guys were going to pass, or when they were going to pull, or run the ball. I mean, we'd watch as much film as the coaches, and we could see a player leaning this way, or I'd notice two linemen too close together, closer than they would normally be, and I knew they were going to pull, maybe the guard was going to pull down the line and the center was going to cut me off. Lee Roy used to tell Jethro where to be, what to do, and it usually worked. We had to play that way, and that's because you've got to make big plays to win, somebody has to, and you aren't going to win if everybody's sitting on their haunches."

The concept of making big plays repeats itself in almost every one of these interviews, from Landry down through the players. How to go about doing that, however, is where the coach and some of his veterans differed.

"Did Tom know what we were doing? Of course. A man as intense as he was doesn't let anything slip past him. You get stale, you know, and it evolved into Tom and a few of us, the veterans, kind of all coaching the defense together. I remember one time during a meeting he smiled and said, 'I know what you guys are doing, but as long as you get by with it, it's all right, but when you quit gettin' by with it, go back to what you know.' Basically, we played the flex defense the way we were supposed to, but there were a few things we knew would work better, and we had half a dozen guys, more, who had been in the league six, eight years.

"We'd free-lance a lot, make those big plays, and we'd say, to each other, don't worry about what the coaches say, let's worry about what happens out here on the field. And then we'd go get the ball and make a lot of turnovers, and that's how you win. You can play almost perfect defense and still lose, because something else goes wrong, maybe somebody on the offense makes a mistake, or gets hurt.

"We just had a very good blend of talent and leadership, offense and defense. And when we retired, Coach Landry seemed to take back a lot of the freedom he had given us on defense. But football had changed by then, too, so changes had to be made in the system. I broke in Harvey Martin . . . I broke in Ed Jones . . . and Randy (White) came the year I left but he played middle linebacker there for a year or two. A guy named Bill Gregory took my place, and of course Larry Cole was still there. Then Coach Landry made Randy a tackle and moved Harvey to the weak-side end and Ed over to the strong-side end and put Cole in at tackle, and when old Larry finally retired they got this big kid from Nebraska (John Dutton) in a trade with the Colts. That was a good, solid defensive line, but they weren't the greatest at playing the flex defense.

"See, Harvey just wanted to rush the passer, and Randy played it well but he was very fast and also a great pass rusher but I never felt he played the run as well as we did in the old days, mainly because he and Harvey were such great pass rushers. They tore things up and made big plays and that's what you've got to do to win."

But even a man such as Lilly, who took a genuine interest in what happened to the Cowboys after he had retired, who tried to help with some of the younger players, who offered advice if asked . . . even Lilly started to make comparisons, to match up the stars of his day with those of the day after.

"There is no doubt Tom built his first defensive team around a few guys," he said. "Absolutely, he built things around Lee Roy, who was very brilliant, a tactician, a student of the game who always knew what was going on and how to deal with offenses. The only thing wrong with just filling spots, replacing a player with another player without affecting the system, is that you've got to find not only great athletes but guys who want to win real bad. There's a lot of great athletes, but not a lot who have a tremendous desire to win. Coaches have a tendency to keep talent, they draft players and hold them two or three years because of their ability, and rarely do they turn out. Coach Landry knew which players wanted to win . . . had to win, to keep happy . . . and I think that's when we did our finest work as a team, drafting those guys who may not have had a great college record but knew how to win and had to win to stay sane.

"Drew Pearson, for example, was just this skinny little bit of a kid when I met him, couldn't have weighed more than 160 or so, and I thought God, he's going to get broken in half. But he was gutty and strong and he knew how to win. And he was very strong. He wasn't real fast, but he just had this desire to be good.

"Even when I was playing, Coach Landry knew which players to bring in, older guys who had already played well for a long time, and maybe they were old and banged up, and slowing down, but they still had this desire to win. Hell, he brought in Mike Ditka, for example, and that old mail horse got another four, five years out of the game because he loved what he saw when he got here, and that old competitive spirit . . . you never lose that, you know, you have to just win at everything . . . just pushed him to play all those additional years."

It remained, because it suddenly was important to both of us, to determine just how good Bob Lilly really was, if he truly was the best defensive lineman of all time, if he is as much a legend as a man, the tall, tough Texan from Throckmorton who never quit and never backed down and never was beaten.

So. Was he? Bob Lilly, are you the best defensive lineman ever to play the game?

"Oh, I seriously doubt it," Lilly said. "I never really compared myself to other guys, and I wouldn't know how. I just played because I enjoyed it and if I didn't I would have found something else to do. I don't know. It's like . . . well, I certainly wasn't the fastest lineman, but one of the quickest, and I was strong. I had a big body, was real strong in my hips, and I could stop a one-on-one block, sometimes even a two-on-one block, and that helped because they didn't pick on me too much. Then, I was quick enough to get off the ball and mess up things.

"Once I got to where I could read the different things, like a lineman backing up a little if he was going to pull, I could defeat what he wanted to do with my quickness. But I watched great, great defensive linemen from the day I learned about football. But I'm not going to brag on myself, I'll let somebody else do that. But I always enjoyed it, and every game was a challenge to me, even in my last year when I was in a lot of pain.

"I felt like a bird dog . . . I don't know if you've ever been quail hunting in this part of the country, the bird dog gets out of the trailer and the first thing he does is start going to the bathroom, about five times before he starts huntin', and it was that way for me from the time I was an eighth-grader until my 14th year of pro football. I mean, I just loved it. I just hated it that I couldn't go on with it. I wanted to be able to do it all my life, I loved it so much.

"But that's the way it goes, and I tried to master every part of the game. I was like a golfer, who practices all the different shots over and over. And when I'd have a game early in my career, they'd try everything on me, cut blocks, blind-side blocks, everything. So I worked on the ropes, hop through 'em, skip through 'em, carioca through 'em . . . until I never had to look down. I just got a sense of where the ropes were and I could go right through them.

"Then we'd start pushing that sled around every day, our own decision. We'd push . . . one guy at a time . . . and Ernie (Stautner) would be the guy on the sled, and we'd push it all over the field, you see, until we got so strong in our hips and thighs that we'd be able to run over the guy in front of us during a game. We worked on agility and strength, so I could go around a guy if I had to or through him.

"And there's another thing. I always heard that the good players had like an extra sense of the game, of what's going on. I heard one time, listening to Ted Williams being interviewed, that when he played baseball and was at bat he could see the threads on the ball. Well, I could do that, when I played baseball, and I know a lot of times in pro football things would slow down so much, visually, it seemed like I had plenty of time to go around the guy while he was waiting, and those things helped me a lot. It was like seeing things in slow motion, and I always seemed to know where the ball carrier was.

"I just wonder if all the great athletes see things like that. I'll bet they do."

Lilly, as big and as strong as he was, has been called by many knowledgeable people the ideal nose tackle—before there was a need for nose tackles.

When this was mentioned, he beamed.

"I would have loved to play nose tackle," he said. "I would have loved to be in the middle of all that action. No way would the center be able to defeat me one-on-one. No way."

Along the way, from the start of the odyssey that would take the Cowboys from infancy to average to competitive to superior, Landry's attitude and work ethic never changed.

"Oh, he took the losing pretty hard," Lilly said. "We all did. We really did. Guys I played with then, guys who are coaches, for instance, now . . . well, they tell me things just aren't the same anymore. 'You wouldn't believe it, Bob,' they tell me, and especially they have trouble with the airplane flights coming home after a loss. They just laugh and make jokes and it's just a lot different. I don't know whether that comes with making a lot of money, or just the times now, but I think I played during the best years, when it was fun to be a player, when we were all in something exciting together, you understand? Now, it seems, it's just a job. Go to work, do the best you can, make the most money you can, then go home.

"It just seems too patently boring for me. And with all the money, it's funny they don't do anything with it, most of them. They spend it but they don't know how to save it, how to invest it. When a kid comes out of college now and signs a million-dollar contract, he's got it made. That's probably what it is. Plus, he's got an agent. I never had one. I didn't think I was allowed to have one, and I didn't want to get anybody angry. You know, I was grateful that they'd let me play. I never wanted to do anything to call attention to myself off the field.

"Sure, I understand now that it wasn't always the smart thing to do, and when I always used to do my contract with Tex (Schramm), I'm afraid most of the time Tex 'did it with me,' you know? Tex was real good negotiating with us guys. I was afraid they wouldn't let me play if I asked for too much money."

Remembering now is sometimes a painful experience for Bob Lilly, because there has been nothing after football that has filled his life quite the same way. "I remember some older player saying that never again could he devote so much of himself to a job the way he did to pro football," Lilly said, smiling just a little sadly. "Now I understand it. Those were the best times, the best years, and honestly, I never wanted them to end."

And through it all, the one constant was Tom Landry.

"He was steady, always steady," Lilly said. "He never gave anybody credit, including himself. We'd come off the field with a 40-point win and he'd start picking at this and bitching about that and never stopping to congratulate anybody. That was the one thing I think we all resented.

"Did I like him? I don't know. I didn't know him that well,

and he never seemed like he was interested. I know different now, that he was just staying a little distant because it doesn't help if you're too close to the players and then have to trade them, or cut them. But since I stopped playing I've gotten to know him well, and now I consider him one of my best friends.

"I always thought he was fair, brilliant . . . but a little bit too critical. Like on Monday, we'd have our meetings, and he'd run every little error that everybody made back and forth, back and forth. You just don't have to harp on something like that. We knew what we did wrong. I never felt that was particularly called for, especially after we became veterans. We knew what to do, how to do it, and Lord, nobody is perfect all the time. But I believe that's the way Coach Landry stayed on top of the game. I never talked to him about it, not even now, but I always felt like . . . after I finished . . . that kept him right in the game. I don't think he ever did it, really, to be critical. We took it that way, but I don't think it was ever a personal thing. I just really believe, knowing Coach Landry as well as I do now, that what he was really doing was critiquing his game, too. We thought he was doing it to be critical of us in public, to make us feel bad, but now I doubt it. He just isn't that kind of person, and I don't think it ever dawned on him, what he was doing.

"In fact, I believe that if we had confronted him with it he probably never would have done it again."

The chemistry of the personalities that made up the Cowboys, Lilly feels, was acquired and not simply created. "It was tough, it really was, because Tom certainly isn't . . . well, he's a lot of things but he is not an extrovert. He's a lot more introverted than most people think, but after football, he's just an ordinary human being, and he was so involved and so engrossed in the game, and he had so much thought going on, that he just didn't have the time for anything else. Nothing. He wasn't going to be friendly because it never occurred to him that he should be.

"But now he's one of the friendliest people you'd ever want to meet, but back then, I never really thought of him as cold, just isolated. Yeah, he'd walk past you a lot, but I think he just didn't focus on anything or anybody."

Such withdrawal just didn't sit well with a few players. Meredith, for example. A wide receiver–turned-author, Pete Gent, for another. "We played hurt because we knew he wanted us to, but he didn't really ask for that. You just knew he needed you to play, because once he counted on you, it was important to be there. After a while we thought of playing hurt all by ourselves, but maybe it was the Cowboy system that conditioned us to do it. Tom was never mean, never nasty. I never felt any fear concerning Coach Landry, nothing bad I can think of, but he wasn't real outgoing and he was real critical of mistakes and I guess there were players who couldn't handle him.

"I know Meredith took a lot of heat after we lost that game to Cleveland, and while I never heard Tom say anything critical about a player in public, I think there were some things he said about Meredith. He never dragged a player through the mud, except that one time. He was as fair as he could be with everybody, and he hated to let players go, just hated it, and he'd keep them around as long as possible. I remember seeing Jethro waddling around in his last year, playing pretty well, but not great, and I knew it was just because Tom hated to let him go."

Lilly, having played through the 1974 season, was thus in a position to watch the evolution of the game and how Landry did—or did not—deal with it.

"I noticed that the Pittsburgh Steelers started taking advantage of the rule changes first," he explained. "It was especially obvious on the offensive line, because as the officials relaxed a little on holding penalties, they started to go for bigger, stronger offensive linemen. I imagine that was the first team in the league that really went into weight programs heavily, and their players became the forerunner of today's players. Like (center) Ray Mansfield. I used to play against him when he weighed 260, and suddenly he's playin' about 285 and he's got arms on him about this big . . . and they were just shovin' defensive players out of the way, because they could do that legally. And that's when the flex defense became ineffectual for Dallas, when teams became bigger, understood the flex better and literally pushed the players out of the way.

"Hey, when a player is so much bigger and stronger and can shove you out of the way, you can't compete. That's how they won those two Super Bowls against us (games X and XIII). Times were changing and we didn't change fast enough. We should have started beefing up the offensive line . . . our linebackers needed to be bigger and faster . . . maybe the flex might have been altered somewhat . . . and we had some bad draft picks, too."

Looking at the modern Cowboys, and Lilly still does see as many of the games as he can, his feeling is that scrapping the flex, as new coach Jimmy Johnson has done, might have been an overdue necessity.

"See, the middle linebacker they have now (Eugene Lockhart) has been around for five, six years (he started his seventh in 1990) and finally started to play well last year, because the flex wasn't his problem anymore. There was just too much thinking, too much reading and waiting, and he isn't that kind of player. He's instinctive."

Lilly remembers that Lee Roy Jordan was the leader of the defense ("he was a holler-type guy"), that others ("Renfro, for instance") tried to lead by performance.

How did Lilly try to help? "I think my biggest contribution was bitchin' about everything," he said. "It was always when we lost, when we made bad plays. I mean, I was just irate. I yelled at the other players, I yelled at the coaches. I mean, I didn't blame somebody for making a mistake, but I just screamed and hollered and it made me wonder, sometimes, tough as we were, how we ever got that reputation of being a finesse team that wasn't real tough. It was probably the flex defense, which was a passing defense, really, and we had to play the flex for about 10 weeks, starting in training camp, to get to the point where we could move and play the flex at the same time, because you had to take certain steps, read certain keys . . . and by the time you did all that, it might have been too late.

"You had to do it quick enough not to let somebody get position on you, and we always got to the point where we cheated a little, like I'd play closer than three feet to the ball, or I'd back off the ball a little . . . lots of things that weren't in the book. If you didn't want to take a chance, you usually couldn't make the flex work for you."

And what does Lilly miss most about this game to which he gave so much of his life?

"I miss the competition, and I miss the camaraderie. And I miss my buddies, miss seein' them every day. Naturally, I miss Coach Landry. I used to look for him in the morning and it became a regular part of the day, just seein' him, knowin' he was there. It was like belonging to a great company . . . all your buddies, you go to work with them every day, have a lot of fun. You know, if I could play again, if I was young again, I'd play football all my life. But that's gone. And as much as I loved the game, as guilty as I felt about actually gettin' paid to play, I don't think you see that today. I don't think the people playin' today . . . well, not all of them, anyway . . . love it like we did.

"I worked a lot harder playin' football in high school and college than I did as a pro. I know players who went to their own doctors, and swore them to secrecy, so that the coach wouldn't find out and sit them down. I think the players, not the game, got away from Coach Landry, because they just weren't the kind of players he was used to seeing, to dealing with. Imagine, hair dryers in the locker room. Man, we didn't have enough hair to need a dryer."

The interview was at an end, but there was a small bit of business still to do.

"Randy White asked for me to give you his new telephone number," the visitor said. "He says to tell you he's wide open, whatever that means."

Lilly smiled. "Right. Ol' Randy wants to go fishin' again. He loves it. We go out into east Texas and get us a mess of bass and I'm sure that's what he wants. Thank you. I'll call him."

He walked the visitor to the front door, made sure to give the proper exit directions, and urged a safe and speedy return to Dallas.

"I'm not going back to the hotel yet," the visitor said. "If I can make it back in time, I have an appointment with Coach Landry."

Lilly's face beamed. "Well, sir, you can cut a little time off the return by goin' another way. Here, let me show you. And don't keep the coach waitin', you hear? And make sure to say hello."

He seemed to want to say more, but nothing happened.

"Just say hello," said Bob Lilly. He paused. "Lord, I love that old man."

As the old Western song says, pretty soon I had Graham, Texas, in my rearview mirror.

CHAPTER 2

LEE ROY JORDAN

THE LEADER

Her name is Aline, but given the peculiar pronunciation style that inflicts those who speak Texas English, it comes out Ay-leen.

In any case, she must be the most efficient of private secretaries, because she knew exactly which days Lee Roy Jordan was going to be in, when to call back to have the best chance to catch him, was able to arrange an interview at Lee Roy Jordan Redwood Lumber Company in northeast Dallas at 8:30 of a gray and raining Tuesday morning and even thought to inquire as to how the visitor took his coffee.

"And you be careful, now, because Regal Row turns into Burbank Street without warning you . . . just stay on Regal, go straight, and you'll find us, y'hear?"

Thanks to Ay-leen, the Regal Row–Burbank Street pitfall was safely navigated, and the visitor turned up at Lee Roy Jordan Redwood to be greeted with a cup of coffee—black, sugar—and a man pretending to be Lee Roy Jordan.

Of course he was pretending. Had to be. He was neatly attired in a stiffly starched white shirt, open at the collar, and crisp brown slacks. He sat at a large, dark wood desk, pictures of Lee Roy Jordan's family on a table behind it. He had huge hands that seemed to be all gnarled muscle knots and massive fingers, one of which carried an obvious replica of the Dallas Cowboys' Super Bowl VI championship ring.

One of those gigantic hands was extended, shook the visitor's, and then this Lee Roy Jordan look-alike said, in a voice that carried at the same time friendliness and authority: "Let's get started, I know you didn't come down to Dallas to ask about redwood, right?"

But there's this problem, see. Is it really Lee Roy Jordan? My God, the man has all-white hair, and everybody knows middle linebackers like Lee Roy Jordan wouldn't be caught dead with all-white hair, certainly not in public. Besides, how in the world could this have happened? Is it really almost 30 years ago that Jordan joined the Cowboys? No, this can't be him. No, sir—no way—not with all that white hair. That's for old guys, right?

A plan is devised. A series of questions will be asked, questions to which only the real Lee Roy Jordan would know the answers. Now we'll see. Now the imposter will be found out.

For instance: Who was the team leader when you joined the Cowboys?

He smiled. Clever man, expected that one. "There was none, and that surprised the hell out of me," he said. You know? That was the right answer.

"I mean, I kept waiting for somebody to come up, to stand up and take over, and nobody did. Hell, I couldn't, not then. I was just a rookie. Nobody would have listened to me, and it really wasn't my place. I was used to somebody taking charge from when I played at Alabama, and Coach Bear Bryant wanted somebody to do that. It was me. I'd be the leader, the holler guy. I'd be the one to yell at players. It wasn't there with the Cowboys, and I missed it. So after a couple of years, when I saw the need for it and just did it, things started to work better, the whole team atmosphere changed, and I was a lot more comfortable."

So we have determined that Lee Roy Jordan—the man they came to call "Killer" in the locker room and on the practice field—felt not only the need for a team leader but to become that leader.

How did he feel about Tom Landry, who provided no team leader?

"I loved him," he said, simply.

And how did he feel when Coach Landry was dismissed—

coldly, arbitrarily dismissed—when the team was sold from Bum Bright to Jerry Jones in February of 1989?

"I was shocked . . . shocked and saddened. Even though I had heard the statements made by the new owner, before he even bought the team, that if the deal went through he was going to make some changes, it still came as a nasty surprise. I thought Mister Bum Bright, who owned the team, was the one at fault. He didn't consult with Landry, didn't consider his feelings enough to make an effort. You know, when they got close to a contract, he didn't say, 'Hey, I need to stop and call Tom right now. This is where I have to talk to him, because even though you told us before that you'd be bringing in your own coach if this went down, that Tom might be replaced, I need to tell him right now before it actually happens.'

"And that's how it happened. One of the television stations kind of . . . you know . . . jumped the gun the night before, and said this is what was going to be announced, and it just wasn't right. I mean, Bum knew for about 30 days that he was going to make this deal, and at any time could have just stopped to get through to Coach Landry. I mean, that old man deserved a lot better than what he got.

"I blame Bright for not seeing to it that Tom was taken care of . . . warned . . . before it happened. And this was one of the first times, probably, that Tex Schramm wasn't involved right to the end in the negotiations, so he didn't really know when it was final, when he should start thinking about calling Tom. Tex must've hated not being involved, since he always was, from the day the team was born. He had kind of gotten put out of the negotiations by Bright and Jones. He was still trying to manage or manipulate the situation, trying to see if he could come out in charge under the new administration. He still wanted control, you understand, but the new ownership made it pretty clear that they were not going to go for another circuit with Tex in charge. They wanted to put their own people in place, do it themselves, and so all of a sudden a three-party negotiation turned into a two-party deal and it worked out smoothly.

"I'm pretty sure Tex didn't know when the deal had been

struck, but I have a strong feeling that Tom knew what was going to happen. But Tom wasn't called, and he should have been, and it should have been Bum Bright who made the call. It wouldn't have taken much . . . he just needed to pick up the telephone, call Tom, and say something . . . oh, something like 'God, we sure appreciate your contributions to Dallas, to the Cowboys, to the state and to football in general, but this man here is going to buy the Cowboys and he's putting in his old, longtime friend as coach.' "

Jordan paused, and a look of semimalevolence flashed for an instant on his rough-hewn, square face.

"I guess if you can fire Tom Landry, you can fire anyone, but I think he was ready for the next season, realized he had the biggest challenge of his life ahead of him, and whether he had the players or the coaching staff or the support, he was going to work 18 hours a day, if he needed to, to get it done. I think what he hated the most was leaving with that last season in the books, that 3-13 thing that just, Lord, embarrassed him. He was a very committed man . . . he could get himself to commit to doing a thing and then nothing else ever crossed his mind. He was still capable of doing that, even when he got into his 60s, and he should have either been given the chance to make up for what he felt was a terrible job on his part or at least be given a more graceful way to leave.

"It was disgraceful, after all that man had given to the team, to just cut him loose like that."

Loving Landry never meant liking him, at least not all the time, and Jordan was quick to make that distinction.

"Do I stay in touch with him? Well, occasionally. See, Tom isn't the kind of guy you stay in touch with, unless you bump into him at a function or a fund-raiser or some community charity dinner. We . . . all of us . . . had a relationship that was a little bit strange. We never became comfortable enough so that we were able to just call him to chat, or visit. If I have something I think he'd be interested in, or if there's something he can help me with, then I'll call him. And whatever it is, he'll do it. He always would, always did.

But as far as just a friendly chitchat, no. I don't think he had that type of relationship with anybody.

"We all played with a kind of healthy fear of him, of what he would do when . . . if . . . we lost. I think we understood that part of it, that it was part of Tom's personality and that I don't think he could get close and still make tough decisions about cutting players, like when a career is finally over . . . especially guys who played for him a long time, guys who were stars, who helped him win. . . . See, I don't think he felt he could make those kind of decisions if he let himself get too close to the players. Personally involved . . . emotionally involved . . . that wasn't what he wanted. He had to stay above the players, away from them, distant from them, in order to do what he felt was best for the Dallas Cowboys. No matter what.

"He was that way when he coached us in the early '60s and I know he was that way the last year he coached. Everything he did in his life . . . personally and professionally and every other way . . . was designed to consider only one thing: What was good for the team? If he felt a move was the right one, then he wouldn't hesitate, would never back down from a tough decision.

"We were an older generation of players, and he was a lot younger, but it was the same then. He was very much removed . . . very much distant . . . the players were there and his contact was to come into a meeting, talk football . . . talk football . . . talk football . . . discuss strategy, maybe. Then boom! he's out the door, gone, to take care of media or take care of his other head-coaching duties, whatever they were. And I feel like that was something he had to deal with. I'm sure he wrestled with it a lot, because I know Tom would much rather have had a friendly, close relationship with the players. But he didn't feel it would work for him, that he'd be able to maintain his objectivity.

"I played for Bear Bryant at Alabama, and it was a much more friendly relationship . . . he was really the opposite of Coach Landry. He motivated by ass-kickin', ass-chewin', whatever. By fear, in some cases. But he also motivated us by affection and love. He was the guy who would get close to the players, but he was also the guy who would get on your unit . . . I mean seriously get down on you . . . and I think Coach Landry kind of stayed away, and by doing that he could discipline and motivate without hurting himself by letting a player get too close to him.

"Coach Bryant loved his players, kept his relationship with them for years after they left school, and showed deep affection. I mean, it was nothing for him to come up and put his arm around you, hug you, talk to you, tell you what a good job you'd done, and then the next day he'd grab you by the collar and tell you what a crappy job you'd done, kick you in the ass, like that. He wouldn't hesitate to change his feelings about a situation, about his players. He was more human, he didn't mind showing you more affection than Coach Landry. It was difficult for Coach Landry to show any feelings whatsoever, because he couldn't turn it on and off and I don't think he felt he could be an effective coach without acting the way he did.

"I mean, we'd come in after winning a game by 30 points and he'd start in with telling us what we did wrong. No compliment, no pat on the back. Just pointing out all our mistakes. That was his way. If you lost a game, and played poorly, he'd come in and he wouldn't be screaming or red in the face or anything, he'd just say, softly, 'You know, such and such happened, and we just didn't play well,' and then he'd just bow out after that.

"But me, I'd come in and throw my helmet through the wall and rant and rave and in 10 minutes it was all over. Gone. I let it out, and then I just started thinking about the next week. Well, Coach Landry would go watch films for a day and a half, and then he'd come in and he'd have a legal pad about nine feet long . . . a pad full of ass-chewin' . . . I mean, he'd chew ass for three hours, and if a guy played poorly, he'd chew him out for three hours, for every mistake. And when he was finished, I mean, the guy was devastated. It was difficult to get through those meetings . . . I called it chewin' ass by the numbers . . . because he had this legal pad with notes on it and he didn't just chew a guy out a few times and then let him off. I mean, he chewed him out for every one of the mistakes, wouldn't let him off. It was pretty tough for some people who were thin skinned, who had fragile egos. But you know, it was never personal. It was just his way of telling us what we did wrong, because more than anything that man wanted us to be perfect, to never make a mistake.

"I don't think he realized that after about 60 times of chewing a guy's ass out he had just ruined him. There were guys who'd throw up, get nauseated before goin' into those meetings . . . because they knew they'd played poorly, I mean guys know when they play poorly . . . and they knew that from the time the meeting started until it ended there was goin' to be constant ass-chewin'.

"Some of the older players . . . man, it's hard to think of myself as younger than anybody these days," he smiled, "they said Tom was just like that when he was an assistant coach with the Giants. He coached the defense and Vince Lombardi coached the offense and they both did it. It was the only way they knew to provide discipline, motivation . . . it was what he learned, and it was how he coached.

"Even after I knew that was his way, it still bothered me because I just couldn't see doin' it like that all the time, not every game, win or lose. I wished he'd show more affection, show more appreciation for good plays . . . show more feeling for the players and be a part of them, of us, when we won. Also, feeling that we were all a part of the losing. It seemed like he separated himself from the losing, that we, the players, lost. And he didn't really include himself with the players when we won. It was like, well, 'I designed the right offense and I designed the right defense and we scored points and stopped the other guys and that's why we won.' It still didn't come together as we all won, or we all lost, and that was the way I was used to it at Alabama. We won. We lost. All of us in it together.

"I couldn't get used to hearing him say, you know, 'Roger had a bad day' . . . or 'the defense played poorly.' Hell, if we lost, all it meant was that we didn't do enough to win.

"But I like Tom Landry very much. He has a lot of characteristics that many of us wished we could have attained . . . in how we live our lives, manage our lives. Once you understood the personality part, where he didn't give out any feelings of warmth . . . well, I just didn't understand that until I got further along in my career and started to realize that was just how he was. The feelings were there, the love was there, he just didn't let you get to see them. He kept everything locked in, so reserved inside himself, that we never saw the feeling he had for the players.

"I had a situation one year, I was in the hospital with a punctured kidney, and he was there early, stayed late, every day. He was judged by us on his lack of making his feelings known, but I think that's probably not justified because the man did have a terrific capacity for caring. I think he just didn't want to let it show that much, and I think it was something he had to work at to make it seem natural."

There were exceptions, of course, and Don Meredith, the Cowboys' first superstar quarterback, was one of them.

"Don had some real problems . . . he really felt like he wasn't appreciated . . . and I think much of this went back to the times when we didn't win games we needed to win. It came down in the press, and to the public in general, as though Don Meredith had a terrible day . . . Don Meredith threw three interceptions . . . Don Meredith did this . . . Don Meredith did that. Well, hell, it wasn't Don's fault, it was the Dallas Cowboy football team's fault. And that was something that Coach Landry did . . . he had a tendency to pick out who played poorly, and he'd say it to the press and I never could understand that. He even did it with Roger (Staubach) later. 'Roger played poorly, it was Roger's fault.' I never verbalized that to him, don't remember if I ever talked about it with him or not. Maybe I felt I didn't have the right, the experience to go to him or not. But I should have. It wasn't fair and I should have tried to fix it. Don took a lot of abuse, and he shouldn't have, and when Roger got all the credit, later on, maybe he didn't deserve all of it, either, but the team was better, you see?

"Between the fans and the press, though, it was Meredith who was just crucified, and it wasn't right. We as a team should have been taking the heat, not just Don. Hey, Don was a winner, a man with great talent. Look, everybody doesn't fit into the same mold, working at the game from 8:00 in the morning to 9:00 at night.

"See, Don could do it, could be his best, by casually attacking football. It didn't mean that when it came down to playing in the game he wasn't as intense as anybody else, because he was, but he had a kind of flippant attitude and personality and it just didn't seem like he was takin' things too seriously. Hell, Don's been an entertainer all his life, you know? Class clown . . . school comedian . . . team comedian . . . that's the way he lived. I mean, he's gonna have fun doin' what he's doin' or he's not gonna be doin' it for long. But I don't think that personality really ever sat well with coach Landry. He thought everybody had to work as many hours as he did, be as serious as he always was about the game, and that was not all of Don's life. He was not consumed by football the way Coach Landry was. I think if Don had played for another team, for another coach, he would never have retired as early as he did. I mean, he was only 31, and he was going to improve and become a great, great quarterback. I think Tom took all the joy out of football for him. He just couldn't play for Tom.

"I guess Tom was so dedicated to winning, and his preparation and life-style was so serious, in meetings or on the practice field, on the bus, on the plane. . . . Don's makeup was all different. He felt, 'Hey, we've got to have some fun or we're going to have tension, and with tension you don't perform well. Maybe he had too much fun. We had some of them . . . Pete Gent, Billy Parks . . . Steve Kiner. Steve Wright, who I knew from Alabama (Packers and Giants). I mean, Steve Wright was the biggest man I had ever seen. He came in as a freshman weighing 320, and he was 6-7, 6-8, but he wasn't fat and he was quick and he had all the talent he ever needed. He could have been the greatest offensive tackle ever. But he had a fun-type attitude, like Meredith's, and then he found himself playing for Lombardi. That didn't work, just like Meredith playing for Landry didn't work.

"But even when he got players who really had problems, guys like Duane Thomas, and Thomas Henderson . . . and Lord, I love the man for this . . . Tom always thought he would make a difference in their lives, not in their football careers but in their lives, that he could make them better people, help them through their problems, show them the way. He was always a good Christian, and he never thought a guy was all bad, or that there was no chance to save a guy, to set him on the right path.

"People didn't always respond to Tom the way he wanted them

to. Some couldn't, just couldn't. We had a kid named Steve Kiner, a linebacker, who was a little more free spirited than anybody we had. I knew he just wasn't going to be able to deal with Tom's way, and he lasted just one year with us but played a long time elsewhere. Those type of people were never going to do well in a regimented situation like Tom presented. I had trouble adjusting to it in the beginning, took me two or three years to feel comfortable expressing myself about how I felt we should play, and practice. I expressed myself as a team leader, and it bothered me sometimes that maybe Tom didn't appreciate my leadership, or maybe didn't appreciate my approach to other players.

"I would confront other players sometimes, if I thought they were people who didn't give 100 percent, or didn't practice hard, or play hard . . . or somebody I thought quit on us during a game. So when they were in my area they were at their own risk, because I let them know I didn't think they were guys we could count on, depend on in tough games. And sometimes Tom thought I was overreacting to that, but I grew up in a winning situation, too. I knew what it took to win. I wanted guys to have the same commitment that I did, because when it got late in the game, fourth quarter, and we're losing by three, four points . . . and we have to hold on a third-and-one, I want to know I've got guys who know what it takes to make the big play.

"You know, a lot of people ask me if I thought Roger Staubach was the greatest two-minute offense quarterback in the world, and I say, 'Yeah, but think about the damned defensive players who had to find a way to get the ball back for him so many times, so that he could work the offense downfield in those last two minutes.

"I always recognized what big downs were, what big plays were, and when we had to have them. I felt like I wanted guys around me whose intensity level rose, and there were a lot of them . . . Larry Cole and Jethro Pugh and Chuck Howley and Bob Lilly and Mel Renfro and Cliff Harris and Charlie Waters . . . we all got in tune together, and we knew . . . I guarantee you . . . that late in the game we had to find a way to come up with a big play. We had to, somebody had to, or we don't win the ball game.

"I'd be yelling in the huddle, screaming at them . . . 'Hey, Cole, are you going to make the big play? Is it you, Jethro?' I called down every one of them, I never hesitated. 'Lilly, is it going to be you?' And every time we got into that situation, I said, 'We got 11 guys here, 11 chances to make the play,' and they knew exactly what I was talking about. Somebody had to make it, and it was amazing how some guy would step up, boom! Like Larry Cole . . . boom! . . . he'd break through and trap the quarterback, and he never was known as a great pass rusher. But the guys just knew that was the crunch play of the game, and with me as the on-the-field leader, it worked.

"After I was here a couple of years . . . you know, I had sat back and waited for some of the older guys, who had been here four, five, six years . . . to come up with some leadership, to show some take-charge ability. Hell, in college, when they said line up, I was the first man in line. When they said it was time to do exercises, I'd be the first guy to do that. When they said run sprints, I'd try to get started first. I loved to be the leader, loved to set an example, and when I got here there was nobody to do that. And I said, 'Shit, I know I can do that, I'm gonna do what I know I can do, be an example, and I think they'll respect me for my commitment to football, to winning, to being the best I can be, and if I can get their confidence in me . . . then I would be able to lead them.'

"I studied films. I worked hard, harder than anybody. I knew if I could show them I knew what was going on, that would give me a lot of confidence. I took films home every night. I knew what Lilly's assignment was, what his keys were. I knew what George Andrie's keys were, how he played his position. I knew how everybody played their position, what their keys were, what their assignments were. Like a coach on the field, I guess. I just made it my business to know. And that's what I did. I'd drag a projector home and after dinner with the kids I'd just study films. The last five years of my contract, I had them write in that I'd have a projector at home, so I wouldn't have to carry one back and forth. That's how important film study was to me.

"I sat in meetings and listened to the coaches and checked to see if they made mistakes. If they did, I'd tell 'em, 'Hey, that's not the way we agreed to do it, that's not the way Coach Landry said to do it yesterday.' Because that's what I did, and they knew I knew what the hell I was doin' and so they never asked me anything, and I talked up only when I heard one of them say something wrong.

"I'd study films for hours, just looking for one little thing that I could use, a tip-off, a clue. It got so I didn't study a particular player, but the whole offense, like I could visualize the whole offensive line and the backs. Boy, a guy could move two inches one way or another and I knew what was coming, what the play was. I'd sit there and watch those guys and I'd be able to call certain plays for Lilly and Pugh and lots of times I'd be right. You know, you couldn't tell every one of them, but there may have been 10, 20 times during the game when I was right, and that's pretty good given that a team only runs maybe 60-somethin' plays a game.

"I used to get beat a few times, and Coach Landry'd say, 'Lee Roy, what the hell are you doin' way out there?' and I had to tell him that I saw something that made me think that's where I should have been. When I was right, though, even if I was 10, 15 yards away from where the flex put me, he didn't complain much. 'Just be right,' he'd say. My guessing percentage was damned good, I'll tell you that.

"See, that's one thing about the flex, about bein' the middle linebacker. You're in that position where you have to take chances, take some risks. That's why Bob Breunig, great an athlete as he was, smart a man as he was, never got to be as outstanding a middle linebacker as I thought he'd be. He never wanted to take those chances and get beat. He never wanted to be wrong, and man, if you're not taking some chances, if you're not wrong sometimes, you can't win those big games where one play turns it all around. You've got to believe in yourself, and what you see on the field, as well as believing in the defense.

"I made a lot of big plays I'd never have made if I didn't take a chance. You've got to take chances, especially if you're a linebacker. I don't think Bob was ever willing to take the chewing that he would have got from Coach Landry if he was wrong. Yes sir, I guess there were some players whose chances for an out-

standing career were diminished because of how they viewed
Coach Landry, because of how afraid of him they were."

It is not surprising, then, when Lee Roy Jordan makes an ad-
mission that, on the surface, just doesn't compute.

"I always wanted to be a coach, always. And when I retired,
when I was 36 years old, I'm sure Tom would have made a position for me on the team if I had gone to him and asked. . . . I
talked to Coach Bryant about coaching, and he told me, 'Lee Roy,
I pay my coaches 25,000, 30,000 a year, and you can't live on that.'
I agreed. I told him I had learned to spend more than that every
year. I couldn't afford that."

Long before retirement became a reality, Lee Roy Jordan—
"Killer"—became an awesome reality for offensive players, both
those around the league and on his team.

The late Steve Perkins, writing in the August 9, 1969 editions
of The Dallas Times Herald, recounted two incidents on the
team's practice field during a summer training camp scrimmage
at Thousand Oaks, Calif.

" . . . (wide receiver) Lance Rentzel happened to be wearing
the wrong-colored jersey Saturday in the Cowboys' intrasquad
scrimmage. He wore white, for offense. The Killer's side was wearing blue. Rentzel had already come zipping across the middle earlier to snare a pass out of the high air and take off like a scalded
cat for a 67-yard touchdown.

"Now he caught another one, and scooted across the middle,
so Lee Roy Jordan clotheslined him with a forearm to the nose.
Rentzel regarded the blow as superfluous and groused loudly. Jordan acted surprised. 'You come through here, you're going to get
HIT, son,' Jordan said.

"Another thing in evidence with Jordan (this year) is his happy
competitive fire. This was also apparent in the scrimmage when
Roger Staubach kept the ball and danced around end. The Dodger
put a move on Ron East and Cornell Green at the sidelines that
you would have to see to believe. They had him cornered, Green
in front, East pursuing from the side, when Staubach gave a head
fake to the inside and somehow made it past both of them a few
additional yards for a first down.

"Staubach has a bad back taped up, and besides, he is that precious commodity labeled No. 2 Quarterback. Jordan ran toward the sidelines at the conclusion of the play, yelling at (defensive line coach) Ernie Stautner. 'Coach, can we hit this guy?' Stautner, who is perfectly in tune with Jordan, replied, 'if he insists on running like that, tackle him like anybody else.'

"Staubach's eyes bulged a little at this repartee. 'I'd already been hit,' he protested. 'That Jordan, you never expect him to let up, anytime. He would rack up his own brother if his brother was wearing the wrong color.' "

Jordan, fully aware of his value to the team, became convinced prior to training camp of 1973 that he wasn't being paid up to that value. There were middle linebackers around the league—everybody used the middle linebacker, and if anyone had suggested a three-man front with four linebackers, he would have been written off as an unfortunate fellow stricken with some sort of rare football dyslexia—good ones, great ones, superstars: Dick Butkus, Ray Nitschke, Willie Lanier, Sam Huff, Joe Schmidt.

"I wanted the Cowboys to show they recognized my value by paying me a fair salary," he said. "My contract was up and I had met with Tex Schramm three or four times during the spring. I wanted to get it done before the two-a-days, before it became a distraction to training camp."

What? No agent? Everybody in the league these days has an agent, at least one per player, sometimes two. But in those days, not really so long ago, nobody hired an agent. The results could be dangerous.

For example, during the glory years of the Green Bay Packers under Lombardi, the team's offensive line was anchored by an All-Pro veteran center named Jim Ringo. His contract was up, and one bright spring day in bucolic Wisconsin he arrived at the team's office in the company of an agent.

They entered Lombardi's office and Ringo introduced his coach to his agent. Lombardi fixed them with a stare and asked if they'd mind waiting outside for a few minutes, that he had an important telephone call to make. Less than five minutes later, Lombardi walked out of his office, looked down at Ringo and the agent and said: "Gentlemen, you are in the wrong part of the country. Mr. Ringo now plays for the Philadelphia Eagles."

So Lee Roy Jordan tried to go it alone with Schramm, the team's most powerful force outside of Landry, the man who did all the player contract negotiations until much later, when he hired an assistant, the man who was as important in the changing of rules and policies in the league as Commissioner Pete Rozelle.

"Anyway, I wanted to get it done before camp, but he wouldn't pay me what I thought I was worth. My choices weren't much. I could play at Tex's salary, play out my option . . . which wasn't that smart because the owners were all together on option players and nobody would sign me . . . or retire, and I wasn't ready to quit yet. At our last meeting, we were still far apart. I got up to leave and said I felt I'd have to play out my option and see what happened. I remember his reaction to this day, and it was the deepest cut I'd ever had by anybody in my whole life. He gave me a backhand wave, like I just wasn't even there, like the Cowboys were saying they didn't give a damn about Lee Roy Jordan, whether I played for them or not."

Jordan went to camp, unsigned, and by his own calculations had the best training camp and best exhibition season of his career. Then, as if Landry was playing to his hand, he cut the only other middle linebacker two days before the season was going to open.

"In my little country mind," Jordan said, unable to stifle the contented smile on his face, "I saw the situation, knew it would work to my advantage, and played my cards. I just didn't show up for the last meeting prior to the season opener. I had never done that, never even thought about doing that, but I did it. Later that day Tex called me and said he couldn't believe I was the type of person to do something like that. In another 24 hours I had a three-year contract. It was my play and that's what I did. I don't think Tex ever got over me doing that."

The rift turned into an open, festering wound for years after, occasionally spilling into public print, evidencing itself by Schramm's refusal to induct Jordan into the team's Ring of Honor, a most select group which now has only seven honored members—Jordan was finally ushered in during the 1989 season by the new owner, Jerry Jones.

"A couple of years ago," Jordan continues, "I was listening to a psychological motivational tape and was prompted by its message to try for a peace meeting with Tex. It said if there was anybody you have had a grudge with, one that hasn't been healed, you need to talk it out with him face to face. So I went to see Tex. I presented my reasons for that brief holdout. He presented his side. He then told me he didn't think my actions were reasonable, that I took advantage of the team. I pointed out that in subsequent years many players, including stars like Randy White, Tony Dorsett and Everson Walls, had conducted long holdouts, but he didn't see it that way. He felt mine was a special case."

It has never really been resolved, and now that both men are far removed from the Cowboys and each other, there is every chance it will never come to a peaceful ending. But for this John Wayne in shoulder pads, it's history. In the past. He had always been organized and far sighted, and even as a player set in motion those things that might somehow, someday, prove to be beneficial.

"Even though I always kind of figured I'd be a coach," he said, "I never passed up an opportunity to meet business people. I always had an off-season job in Dallas. I never went back home, because Dallas was where I was known, and where I might be able to find an opportunity that would lead to life after football. I worked in real estate, in the brokerage business, for an insurance company, doin' public relations work for a moving company. And I took advantage of my status with the top businessmen in town. They were all Cowboy fans, you see. And it was their treat to take me to lunch, to meet me, to talk football with me.

"Sometimes I would be invited to play golf at the Preston Trail Country Club, which is the elite men's club here in Dallas, and hell, yes, I'd go. I'd sit with the men and have lunch, or play golf, or talk football, and I met some very important people. I made this friend, Glenn Butler, and he got these other guys to understand I wasn't just a jock. 'Lee Roy is tryin' to find out what to do after football,' he'd tell them. 'Right now he's working for me in real estate.' I didn't make a lot of money in the off-season, but

I met a lot of important people, and it was one of the best things I ever did.

"It was one of the great things about having been a Dallas Cowboy. Those opportunities would never have presented themselves to me otherwise."

Jordan came to the Cowboys as their first-round draft choice for 1963, and celebrated by having one of the most phenomenal games of anybody's career in his final performance for Alabama. It was the Orange Bowl, and on that New Year's Day night against Oklahoma, in what became a 17-0 Alabama victory, he registered 31 unassisted tackles, and it is probably only coincidental (but don't you believe it) that the last College All-Star team to beat the NFL champion in that once-traditional opener to the season was the '63 team, with You-Know-Who at middle linebacker.

After that success, he flew west from Chicago to join the Cowboys in Thousand Oaks.

"I was another piece to fit into the overall puzzle," he said of the defense he found in Dallas. "We had some of the guys in place. Lilly, Howley, Green, Andrie . . . another linebacker, Dave Edwards, came in with me . . . but we weren't really ready, not yet. We had some great offensive weapons, though. Meredith and Don Perkins and Ralph Neely and Frank Clarke . . . and Sports Illustrated took a chance, tried to get on our bandwagon early, you know? They sent a reporter out to Thousand Oaks and he got the defense on the cover, with a headline that said: Dallas Defense— Good Enough To Win In The East?

"Well, it was just too soon. We had the nucleus, but not yet. We needed another few years, and in 1965 we started to really come together, got to win seven games, and by 1966 we were a damned good football team. We won our conference in '66, played the Packers here for the NFL championship and they scored two touchdowns on our defense before the offense could even get on the field. But we made it close, really close, and maybe should have won it. That was the year that the NFL champion was going to play in the first Super Bowl, only they didn't call it the Super Bowl then (it was the AFL-NFL World Championship Game).

"We really fought back, and we lost it, 34-27, when Meredith threw an interception into the end zone. The safety . . . number 40 . . . caught the pass, but see, that wasn't Meredith's fault at all. You know something? It was Tom, because on that play the tight end is supposed to block on that outside (left) linebacker, then release and drift into the end zone for the pass. But the block has to pin him, as well as make him think it's a run.

"But Tom sent Bobby Hayes into the game at tight end, and he couldn't block (Packer linebacker) Dave Robinson if he wanted to. So he just ran into the end zone, and next thing Robinson is draped all over Meredith like a sack of potatoes, and the ball gets thrown too high. It was supposed to be a tight end there, in that formation."

Being part of the growth of the dynasty brought with it some of the bittersweet memories of being around when it started, when the city and its people were somewhat underwhelmed at the prospect of a football team in town. In fact, there were two—Clint Murchison's Cowboys and Lamar Hunt's American Football League entry, the Dallas Texans. After failing to attract enough fans to make any money, Hunt moved his franchise to Kansas City, where it became the Chiefs.

Lamar was the son of the reknowned H.L. Hunt, one of the richest men in the world, and one day H.L. and an old friend were having lunch. The subject got around to the Texans. "You know, H.L.," the friend said. "I hear that your boy is losin' a million dollars a year on that there football team."

Hunt nodded sadly. "Really? Well, if that keeps up, he's going to be flat broke in just another 350 years."

Anyway, Jordan went through some early experiences that weren't exactly the stuff that legends are made of. "Right there at the start, one time I went to cash a check to buy some clothes," he laughed, "and I told the fellow I was with the Dallas Cowboys . . . and he said, 'Really? I didn't know the rodeo was in town.' But once we played better, like after '65 and '66, it was easier. Then the whole town came alive for us, and I think it was an unusual situation because it really took root. The town was always intense about us . . . I don't know why it was, but there was always something magic about the Dallas Cowboys. And it wasn't just here, it was everywhere we went. It was, well, we might not win, but you wouldn't leave because the Cowboys were going to make it fun. Most teams, they get down by two or three touchdowns, you can go rake the yard or go for a ride or something. But you couldn't do that with the Dallas Cowboys, because even when we weren't an outstanding team we'd always make a run at it . . . maybe we'd lose by a point, or win by a point, but we always made it close.

"See, in Tom Landry's concept of offense, anything could happen, and at any time. He was a creative man, and with Don Meredith and Bob Hayes created long passes, long touchdowns . . . because in the NFL back then it was 7-yard passes and 3-yard runs and keep the ball and eventually make a touchdown. Shit, with Tom's offense, moving people around, getting the defense to make a mistake, suddenly it was a 70-yard touchdown in one play. It was his concept of offense that tried to get the defense into a position where a mistake would be made, and that would give him the big play that he always wanted.

"That created so much excitement that people wanted to watch the Cowboys, whether they were in New Jersey or Georgia or California. And it was that man, with his poker face and always wearin' a hat, that started to become known. But even with all the motion and multiple formations he could be very conservative, go through all that and then just run Perkins up the middle, but see . . . he was always watching to see what the defense would do when he showed them this, or that . . . and suddenly he'd notice something, the linebacker moving in one direction, or a cornerback compensating for something he saw, and he'd remember that. And then maybe 20 plays later he'd show that same formation but this time he'd be going for the big play, based on what he saw the player do before, and most of the time that man was right. It was amazing. When you adjusted in the secondary, you were really giving Tom something to exploit.

"There were a lot of plays run for a reason that didn't produce anything, but the next series, the next quarter, he'd come back with the same formation and set up the same deal and suddenly instead of giving the ball to the fullback he'd go deep downfield to Bob Hayes. That was a weapon, that man. As soon as he became the speed guy who could run and catch, everybody wanted one, had to have one, because Tom's use of him changed how teams played pass defense."

Jordan still watches, still calculates, still, in a way, acts the part of a coach.

"The game has changed a lot, but mostly in the number of people used," he says. "Six, seven defensive backs . . . one guy comes in when it's first down, then another one on second down. Now linebackers are defensive ends. Lawrence Taylor (of the Giants), for instance, he really isn't a linebacker. He's a specialized pass rusher, a 6-4, 250-pound guy who can run like hell and put pressure on the quarterback. If Lawrence had to cover in the secondary, he could never play. And the (Chris) Doleman kid on the Vikings, he isn't really a defensive end. He's a linebacker . . . or a pass-rushing specialist who plays up on the line.

"They're getting a stand-up head start . . . they let him get out, away from the offensive tackle, and he can run past him. They don't give guys like Lawrence Taylor any technique to learn, just tell him to line up and go get the quarterback. Would I like to play this defense now? I don't know. On a three-four, I'd probably still be one of the inside linebackers, but I think I'd probably be dissatisfied by being a part-time player, coming in and out, what the coaches today call situational defenses.

"Shit, when I was playing you knew you had the whole game and there were substitutions only if somebody got hurt. I would think it's more difficult to get into a team spirit feeling kind of thing, any unity . . . to get really involved in the game. You know, when we were out there we only had 11 guys, and we knew it was this 11 that was going to get beat or stop the other guys. I guess they all have fresh legs these days, because they don't really play a full game, but there are a number of plays that have already been run that the new guys haven't seen . . . and maybe the new guy won't make the play, even if the one who's been in was tired or not."

Landry always referred to Jordan as his best middle linebacker, and laughs at the size of the kid he drafted out of Alabama. "He probably wasn't any more than 195 pounds," the coach said, "and even in the early '60s that was small. Huff weighed 225, 230. Joe Schmidt, Chuck Bednarik, Bill George . . . they were all bigger than that. But Lee Roy was as tough as nails, and he had a better feeling for the position than anybody I ever coached."

And coming from Alabama in the early years of the decade of the '60s, was Jordan more familiar with the racial situation in Dallas?

"Dallas was a very restricted city for the black players, no question," he agreed. "You know, that whole business about we win as a team and we lose as a team and we think as a team was somewhat difficult to manage in Dallas then. I mean, we couldn't all go to the same restaurants, for instance. The same saloons. We had our team parties . . . special events or just our after-the-game parties . . . at one of the breweries in town, one of the beer distributor's places. We'd use their facilities and have it catered and we didn't have to be involved with the public problems. That way we didn't have to worry, and everybody showed up, black and white. We were all just the Dallas Cowboys.

"I won't lie to you and tell you I understood how the black players felt, because I can't. But I didn't agree with the situation, because I'm from Alabama but I've never been a racist. I'm a person who looks at individuals, and whether black or white, if you're a good person, I like you, and if I disagree with your values, I'm not gonna get close to you, we're just not gonna be friends. If I disagree with the way you're committed to football, we're not gonna be real friends either. If you just play for half-assed reasons, and not to win every day, we're not gonna be friends.

"But if you were committed to football, to being a good person, to a set of moral values I believed in, then it didn't matter what color you were, you and I could be friends. Honest, I know where I came from, and I know my state has had a lot of problems, and a bad reputation, but I never did look at what color a man was to see whether we could be friends or not.

"I know, for instance, that Mel Renfro had a bad time here, and he would, because he came from the West Coast . . . from

Oregon . . . and he didn't sound black. One summer, we had to play a game in Birmingham, and I know there was some apprehension on the part of the players then. Maybe, being as young as I was, I never realized how tough, how uncomfortable it must have been for those guys. The more mature I got, I think the more I understood.

"Thank God, things have changed in the last 25 years. I grew up in Excel, Alabama . . . and I went to a segregated school system and so forth . . . but my life wasn't segregated. We had some black families that lived with us, we were farmers and had some blacks working for us, working with us. When I grew up, blacks were close to me in my life. They were my playmates when we were kids. We'd go down to their houses and everybody'd come in and eat together, and my mother would cook for everybody working on our place, black and white, and we'd all eat together.

"I never thought about it, except that it was time to eat, so let's eat. But I knew I couldn't have sat down with them in a public restaurant, and that was sad. I know Ted Schramm went to court once on behalf of Mel Renfro, who couldn't buy a house in some development even when they told him . . . on the telephone . . . that there were lots of them available. See, he never did have a 'black accent,' but when he showed up . . . you know . . . 'Oh, my, what a surprise, we just sold all of 'em in this last hour, sir.' "

The miracle of Dallas, in Lee Roy Jordan's mind, was the creation of Tom Landry. Was because of Tom Landry.

"We had the good image from our coach, who was perceived as a very great man, dedicated to his Christian attitude . . . his integrity. We also had a football team that was very exciting to watch, and it was first class. Our management did everything first class, a good, solid operation. We promoted the hell out of the Dallas Cowboys, made them a good marketing tool. It was real progressive thinking. The cheerleaders helped us a lot, we gained a lot of fans . . . and there were a lot of exceptional things about the team, the class we showed, our attitude about our relationship with the community. Most of us got involved with charity groups around Dallas, raising money for groups that needed help, and that was the way the team was perceived.

"An extremely exciting and talented football team, with guys
who were involved, who would help, who would do good things.
Overall, that made us a very appreciated team, not only in Dallas
but all over the state, and in New Mexico, Oklahoma . . . we really
did become America's Team. You know, it was us and the Raiders, the two most popular teams in the country . . . the extremes,
the good guys and the bad guys.

"And if it wasn't for a couple of plays, we could have won four
out of five Super Bowls, or all five. The Steelers blocked a punt
in the one game, and in the next one we dropped a pass in the
end zone. That was Jackie Smith, greatest guy in the world, who
spent 14 years being a great tight end, and now he's remembered
only for that one play, dropping that pass."

Is there one game in Jordan's long and fabled career that he
remembers more than any other? "I guess it would have to be that
Ice Bowl game up in Green Bay (December 31, 1967)," he says.
"We should have beaten them, and the temperature devastated
us because we were a speed team, and everything was predicated
on us moving the ball offensively with movement, and still we
slugged it out with them and had a chance to win until that final
play when Bart Starr . . . an Alabama boy, too . . . scored that
1-yard touchdown with just a few seconds left.

"That game could have been the difference for the next five
years before we finally came back to win a Super Bowl. See, the
next year we had another great season (12-2) and then we got beat
by Cleveland for the league title, we played very poorly, should
have won. Then we lost to Cleveland again the year after that.
Then the press got on us, and we started out the next season losing,
winning, finally getting to 5-3 and then on a Monday night game
we just get blown up by St. Louis. It was 38-0, can you believe
that?

"Then we got together . . . had a meeting . . . said, 'Hey, we
only got these 40-something guys in this room on our side, everybody else is attacking our ass . . . so let them give up on us but
make sure we never do. We started hustling, put together a
streak. . . . St. Louis folded and we didn't lose again until we got
to the Super Bowl. That particular day we had a lot of things go

against us. . . . We fumble on their 2-yard line and Billy Ray Smith yells out, 'I got it' and the official gives it to them but our guy, our center (Dave Manders) had it all along. He never even came in and looked at the pile. So we lose that one on a last-second field goal, 16-13. . . . Renfro tipped a long pass and their tight end caught it and scored with like a 75-yard touchdown. But we were a better team, and against the Colts that day, we should have won.

"But that Ice Bowl game would have put us in the Super Bowl, and we would have won it because we were much better than that American Football League . . . and yes, it did become emotional after that . . . we did start to think about how it was going to blow up on us again. We just didn't recover, didn't do well in big-game situations. I think it kind of killed our confidence. We didn't win the two games against Green Bay . . . the two games against Cleveland . . . that Monday night game against St. Louis. MacArthur Lane ran over me so many times that night, I thought he was a train . . . Jackie Smith took a little pass over the middle and made it a 70-yard touchdown, and outran one of our fastest defensive backs, Mike Gaechter. What a shame about him dropping that Super Bowl touchdown pass, what a shame."

But ever the realist, Jordan reflected on the never-quite-full condition of the Cowboys, even during their Super Bowl years.

"It seemed we were always worrying about two or three positions, or an area. Take the Steelers, for instance. Shit, they had defensive backs, linebackers, defensive linemen . . . running backs, a great quarterback, wide receivers, offensive linemen. They had superb players at every position.

"Seemed like we always had a problem, maybe at cornerback, maybe at offensive line, somewhere. Quarterback. Running back. If we could have had one or two more people, boy, we could have really been something. But through it all, I made friendships that still stand, that are as strong today as they were then . . . with guys like Jethro Pugh, Bob Lilly, Rayfield Wright, Cornell Green. I guess my closest friends are Dave Manders, Chuck Howley and Cliff Harris . . . they're all here, we're all still close.

"Lilly? You're gonna get the thrill of driving down to Graham, right? Chance to see that big city? I don't see Bob all that much, but he's still one of my best friends. And do you know something? I've never seen anybody play defensive tackle better than Lilly. Never. Just think of what he'd have been if he was on a weight program. We didn't do much with that, and he was still the strongest man I ever knew and he weighed only 270.

"Hell, with a program he'd have been 6-5 and would have weighed 300 pounds and been able to bench press the world. We didn't know what it was to lift for certain parts of the body. You know, we'd do a few chins, push-ups and a bench press or two and that was our weight program. We were into conditioning more than most teams, and Kansas City had the first weight coach, man named Alvin Roy, and we hired him. He had been coaching track guys, who did the discus and shot put, and kind of learned on his own how to help football players."

Jordan says he's still a Cowboy fan, but admits that things are a little different now.

"I go to some of the games, give my customers tickets. I took a lot of pride in them when I played for them and, well, even the way the Landry thing was handled it might have turned out the best it could for him. You know, during his last season, they ran a poll here in town and 75 percent thought he should be replaced. But that same group of people, when he got fired, was irate. I mean, irate. It was in the newspapers for days, weeks. Had he been called, had he been given the chance to retire . . . it would have been a lot smoother. But I'm not sure that the love and affection that poured out would have come forth had he been able to do that. Jerry Jones made him a martyr, and they forgot about the 3-13 season and started remembering the Hail Mary and the championship games and the Super Bowls.

"He was abused a little, and the perception was that he wasn't treated fairly, and everybody came to his side. If he had just made a retirement statement, I don't know if the city would have given out that emotion. It was almost fitting, somehow, that after all the things we had been through with this team that his career would end so emotionally, so controversially. I mean, he could have retired and there would have been stories for a couple of days. . . . But this way, the mistreated old man who had won so many championships and Super Bowls . . . how can anybody do that? It went on for weeks, pages and pages of articles, and to me it was fantastic."

And to Lee Roy Jordan, it will always remain the way it was before his hair turned white. It was all sunlight and cheering, Coach Landry and his Cowboys against the world, a new mountain to climb each week, a new war to win each season.

Kind of the way it should be, when legends are created.

"I have talked to players on other teams, who never really won anything," he said, "and I can't tell them what a great feeling it is to have proved that your team is the best there is. It gives you a pride that no individual honor can ever duplicate. And you notice a difference in your relationship with the public, in the special esteem they hold for you. And I think the secret that we had, that made us win, was that it was more important to win for our team and for Coach Tom Landry than it was for ourselves as individuals. Tom inspired that kind of loyalty, and playing for him was an honor. I'm proud of my years with the Cowboys, and I'll never get over that."

The businessman relaxed. It was time to talk about quail hunting—"I just love that, and if I ever get my business where I can, I hope to be able to do a lot less business and a lot more quail hunting between November and February."

And finally, somehow it came as no surprise when he casually mentioned that is favorite movie of all time was "Patton."

No surprise at all, just respect for one great leader from another.

CHAPTER 3

BOB HAYES

THE BLUR

Hi, I'm Bob Hayes. Whooooosh!

By 1964, Bob Hayes was properly billed as The World's Fastest Human. The year before, on June 21, 1963, he had run the 100-yard dash in 9.1 seconds in a semifinal heat at the National AAU championships in St. Louis, Mo. No one in the history of sprinting had ever reached that time. He broke the existing mark of 9.2 set by Frank Budd.

Then, on Oct. 15, 1964, on the other side of the world, in Tokyo, "Bullet Bob" Hayes stood on a platform to accept not one but two gold medals in the Summer Olympic Games. His effort in winning the men's individual 100-meter race has been called the greatest performance in the history of that "headline" distance, and almost 20 years later a panel of track experts from around the world unanimously selected Hayes as the greatest 100-meter sprinter of all time.

Roberto Pariente, then editor of the Paris-based L'Equipe track-and-field magazine, said: "I still consider Bob Hayes' time on a wet cinder track at Tokyo the best ever for that distance."

The day of the race, it had been raining, and the track was still damp. Moreover, the lane to which Hayes had been assigned for the final was the curb lane, next to the grass infield, and it had been chewed up by the 20-kilometer walkers, who had circled it for three laps an hour earlier before proceeding out of the stadium.

The United States' Olympic track coach, Bob Giegengack, tried to convince the officials that since Hayes had run the fastest qualifying time of all the finalists, he be given a more acceptable lane assignment. His plea fell on deaf ears, but they did agree to rake the track, which created a 10-minute delay.

"I remember thinkin' to myself, 'Hey, what's the difference, really?' " Hayes says now. "Man, I knew I was going to run fast, and I figured if I ran as fast as I could, there wasn't anybody in the world who could catch me. Nobody."

The start was predictable. Hayes and his two most legitimate competitors—Canada's Harry Jerome and Cuba's Enrique Figueroa—immediately separated themselves from the rest of the field. But at the 40-meter mark, Hayes just exploded in a burst of acceleration, never slowed down, and hit the tape—without leaning or straining forward—to win by 7 feet, at that time the largest margin of victory in an Olympic 100-meter event.

He equaled the world record and broke the Olympic record in 10.0, and added, in total honesty: "If I had a better lane, I think I would have had a better time." The respected publication, Track and Field News, said in its analysis of the sprint: "It was an almost insulting (winning) margin to an Olympic final field."

Six days later, the United States four by one hundred relay team went for its gold medal. "It was important to us," Hayes recalled, "because our country had always won that event, except for the previous Olympics (1960 in Rome), when Germany took it." And the situation was ripe for another upset when the lead runner for the U.S. team, Paul Drayton, came up with a leg injury—a muscle pull—the morning of the race.

"We were just praying that he'd get through the first leg without pulling the muscle again," Hayes said. "I remember telling him that if he could do it, if he could tough it out, we'd win." Drayton made it, but barely, and in the final step of allowable space he got the baton into the second-leg racer, Gerry Ashworth.

Another Hayes memory: "I told the other guys, Gerry and Richard (Stebbins), that if they just stayed within three or four yards until I got the baton, we'd win," he said. "They looked at me as if I was crazy."

Well, Ashworth and Stebbins kept it close, all right. "Yeah, we were in sixth place, maybe fifth, when I got the baton from Steb," the Bullet said. "And I knew we had to win, so I knew what I had to do, and I did it."

Some say it was the fastest 100-meter leg ever run. One of the Dallas assistant coaches, Red Hickey, was in Tokyo, and he said the time was 8.6 seconds. "But of course," he added, "that would be impossible."

The 19-year-old Hayes had pulled off the impossible.

Exactly 15 years later—to the day—he was in prison, and the only sprinting he did was on the sunbaked ground in south Texas.

"The irony," he said, "did not escape me. There I was in prison, after representing my country, for a crime I didn't do. Fifteen years earlier I was on the awards platform and they're putting medals around my neck . . . the national anthem of the United States was playing, and I was remembering how I used to sing it in class in Jacksonville . . . the flag was rising, my country's flag, to honor me . . . my mother was sitting in the stadium with my idol, (1936 Olympic four gold-medal winner) Jesse Owens . . . a hundred million people around the world were watching me in the Olympics, applauding for me, cheering for me . . . and then I was in jail. Go ahead, tell me about putting things in perspective.

"It was like death."

He paused, and a palpable pain washed over his face, that reflecting pool of the mind and the soul.

"It. Was. Like. Death. And it was unjust."

Hayes spent 10 months in that jail in the Texas State penitentiary in Midway, 20 miles outside Huntsville, and when he got out he found his worlds had changed . . . both the one around him and, more importantly, the one inside him, where Bob Hayes really lived.

"I lost my family, my wife divorced me and took my children," he began. "I had a job. Lost it. I had television endorsements scheduled, signed. Gone. I was really running on empty, man, and it took a long, long time . . . and a stint in an alcohol-abuse clinic . . . to get me back."

It was a setup, a manipulation, and there is a strong feeling that if Bob Hayes had been a white man in Dallas in 1977, when he was arrested and charged with selling cocaine to an undercover policeman, it never would have happened. But there he was, in a city he has come to call home, a city he sometimes loves to hate, other times hates to love, but does.

"Anybody who knows a guy selling drugs . . . somebody will know it. But not one person in America could have said they knew I was selling, nobody. And the guys who bought it, and the guys who sold it . . . they did not go to jail. Only I did.

"You know, I've talked about this so much I'm just burned out on it, but every time it comes up I notice the effect is still there. It is still something I'm paying for, something I never did. Something I'm stuck with because some guy got jealous."

Jealous? Selling drugs? The story, burnout or not, begs to be told once more.

Bob Hayes nods his head—wearily?—and begins to describe the start of the end of his happiness.

"My secretary . . . I was workin' for this company (in Dallas), and I was out of town. Anyway, at the end of the day her boyfriend comes to pick her up, and he's the undercover cop, see? But by now, they're sitting around smokin' a joint, and the secretary has fallen in love with a black former Dallas Cowboy—. . . used to loan him her car, give him money, everything."

He pauses, shakes his head and insists: "No, not me."

"Anyway, so her boyfriend finds out about it . . . yeah, man, they were sleeping together, too . . . and he just made the assumption that it was 'Super-nigger,' which is what he used to call me, Bob Hayes. She also told me she had just gotten a divorce from her husband and needed some medicine, and we had a buddy, a close buddy, who owned a pharmacy, and I'd help her there.

"So they tried to connect this all together, that we were dealing in drugs, you know. Well, the boyfriend comes into my life, makes friends with me, wines and dines me for six months and finally, one night, he asks me if I could get him a gram of cocaine. Well, I had a friend . . . a next-door neighbor . . . who was a user but not a seller. I introduced them to each other. But every time this guy, the cop, would call me, it turns out, he was hooked up to a telephone, and my answering machine, always, was kind of silly.

You know, 'Hi, this is Bullet Bob Hayes, old number 22, the former Dallas Cowboy' . . . that kind of stuff, but it sure did identify me on the tapes, you know?

"I'm tryin' to get this gram of cocaine for the guy, from this other guy I knew, but he (the cop) would never go through the neighbor, always through me. And for 700 dollars on three different occasions . . . two grams here, three grams, two grams . . . one of the times transacted over my desk. One of the guys who owned the company also bought, and the guy who sold it did not go to jail, and the guy who bought it did not go to jail, only Bullet Bob Hayes went to jail.

"And of everybody involved, I was the only black."

Lawyers . . . police . . . judges . . . everybody was told the story. Everybody's response was sadly the same: Tough shit, nigger.

"They had no witnesses against me, nothing but character witnesses came up, and they all said I just couldn't have done it. I don't think it would have happened in New York, but it would have in the South. It took away my family, my pride, my self-esteem. I have caught a lot of hell since then. I'm just written off by a lot of people. They just turn their backs on me. I started drinking, finally had to go to a rehab, just to see what was wrong with me. I did some cocaine after I got out, but I never shot up, never freebased, nothing like that."

It became a time of hard facts, of painful realizations. Bob Hayes learned things about himself he never wanted to know, and how he coped, how he handled this new nightmare, was responsible for the man he has finally become.

"My character defect, everything, was just in a puzzle. I couldn't put it together, didn't know how. It was a bad time, man. I wasn't sure I was going to make it. But then Roger Staubach, and a good friend, Ronny Horowitz, came on board and said, 'Hey, Bobby, let's try it this way, because your life is going down, man.' See, all the stories I had ever heard about people doing drugs and alcohol, how bad they were, I never compared myself to those people, man. I never went that far. But see, you don't compare yourself to others, you compare yourself to your own self in the mirror, you take an inventory and see where you stand.

"So anyway, I found out who I was, finally. For five years, from 1980 to 1985, I was just drifting in my mind, trying to be a human being adjusting to society after being in the spotlight. I was trying to do without that celebrity stuff. I got caught up in the arrest thing . . . just within myself, and I couldn't live a normal life. Folks always treated me special—special good or special bad. They just couldn't deal with me as some guy named Bob Hayes. It was always Bob Hayes, the world's fastest human. Or Bullet Bob Hayes. Or Bob Hayes, the former Dallas Cowboy. You know, 'Hey, Bob, let me see your Super Bowl ring, man . . . let me see your gold medals . . . tell me about Meredith, or Staubach, or does Coach Landry ever smile.' It was just me, man, Bob Hayes. But nobody could see me, they only saw the hero stuff."

Bob Hayes never saw the undercover Dallas policeman again, and it is a sign of his maturity that he never tried to, either.

"What could I have gained? Go after him? He's a law enforcement officer. It's probably what I would have done, see, and I never wanted to get near anything like that again. No more police, no more jails, none of that, man. It ruined my life.

"And it really did, you know. Financially and emotionally, even spiritually. I lost a lot of money. Hershey Foods had me under contract, they voided that out. I had a commercial set up with Miller Lite, and they cut me off on that. I was going to do something with the Olympics, and that was cancelled.

"But now, man, things are a little better. I got my kids back in my life, but I've been divorced for 10 years, so it isn't the same. You know, I see them sometimes, but they live with their mother."

Bottom line truths emerged. Being black and living in Dallas, Hayes insists, is what landed him in jail. So flimsy a case would never have proceeded all the way to a prison sentence in most other places; nor would it have in Dallas today.

"Man, I love Dallas. I'm still here, aren't I, after everything that happened? But Dallas is not exactly ideal, you know. Today, if you're driving your car and you move into the line of traffic a little too fast, ahead of another car, you'll still get a finger, a shout, and usually you'll hear something like 'Hey, nigger, where you goin'?' But at least in Dallas . . . in the South you know exactly where you stand. Some cities up north, Boston, maybe, they won't say a thing, they'll just burn your house down one night, and the next morning the same guy, your neighbor, will come up and shake your hand and tell you how sorry he is at what happened.

"At least I know what Dallas is all about. When I first got to Dallas, it was a problem for blacks. We all had to live in the south Oak Cliff section, all of us. Me, Don Perkins, Mel Renfro, Jethro Pugh, Pettis Norman . . . we all had to live together. Even on the road, man, we had segregation. All the whites roomed together, all the blacks roomed together. And this bothered me, it really did. You know, what President Kennedy had said, 'Ask not what your country can do for you, but what you can do for your country.' Man, I tried. I had gone to the Olympics, I wanted to go. I ran against white boys, I roomed with them, we ate together. But when I came back home with my gold medals, it was the same old thing. Like the guys who came back from Vietnam later on. Nobody seemed to care.

"And it's still computerized that way in Dallas. We have this black college here in town, Bishop College. And with all the money in this town, with all the balls and the testimonials that are held to raise money for education . . . man, here's an institution of higher learning, right here in town . . . to teach minority students. Well, Bishop College ran into financial troubles and had to go into Chapter 11, and you know what? Nobody came on board to help, nobody in this town. Very few, anyway. Seems to me like if you have an institution that old, that has turned out that many teachers, with that credibility, and they let it go down because of a million dollars. There are people in this town who spend that much money on plants for their offices.

"But still, Dallas is my place. I love Dallas. I just know what Dallas is all about. Dallas is getting better, even though there are still sections where you can't buy a house or rent an apartment. I remember one day Renfro saw this ad for a new development of apartments. So he called. And they said, 'Hey, sure, we got a lot of 'em left, come on over.' But when he got there and they saw he was black . . . see, Mel was from Oregon, and he had no 'black-type' accent, they said, 'Hey, no, man, they all gone, just half an hour ago.'

"And even later, Tony Dorsett had a fight in some club because they were hassling him . . . because he got in on his name, on the Dallas Cowboys thing, but a lot of the employees and the other guests just didn't like it. Dallas is still part of Texas, you know. Texas just doesn't stress education, and the way blacks are received in this town is not OK. But it's better. But people here have opened their minds, and the city is getting a lot more aggressive with respect to minorities.

"My all time football hero was Lenny Moore. Man, I laced up my shoes like he did, I tried to walk like he did . . . he played for the Baltimore Colts in the '50s and early '60s, and you always know what he thinks. He said when he got to Baltimore, it was as bad as being in any city in the Deep South, and this was a long time ago, when things all over (for blacks) were worse.

"So suddenly he became a star, and the restaurants he couldn't get into now wanted him to be there, be seen there, he couldn't pay for his dinner, everybody was putting their arms around him. He said he didn't want any of that. If I wasn't good enough as Lenny Moore, then I wasn't good enough as Lenny Moore the football star, either.

"I feel the same way. But you know, life still goes on, life progresses, and you can't change things all by yourself. Coach Landry . . . this was one of the things I learned from him . . . he'd say, 'If you want to succeed, Bob, you got to stay one step ahead of the pack.' I cannot live in the past, I have to look to the future. I have to deal with reality. Grow, mature, self balance. If the bad things about you outweigh the good things, then you work on the bad things to get rid of them, to achieve a balance. That's what I've been doing. There are people who have changed, who have matured, and some of them are my ex-teammates.

"Right now, those are some of the best guys in the world, you know? But years ago . . . like Dan Reeves (the current head coach of the Denver Broncos). He's from Americus, Georgia . . . and he went to the University of South Carolina . . . and he probably never did associate with a black guy. And he and Don Meredith were the fairest white boys on the team, didn't care who was white, who was black. I don't think I can say that about many of the others."

Players of yesterday are no different from those of today in terms of needing off-season incomes. And in Dallas, when Bob Hayes was a star, there just weren't many such opportunities.

"Lee Roy Jordan had work, Bob Lilly had work. All the white guys were driving company cars. But the blacks didn't have that kind of chance. Drew Pearson worked for a moving-van company, loading trucks. I worked for baseball-cap companies. I went to real estate school but couldn't get my license."

There is a sadness here, real and substantial. Bob Hayes has not had an easy life. The ghetto . . . the segregation and bigotry . . . then the American hero experience in Tokyo only to be followed by more of the same when he returned . . . finally the end-of-the-world nightmare in prison.

"You know, the Pepsi-Cola Company has stuck by me. I run the Bob Hayes Invitational Track Meet in Florida, and those people sponsor it," he says. "At Raines High School, in northwest Jacksonville. See, my old school, Matthew Gilbert High School, and everybody was transferred to Raines. I get a lot of athletes there, black athletes. But it's not a black track meet . . . couldn't be, with my name on it. We have over a hundred high schools every year, from the United States, Canada, the Bahamas. You know what's neat? There are displays all over Jacksonville for the track meet . . . with a big cardboard cutout of me . . . and years ago, when I was growing up there, I couldn't even walk into some of those stores and supermarkets because I was black.

"But with a company like Pepsi, knowing the problems I've had, and still supporting me . . . well, that tells me something about that company."

Growing up in that environment, Hayes credits his mother with providing the crucial lessons that kept him from swerving toward bitterness and hatred.

"My mother . . . she was a domestic worker in Jacksonville . . . she always told me, 'Son, whatever you love, you can always bring it home, I don't care what color it is, what denomination.' I don't love a person for the pigment of his skin. From a ghetto called Hell Hole in Jacksonville, man, it was a tough life. I grew up right there by the Gator Bowl, and it was exactly what you'd think a ghetto in the South would be like. It was terrible. It was predominantly black, blue-collar workers. You know, get paid on Fridays, get drunk on Saturdays, go to church on Sundays, be broke on Mondays.

"I saw all the temptations then, as a kid; I was really lucky to get out of that environment. One thing that helped, I think, was that the Milwaukee (now Atlanta) Braves had a farm team, the Jacksonville Braves, and I would go there to stare at Hank Aaron, just stare at him, realize how far he had gone and he was a black man. When he got to the major leagues, he married a girl, Barbara, who was the sister of a friend of mine in Jacksonville, from the neighborhood, and the Braves came down to play the Brooklyn Dodgers. We were Dodger fans, of course, because of Jackie Robinson, and I'd look at him, number 42 . . . and everybody compared me with Jackie. You know, we looked the same . . . got that posture, ass sticks in the air, pigeon-toed. And I was best in my neighborhood in all sports, speed, quickness. Well, my daddy wasn't into education, that wasn't his top priority.

"He owned these shoeshine parlors, pool halls . . . anyway, I got a football scholarship (to Florida A&M) . . . and I didn't play football until the 11th grade. Anyway, I got the offer and my daddy was only worryin' about who would stay and watch the shoeshine parlor after school, so I had to find a friend who would do it. Then I got the scholarship and told my daddy I needed some money to go to college, for clothes, stuff like that.

"He said no, he wasn't givin' me any money for such foolishness like college, but my uncle, he gave me 25 dollars. And it cost me five dollars for a train ticket, so I went to school with 20 dollars in my pocket."

Bob Hayes went to A&M because of the coach, Jake "Pop" Gaithers, who was to black kids in the South what Bear Bryant, who coached at Alabama, was to the white kids. "When he said he wanted me to play for him, it didn't matter where else I had a chance to go. If Jake thought I could play for him, then I would."

Bob Hayes, untrained and unrefined, was embarking on a football-education odyssey that would be administered by two of the most respected minds in the game—Jake Gaithers and Tom Landry.

"You know, Jake sent about 20 players to the NFL," Hayes said. "I mean, guys who wound up playing five, six, 10 years. He was a pro coach, I think you could say, without being in the pros. And he stayed at Florida A&M all his years, because Jake was black, you see, and there just weren't many other opportunities open to him.

"I went to play for Jake because all of my friends, all the kids in the state, really, used to taunt each other, say stuff like: 'Hey, man, you ain't good enough to play for Coach Gaither. You just ain't.' It was a challenge, and as it turned out, the guy who was raised up with me, Curtis Miranda . . . I mean, we were friends since we were little boys . . . he became A&M's first three-time All-America and the first black middle linebacker ever to be drafted by a pro football team . . . the Giants drafted him (in the fifth round of 1962, but he did not make the team).

"We sent a lot of guys to the pros from my teams at A&M, like Clarence Childs (Giants), Carlton Oakes (Raiders), Bobby Phelps (Lions), Herman Lee (Bears), Al Denson (Broncos), Art Robinson (Cowboys) . . . we had a bunch of guys, man. Jake was ahead of his time, football-wise. Just look at that spread formation he put in. The offense was lined up damned near across the field, great big gaps between every lineman, the defenses just didn't know how to deal with it. Jake won every award a black coach could receive . . . matter of fact, in small colleges now, in the black schools, instead of the Heisman Trophy they have in major colleges, they have the A.S. "Jake" Gaither Award. And I know a lot of coaches, college and pro coaches, used to go to see the A&M games—usually we played on Friday nights—to see what Jake was doing with his offense.

"I don't know how many ever met him, but they sure did learn from him. He had a lot of influence on people and he never knew it."

There is the The Bob Hayes Track Meet, sponsored by Pepsico

Inc. It has been one of the critical developments in Bob Hayes's after-football, after-jail, after-rehab life, because Pepsico Inc. stayed with him, record or not, and because he became visible in his home state in the sport in which he first became famous.

Bob Hayes is the man who changed the face of pro football's defenses. He was too fast to cover man-to-man when he arrived for the 1965 season. "Bobby was the only receiver I could never overthrow," quarterback Don Meredith once joked, "and God knows I overthrew a passel of 'em in my time, when I didn't want to."

Hayes smiles when reminded of that statement, and then, serious again, reflects on what Tom Landry really meant to him, to his football career and, more recently, to his personal life.

"First of all, I just can't say how I felt when I heard about the firing," he begins. "I had been following the sale negotiations closely, in the newspapers, on radio and television, because, hey, this is my team, too. I'm still a Cowboy fan. I still go to all the games I can. I think for a long time I was the most notorious of the Cowboys. You know, the advertising used to be something like: 'This Sunday why not come out and see the Dallas Cowboys and Bob Hayes, the World's Fastest Human.' You know, you just don't lose the feeling for what was a major part of your life.

"Anyway, when it happened, and how it happened, I felt like . . . like a member of my family had died, like my mom or my dad. I mean, one day he's leaving his office, with his playbook under his hand, and a reporter walks up to him and says, 'Hey, Coach Landry, I heard the team was just sold and you're out.' All he said was, I don't know, something like, 'Well, I haven't heard anything, thank you very much, no further comment.' And then he just closed the window of his car and drove off.

"I mean, the man had a playbook under his arm, he had been working on getting ready for a minicamp the next month. The coaches had done all the preparation, all the work, and he really wanted that team, that last season. He was really ready to make it all happen."

The 1988 Cowboys had come in with a 3-13 record, so lowly it had stunned, more than angered, the local fans. Not since the first season, the 0-11-1 inaugural year of 1960, had the Cowboys failed to win at least four games. Now, suddenly, the man who had already become a legend became human, vulnerable, the head coach of a collection of castoffs and extremely ordinary players.

"Tom Landry was ready, and if he had coached, I know in my heart he would have won seven, eight games last season. In my heart. He had rejuvenated his feelings, his thinking, his dedication, to the Dallas Cowboys and their fans. But the man who owned the team, Bum Bright, was just in it for the dollars, as a business. He always was. He should have said something to the coach, you know? I mean, how could he have just forgotten all those years, all those championships, everything coach Landry had come to mean to the team?

"Hey, the coach was a tradition, a Hall of Famer, and this man was just some business guy, who looked at it only from a business standpoint. So Tom flew himself and his wife down to Austin that night, and when it was finally official, when Jerry Jones had bought the team, he and Tex Schramm got into a private jet and flew down to Austin to face him, to tell him he would not be returning as the head coach of the Dallas Cowboys. Why not give him an option . . . to resign, to retire . . . why just cut him loose? That old man is deeply hurt, deeply hurt."

Jimmy Johnson, the coach appointed by Jerry Jones, a man who developed national championship teams at the University of Miami, has had no choice but to take a bad rap ever since the firing, according to Hayes.

"Hey, you can't boo a guy who never shows up at games, who people wouldn't recognize anyway," he says. "You can't boo the guy who sold the team and never shows up. So they boo the coach on the field, and I'll tell you this, Jimmy Johnson is a good coach and maybe he's going to make something out of this group, and maybe he's not, but he deserves the chance. I don't think anybody's gripe should be with him. With Bright? With Jones? Even with Schramm? Yeah, sure. But not the coach. He's just a coach, man, and he's the one on the front lines, on the field."

But that, as Bullet Bob says, is in the past. That's history. And yet, history of another sort began to take shape when Hayes reached the Dallas Cowboys in 1965.

"I had learned a lot of football from Jake Gaithers before I got to the Cowboys," he said. "I mean, a lot of football, and I was well prepared when I got to Dallas. But it was nothing compared to what I learned from Coach Landry. He taught me more about football than I ever dreamed I could learn.

"See, I was a football player in college who also ran track. Most of the track guys were just that, track guys, and if they played some football, it was mostly just to try to take advantage of their speed. But I had always been a football player. I mean, coaches tried to change my running style, my form, and I just laughed and told them that I got to be the world's fastest human running my way, why in the world would I want to even think about changing?"

Hayes the sprinter comes with another facet. He did it all wrong, you see. Bud Winter, who coached track at San Jose State and developed such world-class sprinters as John Carlos and Tommie Smith, said Hayes ran "like he was pounding grapes into wine. He really hit the track hard. He was all flapping arms and he ran pigeon-toed and he looked like a crow tryin' to get started."

But there was no way to predict how Hayes would take to pro football, where the hitting is fierce and the margin for error excruciatingly slim.

"All we really knew," said Landry, "was that we had drafted and signed (for three years at $50,000 a year) a kid with 9.1 speed. Now we had to spend the summer training-camp time trying to find out if he had any football abilities we could use, too."

There was genuine concern when the All-Star rookies played the current NFL champions, the Cleveland Browns, in Chicago that July. Hayes was fast, all right, but he kept dropping the ball, and it never occurred to the coaches there that his hand, which had been stepped on and punctured by a teammate's cleats in practice, was too sore, too tender, to take the impact of a football.

"When he came to our camp in Thousand Oaks," Landry remembers, "and when we saw how well he really could catch—not great, mind you, but very good—we started to relax a little. And then he had that catch."

It was spoken of with reverence, as if the words were capitalized and in boldface. THAT. CATCH.

It happened in the final exhibition game of the summer of '65, as the Cowboys were tuning up for the regular-season opener the next week. The game was in Tulsa, Okla., and the rookie quarterback, Jerry Rhome (like Hayes a future draft choice the year before) was on the field.

Maybe Rhome was in the game because he had impressed Coach Landry sufficiently that summer. Maybe it was for a reason as mundane as that he had played his college years right there, for the University of Tulsa, in the same stadium.

Anyway, on a third-and-long, with Hayes split out well to Rhome's left, the hopeful young quarterback dropped back and . . . well, he said the ball got away from him. It flew. It traveled nearly 60 yards in the air and there was nobody even close to it as it headed for the end zone.

"It was so badly overthrown," said local sportswriter Sam Blair, who covered the game that night, "that the Bears' defenders just shrugged and stopped running back. They knew . . . everybody knew . . . that nobody could catch it."

Right. And then there was Bobby Hayes, the World's Fastest Human, sprinting toward the end zone. "Blurring, that's how his legs looked," Blair recalled. And as the ball began to descend, there was Hayes, in a deep, dark corner of the end zone, jogging under it, cradling it in his hands, then casually dropping it into the end zone.

"Even as we were flying back to Dallas," Landry smiles, "I was starting to draw up new passing plays, and I knew I had to start him when the season opened. I knew he was a rookie and didn't have much experience, but Lord, what a weapon. What a weapon."

Hayes remembers that early the following Tuesday morning— usually a day off—the Cowboys' public relations director called him at home. "He told me to come up to the practice field to take a picture, and I asked him what for. He said never mind that, he'll

tell me when I got there. So I showed up and they had me posing
with the football and running with it until they were satisfied.
Then he told me I was going to be starting the next Sunday at
home against the New York Giants."

In the first two regular-season games for the Cowboys that
year—against the Giants and Redskins—Hayes caught only four
passes. Three, however, went for touchdowns, and he would finish
that rookie season with a dozen TDs along with his 46 receptions
and 1,003 yards. It was only the second time in league history that
a rookie receiver had surpassed 1,000 yards. The first had been
tight end Mike Ditka, who had 1,076 yards for the Bears in 1961.

"We had captured something rare," said Landry, "and we had
to figure out the best way to use him. It was almost a revolutionary
concept. We could defeat most pass defenses just by letting him
run, of course, but once they began to adjust to that, we had all
the other players, and we could have him make a move to the inside, to the outside . . . I remember our staff being really excited,
I mean more so than usual, just thinking of the ways we could
put Bobby into the flow of the passing game."

Hayes was an apt pupil, mostly because Jake Gaithers had so
completely prepared him for the pro game.

"I knew about audibles, changing plays at the line of scrimmage. I knew about the pro set, the motion, the pocket-passing
attack, red-right, brown-right, red-left, brown-left . . . flankers and
split ends and all that stuff. Why? Because Coach Gaithers, when
he saw we didn't know something, he'd conduct a clinic, man. He
had pro coaches come in and teach us. Bear Bryant came to lecture. Frank Broyles, who coached all those years at Arkansas, he
came to lecture. Schools in those two conferences (the SEC and
the SWC), incidentally, were starting to accept blacks, give them
student-athlete scholarships, and I guess those two men, at least,
saw the wisdom of doing that kind of thing. So I was ready when
I got to Dallas. I had a choice, too. There were still two leagues
then, and Denver from the American Football League had drafted
me, too. But no, man, I didn't want to go to a new league. I wanted
the NFL, which had all the publicity, which was the one I had
watched when I was a kid.

"You know, in all honesty I wanted to play for the Giants or the Pittsburgh Steelers or the Baltimore Colts, because those were the only teams on television in Jacksonville. And the Washington Redskins, too, but nuh-uh, I didn't want to play for them, because they weren't taking black players when every other team was. But when Dallas drafted me as a future . . . you know, me and Roger Staubach were the two most famous future draft choices the team ever had (Staubach was the 10th-round pick in 1964, Hayes the seventh) . . . I knew I'd be going to the big leagues."

Hayes began breaking ground of his own, too. He was the first black player to take part in the Senior Bowl postseason game in Mobile, Ala. (along with two All-America players from the South, quarterback Joe Namath of Alabama and fullback Tucker Frederickson of Auburn).

"I got more attention when I got to camp than the Heisman Trophy winner would have," he said. "Can he make it? We know he can run but can he take a hit? Can he catch the ball? Will he go across the middle? I figure somebody on the Cowboys had the answers to that or they wouldn't have drafted me, you know?"

At first, Landry included Hayes only as a peripheral receiver, instructing Meredith to use him only for the quick screens and back, quick screens and up, just a few over the middle. Nothing yet, nothing big, because that wasn't the conservative, cautious Landry way.

"He worked me in slowly," Hayes remembered. "Nothing too fast, nothing I couldn't handle. I was impatient, sure, but now I understand why he did it and what he was doing and I was grateful that I didn't have too much of the pressure too soon."

One of the Giants' rookies that day was a strong safety named Henry Carr, who had been on the Olympic team with Hayes, and the two of them had developed a strong friendship. A traveling sportswriter, asking Carr about Hayes on the Giants' charter flight to Dallas, wondered what would happen if a pass intended for Hayes was intercepted on the goal line by Carr, who then raced it 100 yards back upfield. Would Hayes have caught him?"

Carr had responded with bravado. "Nope, I'd score," he had said.

Now, finally, a quarter of a century later, the sportswriter thought to pose that same question to Hayes. "Would I have been able to catch Hank Carr? You damned right I would have caught him," said Bullet Bob. "You damned right I would have caught him."

The emergence of this track star was not a new experience for the Cowboys. Cornell Green, who made several All-Pro teams at cornerback and safety, was a basketball star at Utah State. So, too, was wide receiver–tight end Pete Gent of Michigan State, a basketball-only athlete in college. Rayfield Wright, the All-Pro offensive tackle, played basketball at Fort Valley State. Years later, the Cowboys drafted Olympic record-setter Carl Lewis, but he declined to play pro football.

Matching Hayes with Meredith, Landry set in motion a chemical reaction that burned through the National Football League. "See, I always thought Don Meredith was the best quarterback I ever played with," Hayes said. "He knew when to fire the ball, when to float it, he was always accurate, he was tough and he was always thinking out there. I'm not saying he was the best quarterback, but he's the one I spent the most time with and I guess we got to know each other real well."

But Bob Hayes, the man who made the creation of the zone defense necessary, also became its first victim. "Bob just wouldn't wait for the defense to commit itself," said Landry. "He just figured he could outrun everybody, and maybe in man-to-man coverage he could, but not through a zone. But you know, catching passes against a zone defense is really simple. That kid who just retired from Seattle . . . Steve Largent? . . . I mean, he wasn't fast at all. But he knew where the zone responsibilities started and ended, he knew where there wouldn't be a guy, even for a split second, and he used his head to find the holes in the zone, the creases.

"Bobby just didn't want to wait. I mean, I understood it, because he was a sprinter, faster than anybody who had ever played football, and it must have been really frustrating to him. Even the way I used him must have been frustrating, because sometimes he was just a decoy, and I know he didn't like that."

Hayes smiles, years after the fact, and shakes his head up and down in agreement. "What happened was I got frustrated because I wasn't receiving any passes. I got incentive clauses in my contract, I got two or three guys covering me, I'm not getting the ball, I'm just running around. You know, you decoy for the whole year, you get complacent. It wasn't so much the zone, they just didn't seem to be able to find a way to get the ball to me. I didn't even mind going over the middle, I could take a hit, always could."

There was also Bob Hayes, the punt returner.

His face lit up at the remembrance of punts past, of plainly embarrassing—for there is no better word—professional athletes who are accustomed to pain and perseverance and success, who are inured to the possibility of a season-ending, or career-ending, injury, but who never, absolutely, positively never—expect to be embarrassed.

The odds, if you will, are all in the coverage team's favor. The punt is sailing downfield, high and excruciatingly slowly, for the man poised, frozen and concentrating only on the skies. Meanwhile, a horde of strong, fast, incredibly physical men are hurtling downfield at him. He is their only target, and their mission is to prevent him from gaining even one yard once he catches the ball. A peripheral objective is to make him so nervous, to fill him with such dread of serious bodily harm, that he might, for a second, lose his concentration and—hurrah!—drop the ball.

Scouts and coaches say it takes a particularly brave man, with ice water in his veins, with quickness and speed and strength, to be a successful punt returner in the National Football League. Most of them do not add that they would like him not to be overly bright, either, because anyone with a modicum of intelligence will, after a while, begin to question his role in life and why he seems so intent on ending it during its prime.

There have been a few exceptional punt returners, who may or may not have achieved real celebrity stature in the NFL at a position. Years and years ago, it was Emlen Tunnell. Then Abe Woodson. More recently, it has been such as Travis Williams and Gerald McNeil. But nobody ever returned punts with more flair, excitement and success than Bob Hayes.

One of the more articulate coaches in the league at the time of the Hayes invasion was Allie Sherman of the Giants, and since he had spent years working with Tom Landry on the New York staff, he had all the reason he would ever need to want to beat the Cowboys. But after the first few years, he almost never did, and by the time his coaching career ended in 1968, he had compiled a 6-8-2 record against the new and quickly developing Cowboys.

One day, discussing Bob Hayes and the punt return phenomenon, he phrased the difficulty thusly: "Try to imagine wearing a pair of those asbestos kitchen mitts," he said, "and then imagine trying to pick up a small globule of mercury from a glass-top table. That was how it seemed when you tried to stop Bob Hayes on a punt return."

The one Hayes remembers most came on Thanksgiving Day of 1968, in Dallas, against the St. Louis (these days living in Phoenix) Cardinals.

"Yeah, I remember turning the game around, because it was pretty close until then," he said. "I'm waiting for the ball and so are a bunch of the Cardinals, or that's how it seemed. I guess the punter really put up a good one. Anyway, I turned and twisted away from one guy, made a little move on another one . . . kind of felt two or three others get their hands on me but I kept dancing and jukin', you know, and suddenly, man, I saw an opening.

"Then I had the whole field, except for the punter, who never had a chance, and I ran away catty-corner to the end zone. When I came back to the sideline, the bench area, I remember Dan Reeves saying: 'Man, you really opened up those pipes that time.' That really opened up the game, and that's what we wanted to do."

Landry used to tell Hayes that the first obligation for the big play was his. "Bob was going to get the first chance, whether on a long pass play or a punt return," he explained. "You need to make big plays to win games. You just can't win 'em otherwise. You can't."

Hayes nods his head in agreement. "When you're in the right defense, and the offense comes in and still makes a big play, a long pass, a long run, especially for a touchdown . . . that really brings the defense down, man. I mean, they were doing everything right, you see? They knew what to do and how to do it, and it was the best situation for them to be in, the right one. And we still come out there and make them look silly . . . get them to be chasing a guy and all they see is the back of his jersey, and it's gettin' smaller . . . man, that kills them. Some of the younger guys, especially, the ones who haven't had the experience yet, the ones who are immature, they'll start second-guessing themselves, and that's when you get another one, and pretty soon the game is gone, man. I mean, it's ours, and they just don't really know how that happened to them.

"The big play did it, man. It always does."

What does Hayes remember most about Landry? In most cases, with others interviewed, there were just a few words; labels, perhaps, of perception.

But Hayes saw more, remembered more.

"Religious man . . . the cap on his head, always . . . in the meeting rooms . . . on the (black)board, going over each play, each position . . . offense, defense, the kicking game . . . and he was knowledgeable about each and every position. You could ask him a question for a variation on those plays and he would immediately turn around and answer, spontaneously. The answers were always there, because he had thought about all the possible variations and solved the puzzles before you even had a chance to think of one small adjustment.

"No, I was never afraid of him. He was always the kind who never got real close to his athletes . . . always a thinking man, always preoccupied. He didn't have time . . . very warm man on the field, never heard him use a bad word except for 'hell' and 'damn,' but he could get angry, really angry. And he never got mad if we lost a game, but even when we won, he'd get outraged if we broke down, made a mental error, didn't do what the play called for us to do.

"But I'll change what I said, a little. Everybody had some fear when it got to be Monday mornings, and we gathered together for the first review of the film of the game the day before. Then we all knew he was going to jump on us, we knew it, no matter how well we did, we knew he wasn't going to be a happy man.

"I mean, we could have won the game by 40 points, and he'd come in with that damned yellow pad of his, and he'd go over 60 mistakes I made and 40 that Lilly made and about a thousand that others guys would get called out for, and he always did it in public. And you know what? We're sittin' there and I'm thinking about guys from other teams, all around the country, sittin' in their meeting rooms watching their films and I'm wondering if they're catching the same kind of hell for losing that we were catching after we won.

"Probably not, you know? But that made us win, because guys on Sunday thought of that Monday morning session and we were just terrified to be singled out. He kept us always thinking, always on our toes, always off-balance, somehow. I know he designed it like that. He was a master of psychology, knew how to motivate his players . . . and sometimes he motivated by fear. But it was strange, you know? We were never in fear of him, only of how he could be, of what he would say in front of everybody else. It was very strange, really. We liked him, but we were still afraid of the things he'd do."

And now, faced with, as he puts it, "the rest of my life," what does Bob Hayes do? Where does he go and how does he cope?

"When I was in the rehab," he says, "a lady told me that we have to try to rid ourselves of our egos. She said: 'Bob, ego stands for three words: Easing, God, Out.' And that is going to be my answer. I want to live the rest of this life the way God would want me to, and that's really the only thing I'm going to think about.

"You see guys who are nice, sweet, and then suddenly they go off the deep end. They can't relate, they can't cope. They have eased God out of their lives, as I did when I ran into all my troubles. He got me out of them, and now I am going to make Him proud of me."

And yet . . . and yet . . . there are athletes who reached certain usually unattainable pinnacles, who love to talk about the way it was, those years clearly being the best of their lives.

"I remember how tough it was for receivers when I came up,"

Hayes said. "I mean, playing today is a picnic, the way the rules protect a wide receiver. When I played, everything was legal. I got speared . . . Dick Butkus used to clothesline me . . . head slaps, tripping, everything. Now, man, the defensive players can't touch you after the first five yards (from the line of scrimmage)? Man, if I'm playin' today, I'm gone on every down. If I get by the first man, I'm history. But I played against guys . . . linebackers from the Giants and Packers, Rams . . . they were animals, those guys. I mean, they didn't just take their uniforms off after a game, they ripped 'em off . . . and then they'd lick themselves clean. They didn't even need to shower, man. Guys like Butkus and Nitschke and Dave Robinson and Sam Huff and Willie Lanier and Lee Roy Caffey . . . Herb Adderley, Irv Cross.

"And you know what? I'm sure glad I came in after Gino Marchetti (Baltimore defensive end) retired. I'm glad I didn't play against him, that kid came to play and he was tougher than anybody I ever saw. And Andy Robustelli, and Ernie Stautner. Man, I know those guys were crazy. And those fans who say this guy or that one doesn't want to get hit? Hey, who wants to get hit? That hurts, man. You got to be crazy to want to get hit.

"People around here always said Tony Dorsett didn't want to get hit. Well, I don't blame him. I didn't want to get hit, either. And they accused him of leaving the ball on the ground too much, you know? Well, damn, he was just 190 pounds, and it gets tough to hold on when those monsters are cracking you in half. But ol' Tony used to embarrass the hell out of them in the open field, remember? Whoosh! That man could have been a world-class sprinter. Do you know I saw him run a 9.6 hundred in tennis shoes? Honest."

Sprinting . . . sprinters . . . the world of track and field, where Bob Hayes first became a world figure, has bypassed him now. "It's too far away, too long ago," he says. "The kids know I did something, but they aren't sure what. And I don't think I can coach anybody in the sprints, because I never really did it the right way. I just ran, man. I just ran."

Yeah. Faster than anybody else in the world.

And nobody who was there will ever forget him or the impact he made.

CHAPTER 4

DREW PEARSON

OLD RELIABLE

Even now, six years later, telling the story brings tears to his eyes. His chin starts to quiver and, because he feels he must, Drew Pearson turns his head to hide his emotions.

But he rights himself, and begins to speak, the pain more than emotional now, a visceral torment.

"We had a game in Colgate, Oklahoma, which is about a three-hour bus ride from Dallas," Drew Pearson said. "You see, I was in charge of the Cowboys' off-season basketball team, and we'd get a lot of the guys involved, they'd make some off-season money, stay in shape, and give local charities the chance to raise funds for their cause. It was good for the Cowboys' image, too, because we did it right and nobody got hurt or cheated, so they gave us their blessings.

"Anyway, we took a chartered bus up to Colgate . . . nine or 10 guys . . . and it was a good promotion, everybody had a good time, the local charity made some money. It was fine. So now we're comin' back on the bus, everybody's playin' cards, I'm kickin' (wide receiver) Doug Donley's butt, man . . . he went to Colgate for nothing, because I took his game check.

"And yeah, I had a couple of beers, maybe three, in three hours, and we finally get back into Dallas, to the old practice field where the guys left their cars, and we get there about 1:30 in the morning. I'm not sleepy, at least I don't think I am. I still had a lot to do before I got to bed, because I was taking 18 Cowboys the next

80

day up to Virginia to play a three-game series with the Redskins. All the other guys were bitching. . . . 'Oh, man, when you go out of town you only take the superstars, how come I can't go to Virginia but I can go to Colgate, Oklahoma?' You know, stuff like that.

"So I worked it out where I could take 18, but it would have to be in shifts. Some guys were leaving early, you know, some later. I had to do all that coordinating, make all the calls, tell guys when they were going to leave, their flight numbers, times, stuff like that. And I had to pick up all the uniforms and wash them . . . pick up some other things, too. . . ."

At this point, the voice starts to go. The tears start again, one rolling almost unnoticed down his left cheek. Right now, things are not so good inside Drew Pearson's head.

"My brother was with me, man. He had moved down from New Jersey, to live with me. He was having trouble up there, so he came down and was working for me here in Dallas. See, Carey was always in a shell, kind of, and a lot of the problem was being Drew Pearson's brother. He was an introverted person anyway, and people were always trying to force him to be what he wasn't. So he'd get real quiet, wouldn't talk, nobody knew where he was coming from. So he came down and I was helping him out . . . and when we were riding to meet the bus that afternoon he was telling me how he felt good about himself and how he felt things changing, getting better, inside himself.

"Carey was the ballboy for us, getting all the uniforms, like that. Hey, he was a grown-up, man. He was 28, but we'd kid about him bein' the ballboy. It was really just to get him to go along with me . . . with us, you know?

"OK, now we're back, and I'm taking Carey to my other brother's house. I was awake. I was coherent. We had to clean the bus out, and that took a couple of hours, and I certainly wasn't drunk. So we did all that stuff, finally got in the car and hit the road, the freeway. . . .

"I remember getting on the freeway . . . and that's where I draw a blank—from that moment until I wake up and we've already had the accident."

The accident. The accident that changed Drew Pearson's life—and ended Carey Pearson's.

"I never had any kind of awareness, even at the impact. It was like somebody took me out of the car . . . all right . . . and then it happens and then they put me back in. When I came to, there were ambulances and police cars and the sirens and lights were going and my brother . . . I was in a little sports car that some auto dealer gave me to drive, and I don't know why I took that car . . . it was a souped-up sports car, a five-speed, and I usually hate that . . . but it was sharp and, well, anyway . . . the car was stopped, wrecked, and Carey was lying on my shoulder, and I said 'Moose, Moose, c'mon, man, wake up, wake up.' And he's real limp and everything, and he's not movin'. So I get out of the car, and the paramedic, he was just dumbfounded. He must've thought I was gone, too, and here I was, walkin' out of the car. The car was mangled, no way anybody could have survived.

"What happened is I hit a parked truck. It was parked on the side of the road for service, and some girl who was an eyewitness said she saw me weaving, so I must have weaved into the truck from the passenger side, which is how come I didn't get badly hurt."

Pearson was in a state of ambulatory shock, grief and the realization of death blurring his faculties.

"I remember walkin' up to this paramedic and asking him . . . going into the ambulance . . . and I said, 'Man, please, is my brother dead?' And he said, 'Yes, Mr. Pearson, he's dead, he's gone.' The last thing I remember then was a policeman saying that they were going to have to check me for alcohol and stuff like that, and at that moment it was not a big deal, not really . . . I mean, my brother was dead, you know? . . . but I do remember that. So I get into the ambulance . . . I remember that . . . and then about a day and a half later I woke up in the hospital."

It was revelation time for Drew Pearson, perhaps next to Bob Hayes the finest, most productive wide receiver in the annals of the once-proud Dallas Cowboy franchise.

"As I wake up, after surgery . . . my liver was bleeding internally, that's what ended my career, even though the best doctor in the field up at the University of Pittsburgh said I could play, but there would still be a little risk . . . I felt it had to be 100 percent or not at all . . . and they had to stop that right away . . . as I wake up, the faces I will always remember seeing were my mother, Roger Staubach, Harvey Martin and Coach Landry. And every time they'd wake me up after that, for a test or X rays or something, or every time I'd just turn around and wake up on my own . . . they had me on a lot of heavy sedatives, you know . . . why, I'd see Coach Landry there. Every time, man. Every time. Every day. And I never thought he cared much about me . . . or any of the players."

Pearson shook his head, still finding it hard to believe six years later.

"It was kind of a revelation, man, because he was there, almost the whole time, day after day until they knew I'd be all right, until I was conscious, until I started to deal with the fact that I was driving the car in an accident that killed my brother. Man, that was a tough thing to take, and the coach, he helped me through it more than he'll ever know.

"Not only was he comforting me but my mother . . . and my other brothers . . . praying with them . . . doing all those things to show his support . . . the kind of things nobody knew anything about. Hey, you know, most people thought he was just that cold, rigid old man with the hat and the jacket and tie who never smiled. Including me, man, and I had been with him for 11 years. Imagine, 11 years and I never even had an idea what kind of man he really was. Eleven years playing for the guy and never getting a feel that he cared so much for his players. My mother told me later how they would lean on him, how he would do things for them, make sure everything was OK. How he was a . . . oh, I know it sounds corny . . . how he was a pillar of strength for them when they were in need."

Drew Pearson, a black quarterback at South River High School in South River, N.J. (and the only black on the team in that blue-collar, hard-hat town hard by the Jersey Turnpike), perhaps best known as the high school quarterback who replaced Joe Theismann when he went off to Notre Dame (and changed the pronun-

ciation of his name from 'Theeseman,' which did not rhyme with
Heisman, to 'Thysman,' which did) was signed as a free agent by
the Dallas Cowboys in 1973. He had accepted a dual scholarship—football and baseball—from the University of Tulsa, played
quarterback and wide receiver as well as center field, and was uni-
formly ignored by the 26 teams in the National Football League
(Tampa Bay and Seattle wouldn't be whelped for another three
years).

"It was really for the baseball that I went to Tulsa," Pearson
says. "Tulsa had an excellent baseball program, way ahead of the
football program. My choices came down to Tulsa and the University of Nebraska, and while everybody thought I should be taking the Nebraska offer, I didn't want to be a quarterback. I always
wanted to be a receiver.

"When I was a kid I'd spend hours, hours, just throwing a ball
up against a wall and catching it . . . fielding it, like in baseball,
I guess . . . when it bounced back, thousands of times a day. It's
funny, but I played all the sports where there was something to
catch, no matter what the shape of the ball was, or how big it was.
I'd be a pitcher and fantasize I was going against the Yankees,
or I'd be somebody famous, throwing in the World Series. I only
played quarterback in Tulsa because they needed one, and I only
played it at South River after Joey left because there wasn't another one on the team who could, man. I lost two games in two
years, in high school, but we weren't that good in college. My last
two years we were 4-7 each year, and if I played receiver then,
there wasn't anybody who could throw to me.

"Then nobody paid attention to me in the draft, and when I
finally took the Dallas offer, Coach Landry sat me down and told
me that only free agents who the Cowboys consider special athletes, who they think can make the team, are brought in, and that
if they didn't think I had enough qualifications to make it, they
wouldn't have signed me. He told me he thought all the teams,
including the Cowboys, had made a mistake about me. He said
I had what it took to become an outstanding wide receiver, but
that I had to remember there was a lot going against me. Then

he said he'd appreciate it if I didn't let him down. Man, let him down? I would have jumped off a building for that man."

Pearson said he had turned down a far larger offer from the Pittsburgh Steelers, and an offer from Green Bay that was more substantial than the Dallas numbers. "Did I get a signing bonus from Dallas? Yeah, for 150 bucks. And a contract with a fourteen-five salary, and I had about six or seven thousand dollars in incentives built in, but Dallas had a history of free agents making their team and that first minicamp with the rookie free agents Coach Landry said that once we get into camp, everybody is the same. He promised that to all of us, that free agents and first-round draft choices would all be treated the same, exactly the same.

"That gave me a comfort level, and it was a big reason why I signed with the Cowboys, because they did give free agents a long look and they had that history of free agents making it."

So he signed, went back to Tulsa for his gear—"it all fit in two cartons in a Volkswagen I drove," he laughs—and returned to Dallas in early June.

"You know, June is when all the veteran players get their vacations out of the way, before they take off for training camp. But I had nothing to do, nowhere else to go, so I went back to Dallas and (personnel director) Gil Brandt got me an apartment in town, a job with Merchants' Van Lines, loading trucks, and I worked out with Roger all morning, went to my job at the moving company at 1:30 and worked until 6:00 or 7:00 at night, and then I jogged in the evening.

"After a while, Roger saw I was wearing out, and he asked me what was wrong. I told him I was workin', too, I needed the money to pay rent, and I was married at the time . . . I didn't have kids but I had a wife to support. So Roger went to Brandt and said he thought I had a good chance to make the team, and couldn't he do something, give me something, to keep me from working. So Gil called me in and gave me a check for 500 dollars, and back then, to a kid who didn't have any money at all, 500 bucks was a fortune. So I quit the job, just worked out daily, man, I lived at that practice field . . . and I'd sit there in the morning and wait for Roger and then we'd run these routes and in June, in Dallas, it's like 95 degrees.

"He'd ask me if I was tired, and I'd say, 'No, no, let's run some more,' but I couldn't even talk right because I was so out of breath, just plain exhausted. We had this thing we'd do, as we were wrapping up our practice every day. Roger would throw the bomb, see, and it had to be completed before we could leave. Our thing was that if we didn't complete it we'd have to keep running it until we did it.

"My tongue was hanging out most of those times, but I'd never quit. Hey, here I was, some free agent kid, and I was getting to work every day with Roger Staubach . . . and you know, he really helped me make the team. The coaches saw that he was working out with me every day, they knew he went to Brandt on my behalf . . . they respected his judgment and figured maybe he liked what he saw in me. I realized later that the whole situation resulted in them giving me a longer look in summer camp. Man, it was a long way for a South River guy to work out with Staubach."

Pearson was a Giant fan up until the day he signed with the Cowboys—"I hated the Cowboys, man, they were always beating the Giants," he said. "I won a contest once and had a choice of a jacket or a Giant helmet, and I took the helmet, and I slept in it, honest. But I quickly acquired a dislike for the Giants, especially after they didn't even talk to me when I was a free agent."

So June passed, hot and steamy and profitable. Drew Pearson went on to summer training camp in Thousand Oaks, Calif., on the campus of Cal Lutheran College. When he was cut, he had reasoned, he would go back to Tulsa and accept a job that had already been offered to him, in the recreation department.

"Man, there was a lot of doubt in this head." He smiled. "I just knew I would soon be gone. I didn't think I'd last a week.

"In fact, the first week is all rookies, they need all of them there for practice bodies and stuff, cannon fodder, so nobody ever gets cut that first week. But the coaches know which ones are going to go as soon as the real players show up, and I figured I was just lumped into that category until the veterans showed up. And even then I was comparing myself to the others, and saying, you know, to myself, 'Hey, wow, he looks pretty good, man, how you gonna make the team with that cat there, huh?' And remember, at the end of the second week, after the veterans had come in . . . and when they came in, it was like they had never left football, like there never was an off-season, the minute they hit camp they're in the huddles, breaking out clean, clapping hands, running up to the line of scrimmage. Man, they knew everything.

"But anyway, they had this big scrimmage, a highlight, once every summer . . . it was called the CLC scrimmage, the Cal Lutheran College scrimmage . . . and people come in from all over that area and watch . . . just a jam-packed stadium. I caught just one pass, it was like a 5-yard out and I made a little move, shook one guy and made 6, maybe 7 yards. So I'm sure I'm gone. I even told my roommate, Harvey Martin, that I'm gone by Monday, it's over.

"But in that scrimmage I made two blocks . . . on one I came in on the safety and really annihilated him, and on the other I went down, faked to the corner, set him up and when the safety came up, when he bit to see the run, I cut-blocked him and wiped him out. That Sunday night, after a Saturday night off, Coach Landry singled me out, not for the catch but for the two blocks. He said, 'Hey, here's a guy 150, 160 pounds, and he's goin' in and making those kind of blocks. That's what's goin' to win games here, men.'"

It was recognition, the sort that free agent rookies dream about, crave, and never realize.

"From that point on," Pearson remembers, "I was getting the looks in practice, the reps (repetitions), and the next week when we played the Rams in the first exhibition game they had me running back punts and kickoffs, which I thought was pretty good. I was fourth or fifth on the depth chart at wide receiver so I thought this was a good opportunity.

"But the Rams, man, they didn't punt until like the second quarter, and I'm on pins and needles waiting for the first one, you know? Well, he finally kicks one, and I'm under it, it's right to me, I'm ready, and it hits my chest and goes right through my hands. And they recover. And score. I get up and look over at the sideline and there's Coach Landry, just shakin' his head, and again I figured, well, I'm gone. No more chances for this free agent fool.

"But he gave me another chance, and I took the next punt and went 59 yards down the sideline until they knocked me out of bounds at the 1-yard line. That did it. I figured by then I had made the team."

How did that newly acquired status evince itself? Coaches learned his name. Coaches used him more. And the veterans, who usually ignore rookies entirely, started to accept him, to say hello, to offer pointers during practices or meetings.

"One afternoon, we're sitting in my room, a group of us, and we're all rookies. We've been in training camp six, I don't know, maybe eight weeks. You know, you're only human, and you need a woman, right? So anyway, we're in my room, trading war stories on a Sunday afternoon . . . nothing to do until meetings that night. And Bob Hayes suddenly knocks on my door—one knock, then he opened it, looked around and said, 'Pearson, come here. Put your shoes on and come with me.' So I go with him, and he's got this rented car, him and Cornell Green, and he tells me to get in the back. Man, there was a lady in the back, and as soon as I get in, this chick plants a kiss on me . . . I ain't kissed nobody in eight weeks . . . and all the guys are looking out the window, staring at me . . . I knew I had gained the players' respect. At that moment, I knew I had made the team."

That decision made by Landry set in motion a career that produced 489 career receptions (the Cowboys' all-time record), 7,822 yards (second) and 48 touchdowns. In 22 playoff games, Pearson has all the team records—67 catches, 1,105 yards and eight touchdowns. And he caught at least one pass in every one of those playoff games.

But above all else, Drew Pearson became famous for spectacular last-minute—sometimes last-second—touchdown catches that won games.

Especially playoff games; and while Reggie Jackson became known as Mr. October for his World Series heroics with the New

York Yankees, Drew Pearson acquired the label of Mr. January, and not just in and around Dallas. He became nationally acclaimed as the other half of the Roger Staubach connection.

"Yeah, there were a lot of big catches," he said, "but that was my job, you know? I mean, I was the split end, and after a while Roger, and Coach Landry, got the confidence to throw to me in pressure situations. What else could I do?"

In bitterly cold Minneapolis, on Dec. 28, 1975, the Cowboys found themselves staring down the muzzle of a 14-10 deficit. They had the ball on their own 9-yard line with less than two minutes remaining, the crowd shrieking, the wind howling and elimination from the playoffs becoming a reality as quickly as the temperature was dropping.

Staubach threw five passes in the drive. They amounted to exactly 91 yards, including a key 22-yard gain on fourth down to keep the drive alive.

All five went to Drew Pearson, the final one a 50-yarder with 20 seconds showing on the clock, the one that became famous as the "Hail Mary" touchdown pass. "Roger doesn't like to hear me say this," Pearson smiled, "but the only reason I was able to catch that one is because he underthrew it.

"Do you know, that was the only time in all my years with the Cowboys that Coach Landry ever hugged me. Yes, sir. He did. I was coming off the field . . . hell, we all were, just to get away from those Viking fans . . . and he walked up and hugged me. Now it wasn't one of those wild, emotional hugs, you know, it was kind of (he turns his head, circles his arms around an imaginary body) like this.

"He told me he didn't think I pushed off, either. That was what the Vikings claimed. I couldn't believe it. I was stunned. And I thought I had dropped it, but there it was, with 24 seconds left, and it's in my hands and you know, one way or another, I was gonna hold on. Roger threw it up and I'm running downfield and all I wanted was to be even with (cornerback) Nate Wright, and frankly I was a little surprised he let it happen. So I gave him this little 'in-route' fake, see, Roger pumped it once, and Nate came up, taking the fake. But I kept running, and the ball was a little underthrown, so I could see it all the way.

"And the pump froze (safety) Paul Krause, kept him in the middle of the field and not coming over to help out Wright. Because, you know, we had started on our 9 and I had caught all the passes including that fourth-and-eighteen (when he gained 22). Roger said, before the play, that he had to hold Krause, so he was gonna pump-fake it. And see, Krause wasn't gonna tackle nobody, but he'd intercept the ball if you gave him half a chance.

"So he wanted to keep him in the middle, and he pumped it so good he almost lost the ball, and that's why it was a little underthrown. And I kind of trapped it between my elbow and my hip, and I backed into the end zone and that was it, man, maybe my most dramatic catch.

"I was mad all game. I had only one pass thrown to me before that series. I was mad at Staubach and mad at Landry and mad at everybody, man. But like Landry said later, when the Cowboys needed something to happen, he wanted to have Roger and me, his two big-play guys."

Still, as dramatic as that was, there was another that Pearson thinks of first, when he sorts through his memorable moments.

"The one that really sticks in my mind is the one in my rookie year, in the playoffs against the Rams. I mean, here I was, a rookie. And in those years there was like a traveling squad, a taxi squad, they called it . . . and guys didn't get to make a lot of the road trips. I stayed home a lot when the Cowboys went away that year, because they had drafted Golden Richards, another wide receiver, in the second round . . . and I guess they felt they just had to give him more of an opportunity.

"But we all suited up for the home games, and now we're in the playoffs, at home against the Rams, and we'd had a big lead that was starting to disappear. I mean, at one point I think we were up by like 17 points, and now it's down to three or four and the Rams are really gettin' grooved, you know?

"So Coach Landry sends me in with the play, which is for Roger to throw to me . . . our Sixteen-Cut, which was our bread-and-butter play, where I'd go downfield about 20 yards, make the cut toward the middle, catch the ball and get tackled, but we'd have a first down. But when I get to the huddle, Roger audibled. He said no to the Sixteen, he told me to run a post pattern instead. Man, that's just straight down the middle of the field. And I'm thinkin', you know, this is one hell of a compliment, because I'm a rookie and it's late in a playoff game and we're in trouble and Roger Staubach is changing a Tom Landry play to get me to be a hero. That was some revelation, man. I mean, I was shakin' from head to toe."

But not so the Rams could tell.

"I start my pattern, get to where I'm supposed to be . . . like 40 yards downfield . . . and the ball is there as if it was a line drive off a baseball bat. I mean, right there, right now, on my fingers like he had just handed it to me. And the two Ram guys covering me . . . Eddie McMillan and Steve Preas . . . they collided. They fell. And I'm all alone with the ball in my hands and an empty field in front of me. It turned into an 83-yard touchdown pass. Man, I can remember it just like it happened 10 minutes ago."

Pearson also caught a dramatic, game-ending touchdown pass on Thanksgiving Day the year before, but it wasn't thrown by Staubach. "Roger was knocked out of the game . . . it was probably a concussion, he used to get so many of them . . . and we had this kid, Clint Longley, a rookie from Abilene Christian. Now, I liked Clint, and all, but he was a little different, you know? But now Roger is out and we're playing the damned Redskins and they're winning . . . it was 23-17 . . . and there's less than a minute to go.

"George Allen (the Washington coach) . . . we really hated each other . . . and there's footage of Allen on the sideline, pointing and laughing at guys on our team . . . you know, 'Hey, Landry . . . hey, Schramm . . . hey, Staubach . . . how about this, man,' and then the kid winds up and I'm runnin' downfield and bingo, we got the points, and we kick the extra point and win the game. George never forgot that, you know?"

In fact, it was the only thing Allen spoke to Pearson about in June of 1989 when the city sponsored Tom Landry Day. "He got me cornered," Drew said, "and started talking to me about that game, that catch. 'You were lucky, I wanted to play this defense, I wanted to put a guy on your head, but the defensive coordinator convinced me otherwise . . . and you never would have caught that ball if I played the defense I wanted.' "

In 1980, Sam Pearson died of cancer. "My father died late in the season (November 23, 1980), and I didn't know it until half-time of a game against Washington, when I got a telephone call from my wife," Drew said, "so he never got to see the two catches in the playoff game that year against Atlanta. Roger had retired the year before, and now Danny White is the quarterback, and we had a good season . . . I think we won 12 games. But we weren't division champions . . . the Eagles were . . . so we had to play a wild card game and we beat the Rams. Then we go to Atlanta and it's a close game and I caught one TD pass, I think it was 14 yards, with three minutes and something left (3:40) and that made it 27-23, and then with just seconds left (the clock showed 0:42), I got another one, 23 yards, to win the game. But my father wasn't there for that, and I missed him a lot. I know I wanted to make him proud of me. It was special to me to be able to make those plays, for him."

Growing up in South River, hard by the industrial sector of the mid-Atlantic Northeast, Pearson fell back on sports and friendships and, being that it wasn't the South, he says he never really experienced any racial problems.

"I used to pal around with guys I liked, and guys who liked me, and it didn't matter what color they were. I was like the only black on the baseball team one year, and all the rest of them were on the track team, and my white friends needled me about how I was probably the only black guy who couldn't run fast, things like that.

"Joey Theismann and I were good friends, even though he was two years older. You know, I guess we were the best athletes in school, both quarterbacks . . . or I was his backup while I played defense and receiver . . . so we just kind of hung out together. He always talked a lot . . . I mean, always talked. He was always like that, and arrogant and cocky, but we just wrote it off as Joey, that's how he was.

"And he was an excellent quarterback, excellent. The first pass I ever caught in high school I caught from Joey, and I was 60 yards away, just standing there wide open, and he was rolling out to his left and I was standing in the end zone, all alone. I loved South River, but I've been in Dallas now for 18 years, and Dallas has been very good to me. I don't have any plans to move, I don't want to go anywhere, but I'll always have a special place in my heart for South River and Jersey and all the people up there.

"Look, I know that most of what I've been able to accomplish in Dallas is because of who I was and because I played for the Cowboys, stuff like that. But once my name got around, once people recognized my face, then it was time to take advantage. I don't have any illusions about why I was given these opportunities, but it would be a shame to waste them."

Right now, Pearson is president, chairman and chief executive officer of three companies—Drew Pearson Enterprises, Drew Pearson Marketing and Drew Pearson Manufacturing—and the manufacturing arm of the empire has two factories in Hattiesburg, Miss., with corporate offices for all the companies just outside Dallas in Addison, Texas.

And he remembers where it all started for him, too—on a decision made by Tom Landry.

"You know, we all played in fear of him, in fear of those Monday morning meetings after games, when he would single out guys who made mistakes and embarrass them in front of everybody else. I mean, he did that on purpose, I know he did. It was his way of motivating us, of making us more afraid of peer pressure, of peer exposure, than we were of the opponents. And I understand it, and why he did it, but it hurt, man. It really hurt.

"You know, even when he gave you a compliment it was conditional. Like he'd say, 'Drew, that was a good game, and those six catches were all good ones, but if you had made that block downfield on the cornerback maybe Dorsett would have gone all the way.' He could never just give you some praise and let it go, because he was always thinking of the next game, the next team we had to play, the next problems that we would have to solve or be victimized by. He was a very intense, very driven man, and he made us play better than we ever thought we could.

"Something else, too. He was able to teach us what he meant. Lots of coaches get these great ideas, and they know what they mean, and they know what they want their players to do, but somehow they just don't know how to teach it, how to get it across. But with Tom, it was easy. I can remember lots of times one of the assistant coaches would start explaining some new deal, some wrinkle on what we had been doing because that's what they decided was going to work for the next opponent, and we're all sitting around blinking and staring and not understanding.

"Then Landry would come in, look at the problem, talk to us for five minutes . . . in that dry monotone that never changed . . . and do five more minutes on the blackboard, and we had it, man. It was there, clear and easy to understand, just the way he wanted us to learn it. It was a gift, you know? He was a very gifted teacher, because being a coach is really just being a teacher, when you come down to it. You're just teaching grown men. Not kids in school."

Like the others, when Landry was fired, Pearson was first shocked, then angry, then sad.

"I was in Las Vegas with Too Tall, to see a fight," he said, "and we're walking through the crowd and some fan yelled out that Landry got fired. We just thought it was a bad joke, and then we saw a Dallas radio reporter and he confirmed that it looked like that might happen, or might have happened. I left the fight and called the NBC affiliate in Dallas, where I was working, and they said it was true. It was shock and disbelief, man. I just couldn't imagine the Cowboys without Tom Landry.

"Then I wanted to find out . . . you know . . . what went on. How did it happen, who was at fault, was anybody at fault? Then I heard about Jerry Jones doing it, being the responsible man, how he flew to Austin to tell him, explaining that he just wanted to cover all the tracks and be done with it, start his own program. Look, it was definitely very cold, how it was done, and I know it could have been handled better, but I fault the former owner (Bum Bright), because he knew it was going to happen. He had been in really serious negotiations with Jones, and if that was the case . . . which it was . . . then he should have warned Tom, should have let him know, that there was a chance this was going to happen, that this was going to get done.

"Hey, after 29, 30 years why should Landry have to subject himself to that kind of treatment, and he could have got out smoother. It brought tears to my eyes, that somebody could have brought so much to this organization and then just be thrown out like that. And not Tom Landry the coach but Tom Landry the person, the man I got to know on a really personal basis, to learn that he really cared about his players, really felt for them, and just didn't know how to show it . . . or didn't think he should, because when you get too close it might be tough to make the hard decisions later, like cutting a guy, or trading him, or just telling him it's probably time for him to retire.

"He deserved to be treated better than that, man. He really, really did, and whoever was at fault should be ashamed."

Pearson paused here, and it was obvious he was thumbing through his mental scrapbook of Me and Coach Landry.

"You know, he made me a better receiver just by saying a few things in that rookie season, things I never realized but really simple things. It made me feel like . . . well . . . you know, how come I didn't ever realize that?"

For instance?

"Well, for instance he told me I didn't have great speed but I had great moves and body control, so he said, like, 'Drew, when you come off the line of scrimmage at the snap of the ball, you know? . . . why not pump those arms up and down, act like you're already at full speed, goin' as fast as you can.'

"I thought about that for a while, and it occurred to me that if I saved something, I could lull the defensive backs to sleep. I mean, I had been a wide receiver in high school, in college and now, getting to see the way Tom Landry looked at football, it was like a brand new game.

"You know, he'd tell me on Wednesday that when we were going to play . . . oh, say St. Louis . . . that when I did this kind of move the cornerback . . . like maybe Roger Wehrli, one of the best I played against . . . would back up with his right foot first, and if I took advantage of that, knowing which way he was going to back up, I could gain half a step from the first move. Now, I mean, this was Wednesday, man. How the hell did he know what the guy was going to do the next Sunday? Then he taught me to be aware of what pursuit angles the defensive players are taking after I've made the catch. See, if you know where they're coming from, you can figure out how to get an extra two yards, or 10, and you can see which way to fall so you protect yourself from the career-ending injuries."

And Landry, undoubtedly, had some of the veteran defensive backs on the Cowboys start teaching Pearson little tricks, nuances that would make him a better receiver. Safety Charlie Waters, a three-time Pro Bowl player, taught him about degrees of speed.

"See, Bob Hayes had just two speeds," Waters said, "and his downshift was too great when he was making his cut. He gave himself away a lot of the time. With Drew, once he understood the reason for speed, you never knew what speed he was on. He had four or five gears, and his cuts were so quick that it didn't matter how fast or slow he was. He had a knack of getting away from you, and in this game if you can show yourself to a quarterback like Roger for just a second, he'll put the ball on your chest. Drew made catches that looked hard, but what was hard was the way he got himself clear, gave Roger a clear 'front' to aim at. Drew created a lot of things in the middle of a route that threw the defensive players off balance, or made them go one way while he was going another way. Well, sure we helped him. We didn't have to cover him when it counted, you know. If he burned us in practice, which he did several times, we knew it was just going to be tougher on the next guy that Sunday."

Pearson had a particularly lively relationship with Terry Jackson, one of the New York Giants' better cornerbacks in the late 1970s and early 1980s.

"Man, I'm not even sure how that started, but I guess it was because I had run against his older brother (Monte, a Pro Bowl cornerback for the Los Angeles Rams), and Monte, see, he didn't care what you did to him. You could blindside him, crackback

on him, get in his face . . . didn't matter. He knew it was part
of the game. So now I'm playing against his baby brother . . . it
was late in the '70s, I think (1978), and the first time I run into
him hard, man, just to show him who was boss, you know? Well,
two things happened: I damned near hurt myself because that was
one hard man, strong and wiry; and he went nuts on me. You
know, 'Don't touch me, don't hit me, I'm gonna get you, star.'

"So after that it really began, and one time, I remember, walkin'
off the field at halftime, Tony Hill (for most of Drew's years the
other wide receiver) came up to me and said, 'Hey, man, what
did you do to Jackson? Man, he just wants to kill you. He's yellin'
and screamin' and it's gettin' ugly, man.' Well, after that I just
used to catch everything I could against Terry. I got him for two
(touchdowns) one day in Texas Stadium, and I was really happy
because I knew the game was on television back in New Jersey
and all my people were watchin' it. You know . . . remember? . . .
I was really pissed, hurt, when the Giants never even called me
after I wasn't drafted. It was a little revenge, and honestly, it gave
me a kick when I saw how angry Terry used to get."

Beating another Giant defensive back also gave Pearson pleasure of a different sort—Ray Rhodes (now a successful assistant
coach on the San Francisco 49ers staff) had been a teammate at
Tulsa.

"One time I did a really stupid thing," Drew said, then laughed
at himself and amended the statement. "Among lots of stupid
things I've done," he said, "one game in Texas Stadium I caught
a touchdown pass against Rhodes. Actually, it was even better
than just that, because I gave Terry Jackson a fake to the outside
that froze him, and then I moved into and across the middle and
beat Ray for the touchdown.

"Well, again, I knew it was on television back home, and it was
my second catch for a TD that day, and the fans were cheering
and, you know, it was a happy moment. So I jumped high into
the air and I was going to spike the ball . . . then I thought it would
look neat back home on television if I threw the ball into the
stands, see? So there I am, hanging in the air, tryin' to decide
whether to spike it or throw it into the seats, and by the time I

started to come down I just dropped it, and then I landed on it and sprained my knee and man, it felt like my leg was just broken.

"Next morning it was all swollen and painful, and I've got a big television commercial date . . . with Volkswagen, that I absolutely remember . . . and the man who's comin' to pick me up calls and I can't even get out of bed or put any weight on the foot. Well, I finally got dressed, and before I could go to the studio I had to go for a treatment. And I kept them all waiting, including Staubach, who was supposed to be in the commercial with me."

Pearson was put at the top of the depth chart when he showed up for his second summer training camp, and that, too, was Staubach's doing. "He told Coach Landry that he had the confidence in me, that he felt comfortable in pressure situations throwing to me, and I guess they had to keep their star quarterback happy. But I was too green and too inexperienced . . . and kind of too infatuated with everything that was happening to me to understand what that meant. I mean, Roger Staubach named me, man. Some no-count free agent from just one year ago."

In the 11 years Drew Pearson played, the Cowboys made the playoffs 10 times . . . seven times played for the National Football Conference championship . . . three times played in Super Bowls.

"We were used to winning and the town was used to seeing us win . . . the whole state, actually," he said. "People began to identify with us, because we were the team on television, on Monday night games, the second half of doubleheader games. We got national exposure, and we expected it to benefit us in our own area. We helped make the town more popular, too. I remember one year we went up to Pittsburgh to play the Steelers in one of those off-season basketball games and we drew over 8,000 people. That was how we became America's Team."

Way back, before the Cowboys, before Tulsa, before Joe Theismann rhymed with Heisman, there was South River High School. "We lost two games in three years, and they were both in my junior year, my first season at quarterback," Pearson says. "Oh, hell, yes, I remember who beat us. Highland Park and East Brunswick did. I threw six interceptions against Highland Park and five

five against East Brunswick, but we got 'em back the next year, big time."

Even that high school experience didn't escape Landry and his seemingly endless file of information.

"We were playing the Redskins for the conference championship in 1982," Pearson recalls, "and we were hopelessly out of it. We lost by about three touchdowns (actually, it was 31-17). OK, we never thought we'd win everything, and the Redskins were a really strong team that year. So right at the end of the game, we've got the ball, and there's an offsides call as the final gun sounds. Everybody starts walkin' off the field, but the officials can't let a game end on an offensive penalty, so Tom comes over and says: 'Drew, you go in at quarterback. It'll be like old times, you and Theismann at quarterback again.'

"See, he remembered, I once told him Joey and I were the quarterbacks at South River, and so I went in for just the last play. I didn't do anything, but there we were, on a National Football League field, each of us quarterbacking our team. I think it's safe to say that nothing like that had ever happened before, two guys from the same high school, who played together, playing quarterback in the same game in the pros."

Pearson, like the others, felt racial discrimination in Dallas but accepted it, somehow, as part of how the city was and not as cause for a militant, overwrought reaction to bigotry.

"When I started my businesses, I must have hit every bank in town, for funding, to get capitalized, then to stay capitalized when I had to start spending money and paying bills . . . and I could get into every bank, see, because of who I was, and it was still fresh enough in people's minds so that they wanted to meet me, see me, talk football with me.

"But meeting with the top people, the bank presidents, people like that . . . once I got in and talked to them about the Cowboys, and signed autographs, and all that crap . . . once we set down to talk business, it was different, man. It was different. I wasn't taken seriously, and I'm saying, Hell, I'm the guy who caught all those passes, made all those touchdowns, and I'm finding out how tough it's going to be when I need these people to continue with my life, to make my plans work. Man, if I'm having this kind of trouble, I can't imagine how much trouble the average black guy would have. No chance at all, that's his problem.

"I finally had to go out of town, to Kansas City, to get the financing I needed to start the business, to keep it going for the first two years."

A new look at life, a new direction. Banks and loans and money and bills. Late hours, frequent setbacks.

"In some respects, starting a business isn't unlike playing pro football," Pearson said. "I mean, in terms of the hours, the hard work, the single-mindedness you need. But I miss the camaraderie, the fellowship . . . the team feeling. I get that kind of sense in business, but there's no way to really duplicate it. It's just not the same any more, now I'm just like everybody else."

Just like everybody else. No more Dallas miracles. No more Staubach passes spiraling down from on high, into waiting hands, the blur and the noise of the crowd a faint humming, all senses intent on just that football . . . a time when feelings are intense, when sensations and perceptions are vivid, alive. When the man is more alive than he will ever be again.

"I've been on some kind of team since I was seven years old," he said, "and there was always that closeness, that feeling of togetherness as you get ready to go into battle, when those are the only guys you know you can count on, the only ones you can absolutely count on . . . you really miss that. And I miss being in that kind of physical shape, the condition you have to achieve to play this game on a pro level.

"I mean, I was so confident in myself, not only physically but mentally. I'm still mentally tough, but not like I was then. I put a lot of time and effort into becoming a good football player, into staying in shape, and when I got out my first year I worked with CBS, and everything was flying first class . . . big bucks . . . every time there'd be a meeting with the director in the hotel you'd order stuff from the menu . . . unlimited access.

"You know, I was up to 210 pounds, and I'm the guy who started at 160, remember? Now I'm about 195, I watch what I eat, play some basketball, just do the fun-type exercises. And when I get tired, I stop. I don't have to push myself now. So I don't."

When football ended for Drew Pearson, and after the one-year picnic with CBS, he wanted to stay in football.

"I coached the receivers for a year, and I scouted for a year, to show how I could do anything they'd ask. I don't think the Cowboy organization ever really took us . . . the players . . . very seriously. You know, they'd see us out there running around, catching the football, and that's what we're supposed to do, that's our job. But after 11 years, there wasn't much I could learn about the game. A lot of it I knew after two, three years, and it becomes a 'no-brainer' from then on. You just know what to do and you do it.

"So what do you do with the rest of your time? Just be idle? Turn into a vegetable? What I did was start learning about the business of pro football, how the Cowboys did things, how they spent money, how they conducted the draft, how they negotiated contracts . . . looking to get into the front office. My goal was to become a general manager. I thought I had some kind of 'in' with the Cowboys, with the organization. But that didn't happen. I never got an offer, or even felt any interest. See, I was just a player, and once I couldn't be that, I don't think they were terribly interested in me becoming anything else.

"But I had gotten closer to Coach Landry, so much closer because of the accident, and that has remained to this day. Our relationship now . . . well, I can call him now and feel comfortable, talk about other things besides X's and O's and football . . . talk about life. And that really didn't happen until after I stopped playing.

"But that was OK. See, I didn't need a coach who was going to be my buddy all the years I played. I didn't want a guy who would go out and have a beer with me, tell dirty jokes, chase women. I didn't need that and I didn't want that. I didn't need a coach to say, 'Hey, come on, you need to play better now, hear?' That's bullshit.

"What Tom Landry did for me was prepare me, week in and week out, to play football. I mean, the preparation we received, as athletes, was outstanding. We had a good team because we had great athletes, but lots of teams had that. What we had was Coach Landry and his preparation and his brain and all the stuff nobody else had or could ever have. And the more the things he said came out right, the more you believed him the next week. Most teams in this league have the talent to play about the same, see, but it was Landry, his ability to coach, to be innovative, that brought us up to a higher level."

And, finally, Drew Pearson comes to a realization about himself.

"I wanted to have that fear of him, that respect. It was both, you know. It was the kind of fear and respect you have for your father. You hate to bring that bad report card home because you know he's gonna kick your ass. You hate to do anything wrong around him, because you know he's gonna jump on you.

"It was that way with Coach Landry. I wanted him up here (his hand, palm level with the ceiling, describes a higher plane), I wanted him to be up over me, I didn't want us to see eye to eye. I wanted that motivation through the fear of performing for him, playing a game on Sunday and not knowing whether I did everything I could possibly do to keep him from jumping on me on Monday. He never yelled, never raised his voice, always did it in a monotone.

"But it seemed that would always cut, would always dig so much deeper. I wished the guy would yell at me, just yell and scream and get it done with. All of us felt that way. And he did it in front of everybody, he'd try to embarrass you in front of everybody. And if you had a good performance, he'd compliment you in front of everybody . . . but you really had to have been kickin' ass, you know? Compliments never came easily from that man.

"I think nothing I do in life will ever be as special, as rewarding, as playing for the Dallas Cowboys and playing for Tom Landry, and I think at this point, the thing he misses the most is being with his boys."

And now, looking at the Cowboys without Landry, Pearson is of two minds.

"I'm not saying they didn't do the right thing by making a coaching change, I just think . . . just wish . . . that they had done it different, in keeping some of the old regime intact. I know it would have been tough for Landry to stay if he wasn't the head coach. I know it would have been tough for Tex Schramm to work with Jerry Jones.

"It just bothers me that all that accumulated knowledge . . . gathered over 29 years . . . I mean, for all that time, you had the commissioner of the league and then you had Tex. His experience would have been invaluable. it just bothers me that they tried to push our tradition, the one that I had helped build up with my blood, sweat and tears . . . and they deny this, but I know it's true . . . that they tried to push all of it aside, out the door, and then start their own thing.

"I mean, why do that? If it's not broke, why fix it? It's like they took all our tradition, everything we had built up over all those years, all the glory and all the victories, and just blew it up, man. Just blew it up."

A shudder.

"I never thought I'd ever see a Cowboy team play a season and finish with a 1-15 record. Not in my lifetime. I never thought it would get to that point. Never. But I figured as long as Landry was around, he could turn it, make it better."

But he never got the chance. Tom and the 'Boys all went away together.

CHAPTER 5

RANDY WHITE

"MANSTER"

Manster (man-ster): a nickname originally created for application to one Randy Lee White, professional football player, Dallas Cowboys, 1975–1988; manster, mythological creature said to be half-man, half-monster (hence man-ster); indicates great strength, quickness, speed; flair for life, recreation, freshwater bass fishing, beer; uncommonly loyal, gregarious; subject to swift mood shifts. (Note: The Manster was credited by offensive linemen in the National Football League with the invention of the bad mood.)

* * *

The history: In the middle of the 1974 National Football League season, the New York Giants, then one of the league's funniest jokes, decided they had to have a quarterback. This was the proper decision, since the ones they had were eminently forgettable young men with virtually no professional skills named Carl Summerell and Jim Del Gaizo.

At the same time, the Dallas Cowboys were trying to decide between keeping Roger Staubach or Craig Morton—referred to by some of the more literate local scribes as The Naval Officer and Billy Budd—because the two were hotly competing for the starting position and the longer the competition dragged the more frayed grew everyone's nerves. Players on the team began taking sides, usually according to friendship or the most recent performances by one or both of the principal actors in this cleated morality play.

Morton had been the team's first round draft pick for 1964—the same draft in which Staubach, after a fashion, had become a Cowboy, too. He had been chosen in the 10th round as a future choice, but his particular football future was at least five years away, since the Heisman Trophy winner from the United States Naval Academy had his service obligation to fulfill, the standard method of returning the cost of the marvelous free college education acquired at the Naval Academy (or, for that matter, at West Point or the Air Force Academy).

When he did show up for good, in 1969, the battle that ensued raged for five years.

But Morton was the answer for right now, a 6-4, 220-pounder who eventually replaced Don Meredith but a man whose potential, as it turned out, would always outdistance his performance. He was subject to mood swings, horrendous efforts in crucial games followed by brilliant ones in slightly less important games, but the brilliance was so blinding that the disappointments were forgotten.

He was also subject to bouts of incredibly bad luck; the most perfect pass ever thrown by a quarterback, winging its way toward becoming the game-winning touchdown, would be dropped by a sure-handed receiver who, having run the most perfect pass pattern ever run by a receiver, was standing all alone in the end zone. He tried a hypnotist for a while, in order to be subconsciously reinforced with positive thoughts and optimistic vibrations.

It didn't work. Some said he was too intelligent for his own good, thrust as he was into a less demanding setting than where he had spent the previous four years—the University of California, Berkeley. But some players—Staubach, for example—are equally intelligent. They simply don't spend their time asking "why this" and "why that" and "excuse me, Coach, but what if we did it this way instead?"

But then came the telephone call from the Giants, from one of Tom Landry's best and closest friends, in fact—team president Wellington Mara. The friendship began in the early 1950s, when

Landry was a player for the Giants, a defensive back of Pro Bowl skills who had a mind that helped create specialized defenses, and later as an assistant coach. Mara was always a hands-on owner, the man who once did all the scouting and trading. They became genuine friends, and they and their wives, Alicia Landry and Ann Mara, are friends to this day. But this call represented a surefire problem-solver, totally unexpected but equally welcome. And what a bonanza it was! For the Giants' first-round selection in 1975 and their second-round selection in 1976, the Cowboys were able to move Craig Morton from a situation in which he probably would not have lasted much longer anyway.

And with that first-round pick in 1975, the second choice in the round because the Giants had played through 1974 with the second-worst record in the league, Craig Morton notwithstanding, the Dallas Cowboys were able to claim a defensive line-man–linebacker from the University of Maryland.

The Manster, Randy Lee White.

Before we really get started, how about a little something to show you exactly what sort of person the man-ster is, OK?

His last professional season was 1988 because . . . well, because his neck hurt, because he had "a bunch" of bass-fishing trips scheduled for later in the summer, because the new team owner had fired Tom Landry and the new head coach wasn't exactly prepared to promise him a starting job and, well, Randy White was just pissed off.

But allow him to explain.

"I would have played one more year if Coach Landry had been coming back, but when they fired him . . . well, hell, it didn't much matter anymore. I didn't like it when Tom got fired, I didn't like it at all. To be honest with you, I was never very outspoken or controversial during my career. I didn't really like to talk much at all to anybody but my teammates. I just enjoyed playing the game. I never wanted to start playing the politics that went with it.

"I enjoyed playing football on Sunday afternoons, and that was about it. I didn't care what happened all week, except that we have good practices and get ready to play, you know? I wouldn't let myself get distracted, not by anything. The hell with it. That's not football. But when I heard about him finding out in the parking lot at the office, after he had been in there all day working on a minicamp schedule, when some newspaper guy who was waiting for him to come out ran up and told him, 'Hey, Tom, you've been fired,' you know, that didn't sit too well with me, not at all. It wasn't right, the way it was handled.

"I heard a comment made by Jerry Jones that if he had it to do all over again, well, sir, he would do the same thing, that it was the only way he could have handled it. That's nonsense. That stinks. To me, that wasn't the way to do it. I mean, you know, in this game, or you should, that you're always one day away from going. It's not something you worry about, you just live with it, but it's always there. That's how it works, that's how the business part of it works. But with somebody like Tom Landry. . . . I have the utmost respect for him, as much as I guess I have for anybody in the world . . . to see him treated like that, man, it just wasn't right. They could have done it a lot better.

"Am I a Cowboy fan now? Yes. And no. There are guys still there who I played with, worked with . . . some who I kind of coached . . . unofficially . . . and I wish them well. But it's not the same anymore. I don't know why, but I just don't feel comfortable even going out there. Things keep changing, but I know that, I can understand that, I can deal with that. They're trying to rebuild the team. That's a real good idea, because it sure as hell needs to be rebuilt, considering the last few years.

"But I get the feeling that the new people are . . . I don't know, and I sure don't want to accuse anybody of anything . . . that they're trying to get rid of the tradition of the past, that's the feeling I have. It's like they want to forget all that, and make the fans forget it all, too, and just start this new thing, that's the impression I get.

"You know, I talked to Jimmy Johnson a couple of times, and I like him, I wish him well. I just don't know those people and I don't feel the same about them. But if Coach Landry had been there last season, I would have been there too. It just didn't make sense to risk my neck injury and stuff for a new outfit, for a bunch of strangers.

"Besides, I think it was kind of like a mutual thing. I mean, I hadn't made the decision not to play, I was still unsure, although I was sure leaning that way. But every time I talked with Jimmy . . . well, he kept bringing up my neck every time, you know, 'Make sure you're doin' the right thing, Randy, be sure of it.' I just got the feeling he didn't really want me around. He never once did try to talk me out of it. It doesn't take a genius to figure out when you're not really welcome. It's tough to do, quit like that, when you've been doing something all your life, but I couldn't control it from happening.

"Besides, when you get to that point, it's really time to go anyway. They wanted somebody to play 60 minutes, and I couldn't have done that anymore. But I could have helped them, somehow, I sure could have . . . I just don't think they considered me. Maybe it was because I was part of the old Cowboy tradition, but for whatever reason, they just didn't want me there. But I don't know . . . if I could have still performed, and helped them, why wouldn't they have wanted me around? Because I was part of the old Cowboys, because I was such a fan of Coach Landry? I have to think that was probably the reason. Well, the hell with 'em.

"See, a lot of guys think that if Tom was still there I would have played . . . if Tom had been given another way out rather than get fired so cruelly . . . and maybe they're right. Yeah, if Coach Landry had been there I would have played one more year, I would have wanted to be there, too."

A pause here, a deep, audible intake of breath, which may be the way the Manster shows his emotions.

Then . . .

"I'd probably run in front of a car for that man."

And probably stop it in its tracks, too.

"That's the kind of feeling I had for him, still have. I feel that way about (former defensive line coach) Ernie Stautner, too. Him and Coach Landry, and I'll tell you what, they're probably the two best people you'll ever meet in your whole life.

"Stautner and Landry and the strength coach we had, Bob

Ward, were the three people who really affected my life once I got with the Cowboys. But I never got close to Landry. He always kept his distance, you know, from everybody. But I got so that I was comfortable with him after a while. He's a good person, and once you get past his quiet, his distance, you understand where he's coming from. And he's a compassionate person. I know that for sure."

Another pause, and the big, ruddy, mustachioed face clouded. Not tears, never that, but a sadness reigned, a private flashback to a memory, something. . . .

"The night my father died . . . he died the night before we were playing Denver, I forgot which year it was (1980) . . . well, I didn't say anything to anybody. I just kept it to myself, you know? That's my way. But I'll never forget, right before the game, as we were gettin' ready to be introduced in the tunnel, you know, he came over to me and said, 'Sorry to hear about your father, and you take as much time as you need when you get back home, OK?'

"Now, hell, he didn't have to do that, and it wasn't just me, it was a lot of people. When you had a real serious personal problem, you take all the time you need, do whatever you have to do, then come back."

Sitting with White, across a conference table in Lee Roy Jordan's offices in northeast Dallas, the overpowering impression is of size. Yet he isn't the biggest man in town. He was never the biggest player. In fact, he was somewhat smallish for a defensive lineman, being "only" 6-4 and about 250 pounds. One year he weight-lifted himself up to 270, but lost all his quickness. But he is a big person, big in some intangible sense, big in terms of the aura he creates, of the presence he presents.

He looks like a bear. Really, a bear. Big. Wide. Barrel chested. A dangerously misleading look of softness. You know, you might be able to cuddle up, but you better be sure you picked the right time. But an obviously fun-loving bear, and to women, one assumes, a strikingly handsome bear of a man.

He's wearing jeans and a western shirt, open halfway down his chest. His hands are even more massive than Jordan's and Lilly's, and for a frivolous second the visitor wonders whether big hands

were part of the scouting requirement for draft choices, especially
first-round draft choices. The visitor also wonders how he could
be that big, a towering, imposing man without a waistline.

Randy White was late, he said, because his truck broke down
and he had to get it towed to a garage and fix it. Himself. That
is perfectly in keeping with his image. No sleek sports car, no fat
town-and-country sedan. And, well, it's not exactly a truck, either.
Like a Jeep, or a Ranger, but something else. It's perfect.

And he is friendly. More than friendly. He makes gregarious
take on new meanings. "Hey, let's fish," he says, eyes brightening.
"We'll go out into east Texas and catch us some bass. That's what
I like to do best. Hey, let's go get some beers, eat some Mexican
food. Hey, when I'm up in New York next, call me. Do I what?
Work? Nah, not really. I'm doin' one of those beer commercials
(Miller Lite, if memory serves, where he stands up in the boat,
looks down into the water and yells, 'Hey, fish, get in the boat.'
And they do, hundreds of them) and I took care of myself with
deferred payments and some real estate and stuff. I'm OK with
money, got all I need or want (at one point, near the end of his
career, he was the NFL's highest-paid defensive lineman; no one
will ever have to sponsor a testimonial for Randy White just to
raise him a little cash), and I don't do anything serious, like I mean
no regular job, like that."

I think going bass fishing with Randy White on some east Texas
lake might be extreme fun, and with him along, why would anyone
be frightened of wild animals or snakes? In fact, bass fishing in
east and southeast Texas has become White's passion. He had hit
the creeks from Mount Pleasant to Palestine, Brushy Creek to
Edom, Caddo Creek to Koon Creek, Catfish Creek to Browns-
boro, Murchison to Poynor, Monticello to Athens, Bethel to Cross
Roads, Ben Wheeler to Larue. And don't forget Leagueville.

It was in Monticello, which is public fishing water, that he
caught a bass over seven pounds, and he says he has taken bass
weighing more than 10 pounds from private ponds and lakes. He
fishes on a Skeeter bass boat, and in fact does promotional work
and appearances for the company. He and Jordan, between interview sessions, were discussing Lee Roy's desire to buy his own

bass boat, and White asked the visitor to deliver a message for Bob Lilly: "Tell him it's time to go fishin' and he needs to call me about it."

For a kid from Wilmington, Del., who attended school in College Park, Md., fishing buddies of White's claim he has become more Texan than native-borns . . . much as the most fervent Manhattanites are from places like Springfield, Mass. or Norman, Okla.

This is a clearly uncomplicated man, with simple tastes and simple wants. "Reporters never understood me when I told 'em that my approach to playing football was to go out every Sunday and try to do the very best I could. I couldn't analyze it any more than that then, and I can't now. All I know is that I played football for a living, and grew up believing that you had better damned well do whatever it is you do as well as you can if you intend to keep your job. I never could figure out why people would pay me so much to play football, but I sure wasn't going to argue.

"Now really, how many people get paid to do somethin' they would do for nothing at all?"

And he would have played the game for nothing, absolutely. There is something about Randy White's temperament that rings true when comparing him to some of the old-timers who created the legends . . . before the hair dryers and earrings and agents and "we don't talk to the press" set took over. Like one of his two favorite people in life, Ernie Stautner. And others, like Alex Webster, Gino Marchetti, Billy Ray Smith, Tommy Brookshier, Artie Donovan.

Bill Parcells, the head coach of the New York Giants, calls those kind of people "hard-hat, blue-collar, lunch-pail guys," and insists that if he called them and said, like, "Hey, men, we got a game this afternoon at 2:00 in the parking lot at Bloomingdale's, and we ain't gonna be paid for it but the other guys say you can't beat 'em, you ain't good enough," they'd just ask when to meet and should they bring shoes.

If it wasn't fun, why do it? If it's just pain without pleasure, find something else. And anybody who thought man was meant to go through life without drinking beer had better go back and read the rules again.

"I felt so lousy when I saw what happened to Coach Landry that . . . well, you know, things are just never going to be the same. He knew each guy on the team, each thing about him, he knew when to be rough, when to be calm. . . . He just knew so much about you. That was his style of doing things.

"He used to get to me, man. I mean, in a major way, and he did it for years and years and years. And I knew what he was doin' and yet, I'll guarantee you, he'd get me every time. Every time. Like, we'd have a Saturday morning meeting . . . and I used to take everything personally, and I *knew* what he was doing. And he'd say something, you know, like, 'Well, things didn't go well in practice this week' . . . or like, 'We didn't play as well as I know we can last Sunday,' and I used to think he was talkin' to me, just to me, every time. I'd take everything personally, and I'd say something to myself like, 'Wow, man, what did I do wrong now?' I mean, there were 43, 45 other guys there, and I felt like it was all my fault. He made me think I had lost the game, or damned near lost it, if we had won, and that everybody else on the team had played tougher and harder just to carry my load, like I was some kind of idiot.

"I'd walk out of that meeting room and I'd be so pissed . . . I mean, so pissed . . . I would have punched a hole in the wall. And I wouldn't want to talk to anybody, eat anything, nothing. I'd spend the rest of the day by myself, just sittin' in my room, and I'd think about it and think about it and think about it, and by the next day I just couldn't wait to hit somebody. And that's what he wanted to do, I knew that's what he was doin', and he still did it to me. Every damned time. I went for it, I fell for it every time.

"And now people . . . like the people who fired him . . . are saying he doesn't motivate players, and he didn't pep talk 'em? . . . That's bullshit. You can believe one thing, he damned well motivated me.

"It was better than any pep talk I ever got in my life. All he had to do, you see, was embarrass me a little in front of my teammates . . . that's all he had to say to build a fire in me. I always was comfortable with him, but as I got to stick around, as I became a veteran, I felt even closer. Now, don't misunderstand, you didn't get real close to Coach Landry. Never. Nobody really did that. It was just that you got to count on him . . . expected him, wanted him to be there, beatin' down on you, makin' sure you remembered stuff, not to make any mistakes. Like a way of life. There was me and football and Tom Landry and winning most of our games, and then gettin' pissed off at him when he criticized and wantin' to try harder the next time to make it all right again.

"I remember one day, it's the morning of a game, and we're all sittin' in the locker room, maybe half an hour before we go out, real quiet like . . . just thinkin', gettin' ourselves ready to play, and in the stadium magazine that day there was some article on me as a bass fisherman, with a picture of me carryin' a string of, I don't know, 30 or 40 bass that I'd caught, just carryin' them over my shoulder.

"Now remember, it's like minutes before the game, and I'm not talkin' to anybody, just sittin' in my locker, my head still, picturin' stuff. See, I believed in psycho-cybernetics then, still do, actually. . . . You know, seein' yourself do positive things will make you do 'em. I've been that way for years, since I was in college. I'd do it all week long, building up to a game. So I'm sittin' there, he walks over to me, slaps me on the shoulder and says, 'Hey, Randy, that's a nice picture of you in that magazine, real nice.'

"I mean, he had to think I was retarded, because I just looked at him, couldn't say nothin', because he never talked to me before about anything but football, you know? I mean, tellin' me I looked good in a picture with a mess of fish hanging over my shoulder, right before a game? I mean, God damn, who's nuts, around here, you know?

"Anyway, it got so where I'd feel comfortable enough to talk to him. Not big, important stuff, nothing really personal, no small talk. I mean, just sayin' hello to him first, in the morning. I never even could do that when I first came to Dallas. I tried once, said hello, and he just walked right by me. He didn't do it to be rude, it's just when he got to thinkin' about some football problem, he didn't see and he didn't hear anything else. Damned right, I was intimidated by him. Now . . . man, it was great. I could say hello to him every time I saw him, and he'd answer me."

The year Randy was drafted, with the second pick in the first round, the Cowboys also claimed another player in that round—linebacker Thomas Henderson, from tiny Langston College in Oklahoma, with their own pick, 18th in the round. Henderson quickly became a star and a starter, but then succumbed to admitted drug abuse and was gone from the Dallas roster after the 1979 season, but not before creating scenes and a general circus that was unlike anything the Cowboys had ever had to deal with since the troubled career of halfback Duane Thomas. Henderson was one of the few players who ever really tested Tom Landry's saintly patience.

The Manster smiles. "Hey, let me tell you a few things about Thomas Henderson," he offered.

And then he did.

"Thomas was probably the greatest athlete . . . and that's a damned strong statement for me to make . . . that I have ever seen in my days of playin' football. Thomas Henderson was *the* best, better than Herschel Walker, Tony Dorsett, any of them. The best, as far as havin' athletic ability.

"Lawrence Taylor (of the New York Giants) is a great player, you know. I never played on the same team with him, but I saw him play enough to know he was a great player, in a class by himself. I mean, the things he has done over a period of years is just spectacular. And Thomas Henderson had that kind of ability. He performed that way, too. But he was a loud guy, a jive guy, a colorful guy . . . the kind of guy who could mouth off, you know, but really wouldn't piss you off. I remember he used to say to me, 'Randy White, I'm gonna kick your ass.' He was always pissed because I was drafted number one higher than he was and he didn't like that.

"And I'd say, 'Thomas, look here,' . . . and you know, I liked Thomas, I really liked Thomas. I mean, he had his problems later on down the road, when he went crazy, when he was uncontrolla-

Tom Landry

Bob Lilly: "I think it started to happen in 1962, and we all just started to think of ourselves as Dallas Cowboys, us against the world, and as if we had never played for any other team or any other coach. It was like a mission, a crusade, to get better and win something important for that old man."

Lee Roy Jordan: "Everything he did in his life . . . personally and professionally and every other way . . . was designed to consider only one thing: What was good for the team?"

Bob Hayes: "He never got mad if we lost a game, but even when we won, he'd get outraged if we broke down, made a mental error, didn't do what the play called for us to do. Sometimes I think about guys from other teams, sittin' in their meeting rooms watching their films, and I'm wondering if they're catching the same kind of hell for losing that we were catching after we won."

Drew Pearson: "He was able to teach us what he meant. Lots of coaches get these great ideas, and they know what they mean, and they know what they want their players to do, but somehow they just don't know how to teach it, how to get it across. But with Tom, it was easy."

Randy White: "He helped me not just in football but in life. I admired the way he handled himself during adversity. Everybody can be cool when everything's goin' good, you know? Nobody ever saw him yell and scream, punch a door. Why? Because he put football third in his life. God was first. Family was second. Then football. I really believe that's how he dealt with that stuff."

Tony Dorsett: "He brought out the best in everyone around him, not just players but people who were associated with the team, people who worked for the team . . . the radio guys, the television guys, the newspaper guys . . . it was like anybody who ever came into contact with him was afraid to let him down."

Roger Staubach: "I love that man, I respect him, I admire him, and I will do anything I can for him, but he just didn't give enough of what a lot of the players needed, which was a pat on the back sometime, just that, some recognition of a good job . . . but if you need him for something, if you needed help, advice, anything, he was there for you."

ble and you couldn't really like him. Well, to me that was a different person, that was the drugs, whatever. Anyway, I'd say, to the
Thomas I knew when he had his head on, 'Hey, man, I'm gonna
be sittin' right here, so if you ever want to quit talkin' and do something, I'll be right here.' One day he got to me a little bit, got under
my skin, and I lost my temper just slightly, and I guess I cornered
him in the locker room . . . didn't hurt him or anything, just held
him up, you know? So later, when he wrote his book, he had a
little message for me. It said: 'Randy White, thanks for not kickin'
my ass that day in the locker room.' He finally got under my skin,
but I think that was already when he was gone, man, on drugs
and high and stuff.

"But Thomas was a great player, he really was a great player,
until he started going down the wrong road. He could do things
on a football field, he could make plays, that you just couldn't believe. He could do things that nobody else could, that's why he
was around as long as he was, I guess, even after he started to
be a problem.

"You know, the picture people have of him isn't really the right
one. They didn't know him. You know, they'd see him on the sideline, jackin' around, doing drugs. But that wasn't Thomas Henderson, that's why I want to forget that part. The Thomas Henderson I met when we were rookies . . . you'd just shake your head
at him, at some of the things he'd do. He was a show, man.

"Like that year, our rookie year, we're playin' Pittsburgh in the
Super Bowl . . . and we knew he was goin' to steal the show because that's how he was. You just needed to put a camera in front
of him, and he was on, man. So he said, I mean give me a break,
he says (Steeler quarterback) Terry Bradshaw couldn't spell C-A-
T if you helped him find the C and the A. Remember that? I said,
'Thomas, man, you can't be doin' stuff like that, you're buildin'
us a hole we can't get out of. Thomas, keep your mouth shut, man,
you ain't the only one out there playing you know?' See, we had
to go out and play, too, and there was no sense in getting all of
them pissed off."

That rookie crop that included White and Henderson was the
Cowboys' all-time high-water mark for draft excellence. Of their

20 draft choices, 12 eventually earned spots on the team, and in that glorious season 11 rookies found their way to the active roster of the team that played in Super Bowl X.

In all, the first 10 choices (through the eighth round) made the team—White, Henderson, guard Burton Lawless, linebacker Bob Breunig, defensive end Pat Donovan, safety Randy Hughes, center Kyle Davis, cornerback Rolly Woolsey, linebacker Mike Hegman, punter Mitch Hoopes—plus 13th pick Herbert Scott (a guard who wound up starting in the Super Bowl and sticking around 10 years) and 14th choice Scott Laidlaw, a running back who played for five years in Dallas.

"When we got there, when we went through summer training camp and got to know the Cowboy system just a little," White says, "we just knew we were going to win. I mean, we just knew it. We had Roger Staubach out there, and hey, if things were tight at the end of the game, all we had to do was find a way to give him the ball and we'd win. That was our deal . . . get him back the ball, with a fumble or an interception or something, and if we did that, we knew we'd win. The other teams expected it. . . . I mean, they expected to lose. They were wondering how we were going to beat them late in the game. Somehow it was going to happen, somehow somebody was going to make the big play. When you're thinking right and you're prepared right, you expected it to happen.

"I always felt I had to do it, make the big play, and I guess everybody else on the defense thought that way, too. It was a good team when I got there. I never saw the racial crap they talk about. I don't know where that all happened, when that started, but it damned sure wasn't a problem when I got there. I mean, Jethro Pugh and Rayfield Wright, Robert Newhouse, Billy Joe Dupree . . . they're some of the best guys you'd ever want to meet in your whole life. Good, solid people.

"I remember one time, when I was a rookie . . . just after practice ended I realized I didn't have any cash on me. So I asked Dupree, 'Man, I got to get some money, what time do the banks close here?' He asked what I needed, I told him a couple of hundred dollars and he opened his wallet and handed me the money. Just like that. 'Here, take it, pay me back later.'

"I never saw any of that racial crap. In the city? Yeah, certain places you couldn't go to, maybe. But that was earlier, years before. I like Dallas. I really do. I like the city, the people, east Texas has some of the best bass fishin' anywhere and that's not far from here. I don't want to go anywhere, I'm at home here now."

Home used to be Wilmington, Del., where his father, Gus, was a butcher and an instiller of the American Dream in his son's eager psyche. "For instance, he told me that as soon as you start counting your awards, and believing the stories that say how good you are, somebody is going to come along and knock you on your ass. Never be satisfied, never be content."

There are a few hard truths about Delaware high school football, too, among them that almost nobody comes to scout and recruit. "My father decided where I would go, and since I had only two or three scholarship offers there was no problem. One of them was to Maryland. Maryland was close to Delaware. My dad said I would go to Maryland and that was that. No discussion. That's just the way things were run in my family. Frankly, though, I had my doubts. When I got to Maryland, we were ranked in the bottom 10 in the country."

While in high school, White was a fullback (at 215) and a linebacker. "We never won much there," he remembered. "But we did have a good time." He also played baseball—he was a first baseman—and scouts from the Philadelphia Phillies began expressing an interest in his fielding and his power hitting.

"My father said to forget about baseball, so I did," he said. "When he told me I had to go to college instead of knocking around on buses in the minor leagues, I didn't even think about arguing with him."

One of the traits that Gus White instilled in his son was a dedication to constantly improve.

"I'll guarantee you, I was never sure of my job in Dallas," he said. "I mean, I kept hearing this stuff about how I was the best defensive lineman in all of football, about how I was going to be compared to the great ones of the past . . . like how I couldn't help but get into the Hall of Fame one day . . . but that didn't mean shit to me. I know that every time I got to training camp, every summer, I was scared about losin' my job.

"The only year I didn't worry about it was my last year, when I was hurtin', when I knew I wasn't goin' to be a starter. Ernie (Stautner) told me, and Coach Landry told me, I was an older player and they wanted me to coach, too, so I knew I was going to be around, and honest, in all my years with the Cowboys, that was the only time I wasn't really worried. I knew somebody else was going to start, I knew the staff was counting on me for more than just playing, and it was a lot more comfortable.

"But all those years, when I was all-NFL and Pro Bowl . . . I didn't care. I'd look everybody over, man, especially the rookies, and try to figure out which was was going to take my job. I mean, right after I was Most Valuable Player in the Super Bowl, man, I got to camp fresh from all these honors . . . maybe it was Coach Landry, somehow, who planted that seed . . . he always kept a fire lit under me . . . I was still worried about my job."

A pause for reflection here.

"You know, that Super Bowl (XII, a 27-10 victory over Denver—with Craig Morton the hapless Broncos' quarterback), that was probably the ultimate game for me. I mean, it was my first championship, my first Super Bowl. I was named the co-MVP with (defensive end) Harvey Martin . . . and it was on my birthday, too (January 15, 1978). I guess for a single day in my life, that one had to have more of the high points you could squeeze in, you know?"

An aside: One of the best "leads," or first paragraphs, ever written for a Super Bowl game story, in this writer's opinion, was turned in that day by a man named David Israel, then writing for The Chicago Tribune. "It took fourteen years," he wrote, "but Craig Morton finally won a Super Bowl for the Dallas Cowboys."

Unlike the others, Randy White has tried to convey another side to the portrait of Tom Landry.

"Yeah, we could come in from winning a game by 40 damned points and he'd make us feel like we had lost. He did that, and I can't deny that. But sometimes, when we did lose, and when he could sense that we were really down, then he was completely different. He wouldn't knock you down further, he'd try to pick you up. He was a good psychologist that way.

"I'll tell you what, though. When I played in college, at Maryland, the coach was Jerry Claiborne. And while I was never a rah-rah kind of guy, even though college football was a rah-rah kind of atmosphere . . . I probably didn't say 10 words to anybody on the team, I kind of stayed in myself, did my thing . . . but Coach Claiborne was a real disciplinarian, a no-nonsense kind of coach, kind of like Coach Landry.

"I came from a program that was, in many ways, similar to what I found in Dallas . . . lots of hard work, no foolin' around . . . so from that standpoint I was kind of used to the Cowboy way. I'd see these guys go out there for practice in shorts, Wednesdays, even Thursdays. I never did that. I always played for coaches who believed in scrimmaging on Wednesday and Thursday. Bam! Bam! Just bang 'em all week until you get so damned angry you go out for the game and damned near rip some poor bastard's head off. That's the way it was in Dallas, too.

"Sometimes . . . hell, it's going to sound like I'm bein' critical of Coach Landry, and I'm not . . . sometimes I felt like we worked too hard, like we left a lot on the practice field a lot of times, we'd go into games tired. But then we'd be afraid of letting down because of him, so we just couldn't let down. I mean, playing for Coach Landry was not some high school picnic, you know? I tried to talk to him a couple of times. You know, 'Hey, Coach, how about we slack off a little here, and there? Just for a little while, 'cause we're all tired, you see?' And all he'd ever say is, 'Well, Randy, we'll think about it.' But nothing ever changed.

"You could always tell when a game meant more to him, too. He was pretty level, usually, but he always told us how important it would be to win in New York. He'd tell us if we wanted to get known, to make the Pro Bowl teams, to have magazine stories written about us, then we had better win in New York. He said we had to have a good game against the Giants, because that's where all the publicity was, all the television networks, the big newspapers.

"That's where he was so good in getting us ready for a weak team, too, because most of the years I played we always beat the Giants (the Cowboys during White's career were 19-7 against the Giants, including victories the first 10 times he played them). For the big games, when we played Washington, or maybe sometimes the Raiders or the Steelers, he didn't have to get us up. We knew how big the game was and he knew that if he prepared us the best he could, and if we played the best we could, that we were capable of winning every one of those games.

"But yeah, you could tell when it was a team he really liked to beat, like the Giants. He'd get even more intense during the week, not that he wasn't always intense anyway. He'd tell us when we played the Redskins it would decide who won the Eastern Division championship."

Given the rare level of excellence White reached and then maintained, it is even more puzzling when he recalls his problems of the first two seasons, when the coaching staff wasn't convinced he was a lineman, when they tried to put him at middle linebacker as the next Lee Roy Jordan, when they tried to teach him the finer points and subtleties of the flex defense.

"Hey, one thing I definitely never was was subtle," he laughs. "And man, I tried to learn the flex. I really did. But I really wasn't what you'd call the model flex player, not by any stretch of the imagination. Honest, I wasn't. I tried to conform to a certain extent, but he gave me a lot of freedom. He let me go a little bit, and I'd make a lot of big plays. See, he and Ernie both would tell me that if I could do that, as long as I made the plays, I could be more free. I'd get stuck sometimes, trying to play the flex by the book, and then I'd tell myself, 'Hey, just go. Go. Make the plays.' Once I learned the concept of the flex, and havin' guys around me with the experience . . . see, that's what hurt us toward the end, because we didn't have any more of the veterans, and the guys were trying to play the flex, young guys, and not really knowin' how to do things . . . even though teams adjusted to it, we still had a great defense. See, if you have great players, you can do anything you want. But if you have enough great ones and put them into the flex, it's better, because the flex is better. Because it's Tom Landry's defense. And there at the end, say from 1986 on, we just didn't have the players. They didn't draft good ones, the ones we had started getting too old, or they got hurt and couldn't play. They were good guys, but not the same caliber of players they replaced.

"You know, when you go through 10 years of draft choices and none of 'em, the first-rounders, are around (and with the exception of defensive end Jim Jeffcoat, the statement is correct) you have done some shitty drafting. And if you can't play the defense, you know you can't be successful. In my opinion, that's the answer in a nutshell.

"The Cowboys always seemed to take chances in the draft, and what made them great was how lucky they got . . . and for how long. But it hurt them, too, because they kept doin' it, and the law of averages finally caught up with them. You can't win without the players, and you get them in the draft. If you screw up year after year, you can set yourself back 10 years, you know?"

Growing up in Wilmington, playing football, White should have been a Baltimore Colts fan. But he wasn't. Well, not really.

"You know what? I was a football fan, not really for any one team, just the game. I just loved the game. I played it and I always looked at the sizes of the guys on television and I thought, 'Damn, am I ever going to get big enough to play up there?' Yeah, I always wanted to play pro football . . . man, since I was a little kid. And it never mattered who I played for.

"I was never a fan of any particular team, not at all, never was. I was always playing. I never memorized statistics or shit like that, like the other kids did. I just wanted to play. And I had fun playing in high school, even if we didn't win a lot. When Maryland gave me the scholarship offer . . . I only heard from two others, Virginia Tech and Arizona State . . . I figured my father was right, Maryland was the right choice because it was close to home. Besides, I had a girlfriend who was goin' to the University of Delaware, so I thought that was pretty good, too. I could drive up and see her on weekends.

"Delaware is just overlooked. I should have had a lot more offers . . . even if our team wasn't good . . . I made All-State in basketball, baseball, football. There was a guy named Dim Montero, who coached in Delaware high schools for a while, then went to Maryland as a scout, and he used to come watch me when I was in the 10th grade. He kept telling me to go to Maryland, and I guess he talked to my father, too. If it wasn't for him, I probably never would have gone to college.

"Once I got there and started playing, started making All-America teams, everybody would tell me I was going to be drafted real high, maybe the top draft choice. Well, you know, I've always been funny that way. I've always worried about stuff like that. I never believed that, man. I can honestly look you square in the eyes and say I never believed it. Until it happened, I was never sure of anything. I always thought . . . you know, somebody was foolin' me, that they'd change their minds, something.

"Shit, when I got to Dallas I thought I'd see everybody in town wearing a gun and riding a horse, you know? I had never been any farther away from home than Maryland. But then I got to see they were good people down there, not much different from me, and I figured I'd have a good time."

Landry made that happen, through hard work and dedication.

"Tom influenced my life a lot, not just in football. He used to talk to us . . . you know, he's a real religious person . . . and he'd always try to give us little messages from the Bible. A lot of guys thought that was corny, you know, but I listened to him, I always listened to that man. I learned from him. He helped me not just in football but in life. I admired the way he handled himself during adversity. Everybody can be cool when everything's goin' good, you know? People around, slapping you on the back, shaking your hand. But up until the day he got fired, I learned from him, things like poise and control and consistency. He handled that situation well. Nobody ever saw him yell and scream, kick a hole in a wall, punch a door. Why? Because he put football third in his life. God was first. Family was second. Then football. I really believe that's how he dealt with that stuff.

"I ain't had lightning hit me in the head yet, so I guess I'm not a really rotten person, but I do know I really respect people who can put religion that high in their lives, and I have always been able to learn from them. That's the most important thing I'll remember about being with Coach Landry, that he made me a better person. What I learned from him will last me the rest of my life. It will stay with me forever."

It has not been an easy retirement for Randy White. He has money, he has friends, he has television commercials that go on even now. But he has an emptiness, a void, not unusual with recently retired athletes.

"I miss it a lot. I really do. You know what I miss most? I miss Sundays. I miss just gettin' geared up and goin' out there and, man, just lettin' it loose. Imagine, bein' able to hit somebody in the head as hard as you can and havin' somebody tell you, 'Hey, you did good, you really did good.' And then gettin' paid for it, too? Do that out on the street and do that when you get pissed off and they're gonna put you in jail. I miss seeing the guys every day, dealing with all the little crap you have to deal with, being together like we always were, locker room stuff. You know, if Tom Landry was still there, I might have pursued coaching, but now, in Dallas, I don't think I could."

But if another team expressed interest, if another team said that Randy White might make a fine defensive line coach?

"Yeah, I might listen, I guess. Yeah, I know they (assistant coaches) don't make much money, but what can you do with money if you're not happy doin' what you do? But if somebody else called? I don't know, that'd be a tough decision, it wouldn't be easy to leave now.

"And you know, I'd be on the level of the players, I'd still be like one of them . . . probably will be for another 10 years or so. It wouldn't be like them trying to deal with some old-man father-figure bullshit. It might be a lot easier, and I don't have any doubt that if I was a coach, I could do a good job. Maybe makin' a move would be good. I'm gettin' divorced . . . no, uh-uh, don't say you're sorry, 'cause I'm not . . . and I do my commercials. I have an annuity, some real estate . . . deferred payments. I'm OK, and wherever I go the money will follow me, but I don't want to leave Dallas and I don't think any other team is going to ask me to be a coach."

White's outlook on money is another unusual facet of this man's personality. "I never negotiated any of my contracts with anybody but Tex Schramm," White says, "and I'll tell you what . . . I think he was tough, but he was fair. With me, anyway. Maybe somebody else feels differently. But I always played well, so why wouldn't he be fair? But I played for a lot of years for a lot less money than a lot of other guys were getting who weren't at my level. You know why? I'd hate to be fightin' about money and then it gets time to go to training camp and . . . shit, man . . . I was not about to miss training camp. What's my option, go be a bricklayer back over to Delaware?

"I'm talkin' about a difference of, maybe, $100,000 with Schramm, and shit, I couldn't have made $100,000 any year of my life if it wasn't for football, so what am I really fightin' about, you know? That's the way I looked at it, anyway. You see, a lot of the guys . . . yeah, most of 'em, I guess . . . they always acted like they were doin' the team a favor by playing for them. Me? I always felt like the Dallas Cowboys were doin' me a favor, lettin' me play for them. I really did, honest to God. I felt like it was all vacation time, you know? I'm still livin' in a dream world because of football.

"So if it came down to that 100,000, and if I wanted to start thinkin' about gettin' ready for training camp, you know, no distractions in my mind, I'd say, 'Hey, what the hell, the hell with it, let's go for it the way it is,' and I'd sign the damned thing and be done with it. My last year, my last contract, I held out and went fishing. It came down to the wire, I missed the whole training camp, but it worked out. I missed all the preseason games, too . . . hardest damned thing I ever did."

And now, with nobody to hit on Sundays, what does Randy White do?

"What do I do now? I watch the games. I went to all but two of the home games, but I'd get too wired up, man. I'd be walkin' into the stadium and I'd get butterflies in my stomach, and people recognized me, asked if I was playin', asked if I was planning a comeback. But I sat with a friend of mine, he has a box, and that made it a little easier because I wasn't just surrounded by fans.

It's tough. I'd jump around and cheer and I'd have to calm myself down. You know, 'Hey, take it easy, you don't do this any more.'

"You're not playing, you're just a spectator. Shit, when they were out in training camp and I was home, I was a little crazy. I was liftin' weights every day, running, getting in condition. I was in better shape than I ever was. Do I think I could play now, a year out? Shit, yes. I could play, if my neck was OK. And maybe it is, but I'd never call Jimmy Johnson and ask to go to training camp. But if I ever got there, I'd have to have some conditions. I just can't go out there and beat myself to death doin' two-a-days now. Shit, I just got so many bullets left to shoot. Might as well save 'em for when you get a real good, nice, clean shot. And I don't think that would sit well with them, they'd need somebody to go full time.

"You know, when I first came to the Cowboys, I felt like I was becoming part of a legend. I mean, they had always been winners, far back as I can remember. It was kind of special, thinking about the Dallas Cowboys, and them making me their first draft choice. Lee Roy Jordan was the team leader and very helpful to me. He was kind of like the perfect Dallas Cowboy, the guy who set the example. And he was a pretty outgoing guy, but strict, no nonsense, no bullshit. Have a good time, but I tell you what, when you're playin' football, nothing else is that important. Not nearly.

"I bounced around my first few years, playing special teams, not being sure what the coaches wanted. Lee Roy was starting to groom me to play middle linebacker, but I didn't think that worked. I knew it would never work. Lee Roy, and the rest of the veterans, they kind of thought it was their job to groom the rookies, to make sure things were set in motion for replacements, because they knew when they were about to retire, when they couldn't play anymore, they wanted to know the Cowboy tradition would continue. I don't know, of course, how it is anywhere else, but I thought that was kind of unique, kind of special.

"Looking back, I wouldn't have wanted to be anywhere else, for sure. I wouldn't have wanted to play for another coach and I wouldn't have wanted to play in another city, or with another bunch of guys. These were the best years of my life, and I don't think there's gonna be anything better coming ahead. The flex was tough, the work was hard, I found myself once covering Dorsett on pass coverage one-to-one, and I knew that wasn't for me.

"But as soon as Coach Landry moved me to tackle, I felt natural, just like, boom, right away, like somebody took the handcuffs off me. On a three-four team, I could have probably been an inside linebacker. Or a nose tackle. I would have loved nose tackle, I think, bein' in the middle of all the action like that. But a lot of the inside linebackers in the three-fours today are just a little bit more mobile nose tackles.

"I came down to Dallas when I got drafted and I just felt a chemistry, a warm, comfortable feeling, and I guess from the first minute there I knew I was sort of home. A second home. And I loved all the years with the Cowboys, the real Cowboys. I loved the people and how they reacted and I loved the excitement and the electricity you could feel just walking around the streets, being in the restaurants and shops. It was a special, magical time, and it just ain't gonna come back again, at least not for me, you know?

"And these new Cowboys? If they called me back, asked me to play? Nah, shit, no more. I'm done. I thought it would go on forever, but in my mind I knew it had to end. I'd see guys like Lee Roy, and I knew that'd be me one day. I knew it would end and I didn't want it to end. But I walked away, on my own. I didn't go through that bullshit of gettin' cut and tryin' to sign on somewhere else. I'm glad, in a way, that it worked out this way."

Why?

"Because me and Tom Landry walked away at the same time. That's the way I would have wanted it, and it sure isn't a bad thing to be remembered for."

CHAPTER 6

TONY DORSETT

THE NATURAL

Anthony Drew Dorsett sat at the dining room table in his ultra-modern single-level north Dallas home, on a cul-de-sac called Kettering Court, swimming pool in the back, circular drive in the front, where everything inside is spotlessly clean and meticulously arranged despite the fact that he lives alone, and said the most amazing thing.

"No doubt about it. Some of the moves I see myself making when I watch game films are absolutely incredible. They were never planned, they just happened. And now, when I see them on film, I wonder how I did it."

And that, friends, should dispel any lingering doubts that running with a football in your hands is instinctive. Nobody can teach it, nobody can capture it . . . and nobody can ever match the gliding, slip-sliding style that set Tony Dorsett apart from everyone else in the game.

Players remember problems they had with Dorsett, because on their particular world-class plateau of athleticism, their failures are far more bitter, as well as infrequent.

"He never gave you a fair shot at him," said linebacker Rich Milot of the Washington Redskins, now retired. "You were always grabbing at him after he was past you, you know?"

Harry Carson, who should find himself in the Pro Football Hall of Fame one day after a storied 12-year, nine–Pro Bowl career with the New York Giants: "I hated to play against Dorsett. He made you look bad, and players hate that. I mean, I'd have the guy, dead to rights, and suddenly I'm grabbin' air and he's prancing downfield someplace."

Former Philadelphia Eagles head coach Dick Vermeil, who once said his admiration for Carson was so intense he would pay money to see him play: "Dorsett is the only running back I ever saw who could make Harry Carson look like a normal human being. One day a scout told me he thought Dorsett had started to slow down. I asked him, in all honesty, how he could tell. I mean, how much faster is invisible than almost invisible?"

Tony Dorsett smiles. He is recently retired, having spent the final two years of his 13-season career—unsatisfactorily, he admits—with the Denver Broncos. But the first 11? Aah, those were, as the poet said, the stuff of which dreams are made.

First of all, it should be said that the Dallas Cowboys fooled the Seattle Seahawks. Bamboozled them. Tricked them. Sold them a bill of goods and the exclusive rights to the Brooklyn Bridge, the Golden Gate Bridge, the Lincoln Tunnel and O'Hare Airport. It happened in the spring of 1977, when two blue-chip running backs were coming out of the college ranks into the world of megabucks and the National Football League. They were the late Ricky Bell of the University of Southern California and Tony Dorsett of the University of Pittsburgh.

The teams holding the first two picks were the Tampa Bay Buccaneers and the Seattle Seahawks. Everybody knew the silly old Bucs were going to take Bell, because as an expansion team the year before, their owner, Hugh F. Culverhouse, had hired a college coaching legend, the acerbic John McKay—head coach at USC.

McKay said he would take Bell if he wound up with the first choice in the round, and then his patch-quilt new team locked it up for him with a winless first season.

Seattle wanted Dorsett, of the pair the one most scouts felt would be a better and more effective professional, but despite the obvious difference McKay would not allow reason to blind him to old Trojan loyalties. Dorsett, you see, never played for him at USC, so how good could he really be?

But Dallas wanted Dorsett even more than Seattle did, and "TD" made things significantly easier by telling Seattle management that under no conditions would he consider playing for the Seahawks. Normally, this sort of declaration has as much effect on a team as the weather. The college player signs with the team that has drafted him—or he doesn't play at all. And, as one general manager in the league once noted, quite cleverly: "Football players tend to play football."

But the Seahawks, equally as new as the Buccaneers (both franchises had been whelped in time to start the 1976 season), weren't in the mood to woo and cajole. And when Dallas made its offer—a swap of first-round choices plus three second-round picks—the eager Seahawks said yes.

It is immaterial, in the final analysis, which players turned into Seahawks, because the Cowboys were able to land Dorsett. But, for those who keep records, they were guard Steve August of Tulsa in the first round; offensive tackle Tom Lynch of Boston College, linebacker Terry Beeson of Kansas, and linebacker Pete Cronan of Boston College in the second round. The Seahawks then traded a fourth second-round choice—oh, sweetest irony of ironies—to Dallas for wide receiver Duke Ferguson, whereupon the Cowboys immediately claimed quarterback Glenn Carano, who would serve as a competent backup for the next seven years.

The scoreboard, then, shows that the Cowboys traded Steve August, Tom Lynch, Terry Beeson, Pete Cronan and Duke Ferguson to the Seattle Seahawks for Tony Dorsett and Glenn Carano.

There are people sitting in jail, even as you read these pages, for masterminding far less flagrant scams than that.

Dorsett retired as the second-leading ground gainer in the history of pro football, behind only Walter Payton of the Chicago Bears and ahead of Jim Brown, who for two decades was the league's all-time leader. In his 11 Dallas seasons he led the team in rushing 10 times, holds team records for career yardage (12,036), single-season yardage (1,646), single-game yardage (206), career attempts (2,755), career rushing average (4.37 yards per carry), career rushing touchdowns (72) and career touchdowns overall (86).

In addition, he has four of the five longest runs from scrimmage in team history, including the 99-yarder against the Minnesota Vikings before a Monday night national television audience that stands as the league record as well and that earned most-favored status with ABC as promotional footage.

Through it all, through this remarkable career, as one of the sportswriters said, Dorsett "spent most of his time apologizing for things he said the day before . . . and the rest of the time in trying to explain bad decisions he made concerning his money."

At one juncture in the early and middle 1980s, Dorsett defied the best judgment of everyone he asked—and several who offered unsolicited advice—and sank more than $600,000 into a questionable oil-options shelter in Oklahoma. In order to raise the money, he cashed in all of his deferred money contracts, which would have paid him upper six-figure salaries annually through the year 2000. He lost it all, and the team helped by advancing loans, arranging manageable payment schedules with such otherwise unforgiving institutions as the Internal Revenue Service, and managing his money for a while.

The Dorsett-Landry relationship, which never came close to matching the bitterness that flared between Landry and quarterback Don Meredith a decade earlier, did test Landry's patience more than a few times. But through it all, Dorsett remained wonderfully respectful of the man.

"What I learned from Coach Landry off the field was just as important as winning games," he began, and while contrite is not a word normally used to describe his persona, it might come close. "We didn't always get along . . . I know I wasn't the easiest guy to live with . . . but I always respected him as a coach and a man, and I wouldn't have wanted to play for anybody else. Even when I was traded to Denver, it had nothing to do with Coach Landry. It was other things."

Those other things were, in order, Herschel Walker, Herschel Walker and Herschel Walker. When the Cowboys signed the fabled back, after the death of the short-lived, poorly run and ill-advised United States Football League, there simply wasn't room enough in the backfield, nor were there enough footballs used during a game, to give each of them the number of carries they expected and deserved.

"Tony pushed and pushed," said Frank Luksa, columnist for The Dallas Times Herald, "and it was a mistake, because he was 33 years old and Herschel was seven years younger. And bigger. And healthier. And just as fast. And, well, the new kid in town, the new excitement. What did he think would happen?"

In truth, it wasn't much of a trade. The Broncos offered the Cowboys a fifth-round draft pick for 1989, which turned out to be the third of three fifth-round spots held by Dallas, and the draft choice . . . in effect, the man who was "traded" for Tony Dorsett, was defensive tackle Jeff Roth, who made the team as a bench reserve.

"You know, what always impressed me most with Coach Landry was his ability to bring out a guy's talent . . . to know how to get the most from his players, to know each of the players, what it took for them to play at their best, sometimes to make them play better than they ever thought they could play. We knew that if we didn't get the job done that we'd have to be looking for a job elsewhere, and while that's true anywhere, Tom had a certain aura about himself because, well, you know, he was a legend, man. A living legend. You knew he wouldn't accept anything less than what he wanted, than what he expected from you.

"He brought out the best in everyone around him, not just players but people who were associated with the team, people who worked for the team . . . the radio guys, the television guys, the newspaper guys . . . it was like anybody who ever came into contact with him was afraid to let him down. It was just the way he carried himself, drove himself. It was his personality."

Dorsett, perhaps because he was no longer a Cowboy, and hadn't been for two years, said he didn't really feel one way or the other when Landry was fired . . . and then proceeded to prove he didn't mean that at all.

"I thought the guy deserved better," he began. "But, you know, Tom was a very intelligent guy, and he understood the nature of sports, in particular that . . . well, he'd be the first to say it . . . that if you stay around long enough, eventually it's going to happen to you. Even to him, but nobody ever thought it would happen that way to him.

"Sure, players are here and gone. We have always been treated in a similar fashion, one way or another . . . all the time, and usually a lot worse . . . but this guy was around the league for so long, had been the head coach since Dallas came into the league . . . and such a figurehead in and out of the game, such a proper man, with his lifestyle dictated by his Christian beliefs. . . . You just never thought a guy of his magnitude would get the kind of treatment he got. But that's the nature of sports, and we as athletes sometimes feel we're invincible, that things could never happen to us, and then it does.

"I felt for him, I guess I really did. It was such a lousy way for his career to end. He deserved better, regardless of how I think other people were treated when they came through the Cowboy system . . . and I guess what proves that is how the people here showed their displeasure with how he was treated. They were upset, angry, and they should have been. And nationally, I mean, they accepted him right away in the Hall of Fame, that should show you how much people around the country felt about him.

"I had my problems with him, so did other players on the team, but those problems seemed to stay mostly behind the doors, private. The Cowboys did one hell of a job in marketing the team, Tex Schramm in particular . . . that America's Team rah-rah stuff. But remember, Tom was really the figurehead around whom everything was based. They painted the picture for so long about how clean-cut and American the Cowboy players were, when in reality it just was not that way. But give credit where credit is due, they did one hell of a job.

"And with Tom, well, he was different. There's no way to get around that. You see coaches today, all of them, and coaches of tomorrow, they're all going to be regular people, they're going to react similar to how I reacted, to how other players, people in all walks of life, are going to reach sometimes. They just lose it once in a while, just go off, you know?

"But Tom Landry never did. He always stayed just the way he looked. He stayed cool. Poised. I have often wondered how he handled things, pressures, tensions, frustrations. Did he take all this, all of this human reaction stuff, and go home with it? I just can't see him venting all his frustrations out on Alicia, because she's a very beautiful woman . . . it's a great match. I don't know where he released this, I really don't. You know, he was a politician in a way, especially with the media. He knew the politics, who to talk to, what to say and what not to say. He never got flustered. You see other coaches go off, just like players, but Tom never did. I always wondered about that, and envied him, and respected him because of it.

"I mean, how can a guy never lose his temper? Never. I guess we all saw him, a few times, almost break, start to get excited, but then he'd always catch himself and hold back, keep it in. How can a guy hold all this in when there's thousands . . . millions of other people just going berserk? How can he not even get excited? We had some run-ins, I guess I got under his skin a few times, but he never came out publicly and said things about me, as I've seen other coaches do, and if we had some differences, it was between him and me, that's all. There were times I chose to make it public, and then I would usually regret it, but he never did, never would."

Looking back at the 11 years spent with Landry, Dorsett, perhaps the greatest all-around running threat in pro football history, holds one trait closer than any of the others in his remembrances of the fabled coach.

"His work ethic, his preparation. I just always thought that there was no team we could ever come up against that could be more prepared, better prepared, than we were. I was amazed, when I first came up, at his intelligence as a football coach. Hey, everybody can put X's and O's on a blackboard, but he knew situations . . . the short-yardage situations, goal line, third-and-long . . . he could almost predict what could happen and I always found it amazing.

"It was one of the ways that he used to teach football but some of us found could be applied to life, too. Like there's always a goal, one way or another, but you've got to have a method, a way of accomplishing that goal. I'm quite sure all the players who have come through the system took that, at least, with them. It isn't enough to just set yourself a goal, you have to come up with a method, a solution, a way to get it done.''

Most of the players, perhaps intentionally, came up through the system and left and were remembered only as a series of faceless blurs. All the running backs, all the quarterbacks, all the offensive linemen . . . with some obvious exceptions, of course, were more than just similar to each other. They were clones, as close as the Landry-Schramm consortium could make them.

Doug Dennison was a halfback. He started for a while. So, too, was Scott Laidlaw a halfback who started for a while. And Ron Springs. Timmy Newsome. Robert Lavette. Darryl Clack. Les Shy. Even Dan Reeves, who has gone on to head coaching success in Denver. They were all of a same cut. About the same size, same weight, same speed, same specialized movements. They fit the pattern. Others didn't. Those others were never drafted.

"It was a lot like, or so it seemed, anyway, that the organization tried to create interchangeable parts," Dorsett said. "I don't know for sure about that, all I know is that they did a very good job of finding talent, the kind of talent that fit into what Coach Landry was trying to do. Maybe as time passed they got caught up in the process of trying to find the, quote-unquote, 'good guy, Cowboy type of guy,' and they'd maybe pass over some other guy who they didn't think was smart enough, or whose reputation wasn't good enough . . . and as a result you started to see a decline in the quality of their draft choices, because I thought they really got too much involved in that psychology of it all, you know, the Cowboy way, America's team, stuff like that.

"They tried to keep the 'good old boy' type of image, instead of goin' out there to get the kind of players who could have helped right away . . . impact players. They'd pass on them because of what they felt were traits that weren't in the Cowboy image. Guys with a bad reputation coming out of college, even guys who got better later on, who just had to get past stuff lots of young men have to deal with . . . they got signed by other teams, drafted by other teams, and the Cowboys forced themselves to pass on a lot of talent."

Running backs such as Dorsett, who weighed maybe 190 at their peak, always took special care to learn all about other linebackers. They are the ones who can inflict the most pain and do the most damage.

"I guess there were a lot of linebackers coming out of college the last few years, the last five or so years, because most of the teams had gone to the three-four defense and just needed more linebackers. That seemed to be an area where the Cowboys didn't seem able to find great players, while other teams, like the New York Giants, the Rams, Chicago, others, just did.

"Like, I always had the greatest respect for the Giants' linebackers, even before they got Lawrence (Taylor). Harry Carson? I'll never forget, we were playin' them, and I was breakin' through the line almost every time, and when I did, almost every time, there's this big black forearm stopping me. I remember at halftime our offensive line coach, Jim Erkenbeck, saying, 'Hey, we could run for a lot of yards if somebody would just block number 53, OK?' Harry was always one of the true competitors in this business. Every time we played them . . . and they almost always lost to us, you know? . . . I'd look to see where Harry was, what he was doing. Out of all the guys on the team, it seemed like it always bothered him the most. A lot of the times, they'd actually have us beat, late in the game, and then something would happen. You know, (quarterback) Phil Simms would make a costly mistake and we'd end up pulling the game out. And Harry always looked absolutely devastated. I would always try to find him . . . not to talk to him, but from a distance . . . but he would always show a lot of hurt.

"But it's true, or I believe it's true, anyway, that the Cowboys got caught up in their own image . . . so caught up in it . . . that they let good players get away. And my evaluation of it, the reason for the demise of the Cowboys and for all the stuff, like this Landry firing, that it caused . . . you blame whoever you want to blame, but the drafts started to hurt them. Was it the scouts, the personnel people, the coaches? I don't know. Landry had a lot to say about the draft, too. That's not important. When you can't get the good players . . . when you let other teams draft them . . . then you can't win."

The Dallas image, in its silver-and-blue glory, was already well in place, firmly established, when Dorsett twinkle-toed on the scene. But his arrival, or the arrival of someone like him, had been eagerly anticipated by the veterans for years prior to the event.

Safety Charlie Waters remembers the need. "We had gone to the Super Bowl (just two seasons prior) with running backs like Doug Dennison and Preston Pearson, and while they were wonderful players we still needed somebody who could break it any time. I liked Tony immediately. He was cocky, but he was good-guy cocky."

He was also an immediate sensation, leading the team in rushing with 1,007 yards, a 4.8 per-carry average and a dozen touchdowns. But even then, as he began to slip-slide through the NFL's defenses, he began to question Landry's scheme. "Speed has always been one of my greatest assets, and I started to wonder why they didn't use me more on quick-hitting plays, traps . . . and why I wasn't used more as a receiver."

In Landry's defense, it might be noted that several skilled observers feel the coach's judicious use of the somewhat undersized Dorsett was the real reason he was able to last as long as he did without injury. In the world of pro football, one of the magic words is durability. Athletes of Dorsett's stature—barely 5-10, sometimes weighing as much as 190—who are asked to slice and slash through the mined fields of defenses, don't normally last very long at all.

"The image was here, the legend was underway when I got here," Dorsett agreed. "Tom Landry was here, Roger Staubach was here . . . and they were pretty much the focal points of the organization. They had these squeaky-clean lives, they played on it and built on it and it paid off for them. Hey, America's Team? How else would that name have worked? There were problems within, of course, but nobody was saying anything about them, and I think when I started to play, I moved the team up to another level. I know that. I also realize they pulled a fast one on the

Seahawks, and I'm more than happy that they did. I was extremely delighted. I knew what the first pick was all about, McKay needed to take Ricky. I didn't want to go to Tampa or Seattle, in fact that was part of the psychology of our negotiations. We knew Tampa was going to take Ricky, and so we went to Seattle, which had my rights, to tell them I had no interest whatsoever in playing there, that if they drafted me I'd consider taking an offer in Canada (the Canadian Football League is usually more threat than substance), sitting out a year and being drafted again. No, I don't think I really would have crossed the border. That would have taken an awful lot.

"When I was at Pitt, I wanted to play for the Steelers. It's home, man. I'm from Aliquippa. I would have loved to stay home and play for the Steelers, and maybe that could have turned out to be some kind of headache, you know, with family and friends all over. . . . I had always dreamed about wearing the black and gold. I always liked the Dallas Cowboys, though, and it was an amazing thing that their popularity was all over the country. Once I got here, it seemed like there were great gobs of people waiting for our bus in every city we went to, and in talking to other players around the league, it just wasn't the same for them. Maybe today's 49ers. But we had fans all over, it was unbelievable.

"I remember when I was a kid, a friend of mine and I got into a fight because he was for the Packers and I was for the Cowboys and Green Bay always won those games. But I think if the Steelers had found a way to get me, that would have probably been the best thing. In fact, I won the Dapper Dan award (a Pittsburgh tradition, which bestows an annual award on the outstanding local high school, college and professional athlete) my senior year at Pitt, and I remember, at the end of my speech, I said, to the Rooney family (which owns the Steelers), to please not let me leave Pittsburgh.

"From what I understand, they were one of the teams that were in the sweepstakes with Seattle . . . tryin' to work out a deal, but supposedly it got too high, too expensive, and they dropped out. It didn't really matter, otherwise, where I played, except I just didn't want to play for an expansion franchise. To a running back, that didn't sound too healthy, you know? Young, inexperienced offensive linemen trying to block for me against those old, experienced killers on defenses around the league? Not me, man. I'm not big enough to be able to deal with that.

"And I would have loved to play in New York, too. Can you imagine, a guy like me in a city like New York? That would have been a great place for me. I guess it's possible I might not have gotten to all the games on time . . . but it sure would have been a great spot for me."

As a collegian, the wiry kid from the coal town won the Heisman Trophy in his senior year, became the first player in college history to put together four consecutive seasons of 1,000-plus yardage, set an NCAA career record (since broken) of 6,082 yards and was named to the first team All-America squads as a junior and senior. This, after being a High School All-America and one of the nation's most heavily recruited players, gave him an instantly recognizable name.

And when he got to Dallas, he found out it was also important that he was black. At least to some people.

"I guess it was less pronounced than it had been 10 years before," he said, "and I suppose it wasn't as bad for me because of who I was, but it was there, man. No question, it was there. Hey, I know it never reached the magnitude of what the everyday black citizen had to go through . . . still, you know, it was pretty obvious. But it was here, Dallas was not immune to racism, to prejudice, no doubt it was here. I experienced some things I wasn't used to experiencing.

"But when I first got here, I'd sit down and talk to some of the older guys, like Rayfield Wright and Jethro Pugh and Mel Renfro, and they'd tell me things . . . like about north Dallas, where the old practice field was, and the black players couldn't rent or buy a place to live near there. Blacks just were not allowed. Nobody said that, but you didn't see any. Some of those guys went to management, told them they wanted to live near the practice facility, and they were told there was nothing anybody could do. So they had to live way out to the south.

"Renfro was telling me about calling on the phone for an apartment and was told there were a lot of vacancies, but when he got there they said everything just rented out, you know? I think Tex Schramm went to court for Mel over that one.

"And there were clubs you couldn't get into if you were black . . . and I had an altercation there, too . . . the first week I was here. I had been to the place earlier that year, with ABC people, working with the NCAA on an anti-drug campaign . . . I think it was six players goin' to six cities to make speeches. Anyway, Dallas was one of the cities, and I got to do Dallas. So now, when I was back in town as a member of the team, I knew about this club, and I knew this particular night was going to be Ladies Night. So I went.

"I wanted to let the people know I was in town, and so I'm by myself and when I get there I'm stopped at the door. I want to know, hey, what's goin' on here? The guy said he wanted identification. So I gave him some I.D. Then he wanted another I.D. And then he wanted another I.D. He says you've got to show three proofs of identification, and maybe surprisingly to them I had what they wanted.

"So now they start questioning the way I was dressed. So I'm saying, 'Hey, look at these other people walkin' in, and look at these people walkin' out,' you know? I was dressed better than they were. So then they get to my sunglasses, tell me I have to take off my sunglasses. I say, 'Hey, come on, man, let's cool this,' but in the meantime I'm gettin' a little upset, but I wanted to go in to that place. So I finally get in, and yes, it was an all-white establishment, except for this one black lady, but she came in and disappeared. I ended up dancing with a lady, got off the floor, went for a drink. So she ordered a drink, and I ordered a drink, and she paid for hers with a ticket, the kind the club distributed. It was Ladies' Night, so she got the tickets that way, I guess.

"This bartender took care of the drinks, she excused herself and went to the ladies' room, and while she's gone this other bartender came up and asked me if I paid for my drink. I said, 'Yeah, I paid for my drink.' He said I didn't but then the first one came back and said, 'Yeah, he paid for it.' So now this other bartender tells me, he says, 'Well, I don't want you standin' here drinkin' your drink, you hear?' Now come on, there were people all over standin' there drinkin', so I asked him how come I can't. One thing led to another, he started yellin' a bunch of racial obscenities at me, I got upset and grabbed him and punched him when he tried to come across the bar, another guy jumped on my back and I got him off and next thing I know I'm standing outside talkin' to the police.

"And later, when the Cowboys kept winning, when we became really popular . . . well, yeah, we were highly visible, we could go places, that was the thing about it. But, you know, it was like the people all loved you, but then they'd do something that would bring you right down again . . . yeah, this is still America, I'm still black, and this is the way I'm going to be treated.

"Over the years, I've seen Dallas grow into a different city, but things have changed. Still, it's here. Hell, it's everywhere. Dallas is one of the few major cities in this country that has never had a race riot, and I'm not sayin' that race riots are good, but when everybody was going through the struggle, the civil rights movement, nobody here was angry enough to do that, I guess. Maybe they were afraid, or supressed, and man, they were rioting in Alabama and Mississippi, and not here?"

Landry even took a hand in the racial situation in Dallas, played a part in trying to smooth things out for the players.

"When things got really bad, he'd come in and say, like, 'These places are off-limits . . . you don't need to go to this place . . . you don't need to go to that place' . . . and he'd name them, see . . . because only bad things can happen to you if you do. He'd tell us some of those things, but mostly it was (personnel director) Gil Brandt who took care of that. Man, he knew everything. There were places I'd go, places I'd be at one night, and the next day at the practice field he'd come up to me and say, 'Hey, Tony? I hear you were at such-and-such a place last night, and maybe you shouldn't be, you know?' God damn, how'd he know so fast? I wasn't that popular, and I sure tried not to be that visible. I was single, and I wanted to go out and have fun, and what was wrong with that?"

It is entirely possible that no running back since Tony Dorsett came out of the college ranks with such fanfare and electricity as Herschel Walker, and it was to Dorsett's extreme discomfort that he, too, gravitated to the Cowboys.

Dallas had taken a chance in the 1985 draft, and in the fifth round—still a relatively high pick and one that had produced Pro Bowl players for many teams—they claimed Walker, who had left the University of Georgia with two years of eligibility still remaining to accept a multimillion-dollar deal from the USFL's New Jersey Generals.

There is some thought, and there were some accusations, that the Generals "tricked" Herschel into leaving school early, or at least into disqualifying himself from further NCAA-sanctioned athletic eligibility. They made him an offer. He refused. They made him another offer. Again, he refused. Finally, they sent a small group of team representatives to talk with him, and when he agreed to the meeting, when he agreed to discuss contracts and money and professional involvement, he was in violation of the rigid policy the NCAA applies to players and schools when it seems like the right thing to do and, at the same time, is politically appropriate.

So Herschel Walker, a man with great size and speed, became a member of the Dallas Cowboys in the summer of 1986. It was an extremely delicate situation. Dorsett, with an ego as large as his impact on the game, was offended. And, quite frankly, he was concerned that his future as a Cowboy was imperiled. Walker, variously 30 to 40 pounds heavier than Dorsett, was just as fast and clearly a superior pass receiver.

To be effective, Dorsett needed to carry the ball 20 to 25 times a game. To be effective, Herschel needed the same attention. That, of course, isn't possible, and Landry wrestled with the dilemma night after night, finally opting for a split-backfield situation in which Walker would carry the ball a considerable amount of time but be the pass receiver he never felt Dorsett could be, while allowing Tony to remain the "featured" ball carrier.

In the 1986 season, Dorsett gained 748 yards rushing. He was the team leader.

Walker gained 737 yards—obviously, just 11 less—and was the

Cowboys' leader in pass receptions with 76, a team single-season record that still stands, and the 837 yards he accumulated made him the team's overall yardage leader. He scored 14 touchdowns. The pendulum had swung, and Tony Dorsett could feel himself being eased out.

He would put up with just one more season before demanding a trade, and it came as no surprise to anyone involved when the Cowboys did not try to talk him out of that decision. No one but Dorsett, that is.

"I was a little unhappy with the treatment I got in Dallas, and then last year (1989), I was unhappy with the treatment I got in Denver. I mean, after 13 years they said this guy has to learn to catch better when they don't have anybody who can run as well as I can. When you do it as well as I have for as long as I have, why not just use me at what I do best? I even offered to stay in Dallas last summer and not go to training camp. I spoke to Dan (Reeves), and asked whether the verdict was already out on me, whether I'd just be wasting my time going there.

"But I was assured the decision would be made based on training camp, so I went. Hey, I'm the second all-time leading rusher, who can you get who's going to run the football better than me? I can still play, too, and if somebody gave me some guarantees, I'd play again. But when Dan said, 'Tony, we don't have any problems with your running, we want you to be able to catch the ball better,' maybe he should have sat down with his quarterback and said, 'Hey, John (Elway), take a little bit off when you throw those 5-yard outs, man.' Hey, my career has been so good, all the things I've accomplished have been so meaningful, that my career dictates I go out with high fashion, not with somebody cutting me. But I'm not going to put up with anybody's bullshit. My mindset is done. I'll never play football again, and a lot of business deals are coming my way, I've got a lot of irons in the fire. I'd like to get into communications, stay in sports, do some broadcasting, maybe.

"Coaching has never been an ambition of mine. I don't know if I have the dedication for coaching. That takes a very special individual, a very committed individual, like being a schoolteacher, and I don't know if I have the patience, either. Coaches are special people, and while I know I can do it, I don't think I can deal with all the personalities today, they'd probably just make me gray before my time. They're coming out of college with problems. It's tough, they're a new breed of athlete. And I admire the hell out of coaches, especially head coaches, who can still get their message across, who can make these kids play. On this level, you're dealing with 45, 50 different personalities, and if one of them does something, you're the one who has to answer for it, to the media, to the owners."

That comparison brought Dorsett back to Landry again.

"I think he had all the qualifications a perfect coach has to have," he said. "He had endless patience. He was a great teacher, I mean, he could explain some football thing to you better and in less time than anybody else I ever played for. He was perfectly prepared, always knew what to do in any crisis situation, and he respected football players more than anything. You know, I think that's what gave him the patience he had with Thomas Henderson."

Henderson, of course, was one of two first-round draft picks in 1975, the other being defensive tackle Randy White. And Henderson—the self-proclaimed "Hollywood" Henderson—seemed on the verge of becoming an all-time great linebacker until he went down the path of drug abuse and brought his career to a premature end.

"In all the image-making stuff about the Dallas Cowboys, people ask how Thomas could have been allowed on the team. Well, see, I don't think Thomas was a problem at first. I think Thomas was a guy they thought they could handle, and he was a very personable guy. Very charismatic. He was good for the Cowboys, I think, until he got led astray. Tom was able to deal with Thomas a lot longer than I ever thought he would, because Thomas was a player, and when you were a real player for Landry, you could get away with a few more things. You know, you had leverage.

"But when things started to go bad, and you're still carryin' on the way you used to, then it hurts you, and that's what happened to Thomas. He got caught in it. He was a self-made star,

had the gift of talking his way into publicity, notoriety. I think
Thomas was one of the best linebackers I ever saw, and if he had
been a different kind of person, he'd maybe still be playin' today.

"But that's what he chose to do, and it was his decision. I saw
it all take place, watched it happen, and through it all I got a new
sense of respect for Tom Landry, how he handled it, how he kept
his composure. I think many of us did."

The Dorsett personality—more properly, perhaps, the Dorsett
temperament—exhibited itself in contract negotiations, too. He
was, it seemed, constantly at odds with Tex Schramm. He wanted
more money, more than anyone else on the team, and grew dissatisfied when, one year, Randy White signed for more money.

"Landry said, once, that there were only two people on the team
guaranteed of their jobs, Tony Dorsett and Randy White. Well,
why didn't that translate into equal value? So when White signed
a multimillion-dollar deal, complete with a healthy annuity and
a real estate participation deal, Dorsett held out for equal treatment. Right, my contract wasn't up, but when I looked at what
they had given Randy, it seemed so lopsided that it had to be cor-
rected. If I'm as valuable as he is, then how come we don't make
the same kind of income, you know?"

The fact that the bitter holdout occurred immediately after
Dorsett's $600,000 tragedy played a large part in his determina-
tion to successfully pursue renegotiation, but cornerback Everson
Walls, who would also experience contract difficulties that would
lead to a summer camp holdout, seemed to put it in a proper perspective: "Do you think Tony Dorsett is worth as much to the
team as Randy White? Then they should quit messing around and
give him what he wants."

It is said that Landry was instrumental in getting Dorsett the
financial help he wanted, and in convincing Schramm to renegoti-
ate the contract that was in place.

"I don't want people to think that I only had problems in Dallas," Dorsett says. "I have a lot of very vivid memories, the kind
that will stay with me always. I remember . . . maybe this was
the most exciting game of my career . . . and I didn't even play
in it, I was hurt and sitting on the bench . . . the final game of

the 1979 season. It was in Dallas, we were playing the Redskins, and whichever team won was going to be division champion. So it gets real late in the fourth quarter and they're leading us by two touchdowns. We came back late in the game . . . (defensive end) Larry Cole made a big play on (fullback) John Riggins, stopped him on third down, we get the ball back and Roger's throwing to Preston Pearson, Ron Springs, and we wind up scoring. Then we get the ball back again, Roger puts together another long drive and he throws the touchdown pass to (wide receiver) Tony Hill. The winning touchdown, in the right end zone, right at the tunnel where the visiting team comes out, and I saw Tony, standing there, spreading his wings like he always did when he caught a touchdown. He caught it against (cornerback) Lemar Parrish. I knew it was (going to be) a touchdown when I knew what play was called and Lemar was up on the line, man-to-man, bumping Tony as he got off the line. Tony shook him at the line and it was a perfect pass. That was a very memorable game, and I was just standing on the sidelines, cheering the guys on. I wasn't involved in that one."

The Cowboys won it in the final minute, the Staubach-to-Hill pass and the subsequent extra-point conversion forging the 35-31 score.

"I remember my first game . . . regular-season game . . . it was up in Minnesota. I didn't start, Preston Pearson did, and there we are, up in Minnesota, playing the Purple People Eaters, and I was just in awe. And first time I get in the game, my knees are knockin', you know, and the first time I touched the football, bam!, I fumbled it. I was just a little kid out of college, you know?"

Preston Pearson, who played for the Cowboys for six years after a similar stay in Pittsburgh, was the object of some earlier hard feelings. "When I was a senior in high school he came to see a game. He was with the Steelers then. And after, he told me I was too small to be a running back. I remember stuff like that. All four of my brothers were outstanding football players, and they were all small, like me. Tyrone was the original 'TD' and I remember people telling me stories about what the teachers would say to each other about each of them, and then me: 'He had his one good year, and now he's going to start falling apart, just like his brothers.' Those kind of things stick in your mind—they are motivating tools, baby."

Dorsett picked the scholarship offered by the University of Pittsburgh because . . . well, because it was Pittsburgh.

"Oh, I had a great time playin' at Pitt, I was home, my family was there and that was my biggest motivating factor. They were there. That's what it was all about. My mom and dad had the chance to see me play at home, we had a lot of games that were on the road but on the East Coast . . . you know, Boston College and West Virginia and Penn State and Syracuse. My sister worked for the airline and they could fly to all the games. All that was very important to me.

"I turned down a lot of schools. I did. I turned down an awful lot of schools to stay home. We had a real close-knit team, too, I made friendships I still have. Nobody could understand why I stayed home, but first, I was a kind of built-in stay-at-home anyway, and then Johnny (Majors) and Jackie (Sherrill) did a great job of recruiting me."

(Majors was the head coach and Sherrill was an assistant on the staff, the man who later took over as head coach and subsequently moved on to a similar position at Texas A&M.)

"They didn't really have to recruit me that hard, you know? I wanted to be there, I really did. I wasn't going too far, no matter what. Also, I wanted to help get the program back up to where it had been 10 years ago. I wanted to help it win.

"I'm loyal to the Panthers . . . and I'm still a Cowboy fan, too. I'll follow them, probably until I die, but it's not the same now. It's just not the same anymore. I don't know what's going to happen. Will they keep any of the old traditions? Will they keep inducting people into the Ring of Honor? (Yes, apparently, because linebacker Lee Roy Jordan was inducted during the 1989 season, after Jerry Jones had long since become the new owner and fired Landry.) Will they have the alumni weekends, when all the old players come in? (Apparently not, because for the first time in more than a decade, there was no alumni weekend during the 1989 season.)

"It's different now. It seems like the new regime . . . and I like Jimmy Johnson, I think he's a good coach and he'll do a good job . . . but it seems they're just getting rid of all the old players who were here under Landry and the old traditions and all of it. You've got to have an influx of veterans, and I think they tried to run off too many of the veteran players too fast. You know, Tom's last season . . . when they were 3-13, I said to all my friends that there was just no way it could get any worse, it could only go up. But I was wrong. I never would have dreamed that a Dallas Cowboy team could be 1-15. I never would have dreamed it. You know, they got a few bad breaks along the way, but they never should have been a 1-15 team. It should never have happened.

"I don't think Tom Landry would have allowed that to happen, and I'm not knocking Jimmy Johnson or anybody else, I just can't conceive Tom Landry having a team that won only one game for an entire season. Now? I don't know what he wants to do. I don't think he wants to coach anymore. I think he should do whatever he wants to do, and honestly, I think he's probably enjoying himself now. He must feel like a ton of bricks has been lifted off his shoulders, there isn't any pressure anymore, just being so consumed with the team, with the different personalities, now he has the chance to be with his wife, to spend time with his family, to travel.

"I haven't visited with him. I haven't talked to him since Tom Landry Day (in July of 1989), and I never got real close to him. How close? About as close as I am to you, and I don't know you. So I don't know Tom Landry, I can't say I do. I've seen him change over the years, seen his personality change, seen him become a little more lenient to the players, seen him joke around a little bit more, but I can't say I know him. I never got close enough.

"And of all the things that happened to me . . . throughout my career, that's maybe my biggest regret. Wherever I was, I always had a closeness to my coach, and it just never happened here. He had a way of humbling people, and as a matter of fact, that's probably one of the things I had to go through when I first got here, not starting right away. I wasn't a spot player, I started to get upset. And Billy Joe Dupree and Harvey Martin sat me down one day . . . they told me about the mind games that Landry played, and I think it was a good thing they did, because with my personality it could have gotten out of hand. You know, I kept askin' what's goin' on? And at meetings, I saw Tom embarrassing other players, and wow! if it was me, I thought, would I let him do it? But I never had fear of him, like some players did. I respected the man, but I wasn't afraid of him, and later on, younger players who were having a problem would come to me, asked me to go talk to the man. I'd get angry, tell them to do it themselves, why did I have to? And they'd tell me, 'Hey, man, you're closer to him, he'll listen to you.' So I'd call him for the guys about this and that, but I've always felt I had an understanding of why certain guys were so afraid of him, but I never was. You have to be a man as well, keep your own individuality, and over the years here, I was like a wild stallion they tried to break, but they never really did, they just tamed me a little.

"You know, they put a saddle on me, maybe, but they never broke my spirit."

A pause. A false start, then another, and another. Finally, a disclosure.

"It would be hard for me to say I liked Tom Landry. Let's just say I didn't dislike him. I didn't like some of the things he did, but I didn't really dislike him. I felt emotionally closer to my college coaches, but I admired Tom from a distance. Some disciplinary actions that took place I didn't like, and I'm sure a lot of the players didn't like them, either. On the other hand, I'm sure a lot of players liked him better than I did.

"I had an experience with him once, I think it was kind of telling, you know. I was at a banquet in Washington, and he was there, and we were both flying home the next morning. But he didn't realize there was an earlier flight, the one I was on, and I knew how much he wanted to get back so I told him about it. He was glad I told him, said he'd get on the flight . . . and so we're in the limo going to the airport and I'm trying to talk to him, you know, I never had the chance, one-on-one like that, but he just didn't have any small talk. We got to the airport, had to wait a while, and he still didn't want to talk. So I just gave up. I don't know if he was doin' it intentionally, or just had so much goin' on in his mind, but I got the idea he just wasn't interested."

(Hall of Fame defensive end Andy Robustelli, who spent the bulk of his career with the New York Giants, remembers driving to work every day from Connecticut with Landry. "He'd just sit in the car, staring straight ahead, and not really say anything. I learned that it didn't mean he was unfriendly, he was just so wrapped up in the football that he didn't have time to talk about other things.")

"You know, I have wondered, sometimes, if Tom was hiding something? Maybe he was a shy guy, just real, real shy, and was hiding it by not talking. You know? I've always thought that, and like that old stereotype Western hero . . . you know, doesn't talk, doesn't have anything to say, answers in one-word stuff . . . maybe that's really Tom Landry. Maybe he was just shy.

"I know he didn't understand a lot of the players, especially the younger ones. I think he was naive to a great extent to the things that were going on around him. He just wasn't the kind of guy who was out and about all the time. You'd never go have a beer with him. I mean, I like fine wines, and when the season was over, it was time to do that. I think he was really sheltered, did it to himself, didn't know a lot about what was going on.

"He just knew about football, man. It really consumed his life, and no doubt that was why he was so successful. The man didn't have the social graces, not so I could see, anyway. If anything distracted him, he'd make sure to fix it, because he didn't want, couldn't deal with, disruptive forces. He didn't want his players around that, or want his players like that. One of the older players said that the first time Tom really lost control of anything was with Duane Thomas.

"I wasn't there when that was going on, but I did see the Henderson stuff. One game, in Washington, Thomas was doing his thing, not playing the position right, arguing with the coaches, and we lost the game . . . see, I knew that would make something happen . . . and we had lost like three or four games in a row during that time (it was three), and Thomas was doin' all the crazy stuff that he did right near the end. Anyway, we lose the game in Washington, and by the way things were going I told people that by the end of the season he'd have to be going. It just got a little messy in the locker room, screaming and yelling, and I never saw anything like that on the Cowboys.

"I'll never forget, I was tellin' (defensive back) Dennis Thurman, I said, 'Man, Tom's gonna get rid of this guy, he ain't gonna put up with much more of this shit.' So we get to the meeting the next day, and Thomas, man, he isn't there. I couldn't believe it had happened that fast, not before the season was over, but then Tom told us what he had to do. He had released him, just like that. It finally reached the point where he had to do something, and he did it.

"The man was always in control, and it was an experience being with them, and with Tom Landry. I loved it . . . and there was so much other stuff, too, but during the off-season I'd talk with guys from other teams and they'd say all they wanted to do was beat the Cowboys, beat the Cowboys. But sometime after a game we'd go in and Tom would be so hard on us, you'd say, 'God damn, did we win this game or not?' And if we lost a game, the people who worked in the front office, like, they wouldn't talk to you in the halls, nothing. Come on, give me a break. It was a game, not a war. We still won a lot more than we lost. A lot more. You know, come on, give us a pat on the back sometimes, and you just didn't get much of that, and guys would bitch about that all the time, and we won, yeah, but we'd still have to see those damned films in the morning and get yelled at and criticized.

"But it was a special time. I wouldn't change anything, and I would never trade those years. It was a great city, too, or it became a great city, and being a part of it was special, too, growing with Dallas. I had a great time in Dallas. It was a very enlightening experience, a wealth of knowledge, and being able to play under Tom Landry is something that I'll never be able to forget."

Friends? Many, many of them, almost all former teammates, men who went through the process together. "I see Drew (Pearson) and Harvey (Martin) and Ed (Jones) . . . (linebacker Mike) Hegman . . . Tony Hill and I are very close, do a lot of things together today . . . Ron Springs. Dennis Thurman. You know, we created a bond, and those are friendships that are everlasting.

"Sure, we had cliques. Black-white. Guys who liked Landry, guys who didn't. Black players thought white players were getting better contracts. But those things . . . when we stepped on the field, they were put behind us. We had a common bond, the Cowboy tradition, and as players we were united."

But off the field, there were tensions rumbling just under the surface of the allegedly placid team psyche.

"I remember one confrontation, that was because a guy thought I was laughing at something Coach Landry said. It was on a plane, and I'll never forget this. Look, I have always been a guy who looked at football as a game, just a game. You can't win 'em all, but I wanted to win as bad as anybody else. You know, the man next to me can't want to win more than I do. Anyway, I forget where we were coming from, maybe Washington, and we're playin' cards, jokin', having some beers. I get up to go to the back of the plane, and a couple of guys (defensive tackle) Don Smerek and (linebacker) Jeff Rohrer, they're standing there by the restrooms. I thought they were, like, waitin' in line. So I asked, and they said no, nobody was in there. So I say, 'Great, can I get in? Can you let me squeeze by?' And they said no.

"They said, 'Dorsett, you're the ringleader, you're up there laughing at what the coach said.' I thought they were crazy, man, and I said, 'Hey, we're just tryin' to get over the game, play a little cards, that's all.' And I pushed my way past, told them we'd continue talking about this matter when I was finished in the restroom, after I made a water deposit.

"So I did what I had to do, came out, and this turned into a big argument. I told them ain't nobody on this team wants to win worse than Tony Dorsett wants to win, but it's a game, and I don't take this shit home like some of you guys do and abuse my dog or my wife. I leave it on the field, or at the stadium, but I don't get overly consumed with this. Man, it got into a big argument, and people are comin' back, tryin' to break us up, to mediate and get between us, and some of the guys thought it was going to turn into a black-white thing.

"Man, they had me surrounded . . . and I'm so little, man. I told Smerek he didn't scare me, that evidently he didn't know where I came from, and he wasn't about to put any fear in my heart. He made a little move, you know, trying to get me to flinch? And I said, 'Hey, what are you doin', tryin' to scare me? It won't work, brother. You may jump on me, and you may beat me up, but I'll shoot you, I'll just take you out. He said, 'Hey, I got shot before.' I said, 'No, Smerek, the way I'm gonna blow you away you ain't gonna be standing here talkin' about it, you know? You won't live to tell anybody about this shit.'

"See, it all happened because a guy didn't like to lose and he thought it didn't matter to me. You know, it's possible that if I was a white Tony Dorsett it might never have started. Might never have happened."

The telephone rang, and rang and rang. Finally, looking uncomfortable, Tony Dorsett got up to answer it.

"Are we through here? I don't think what happened to Tom Landry was right, and while things happen to people all the time that aren't right, in football and in life, I think he deserved better. And yes, it was a privilege to play for him and the Dallas Cowboys, no matter what kind of trouble I was involved in, no matter what kind of stories we produced.

"There were special times, special years, and I don't believe they're ever coming back to this town again. They left for good with Tom Landry."

CHAPTER 7

ROGER STAUBACH

THE QUARTERBACK

When Jack Armstrong retired, Roger Staubach replaced him.

You remember Jack Armstrong, don't you? The All-American Boy of song and story? The hero? The one who would stand up, even if alone, for the American ideals of life, liberty and the pursuit of happiness?

Well, even heroes get old. Tired. Retire. And when Jack went to the farm, it was only because Roger had turned up.

Talk about American heroes, this was direct from Central Casting in Hollywood. This was Ronald Reagan, James Cagney, Fred Astaire and John Wayne wrapped up, bundled, given athletic skills beyond the imagination of scriptwriters, and renamed. After all, he couldn't be Ron-Jim-Fred-John, not even in Texas, where the legend was going to reach full fruition.

So they called him Roger Staubach.

But first, they had to get him born, which they accomplished on February 5, 1942, in Silverton, Ohio, which has its own post office and zip code but is really a part of Cincinnati. The main road leads into Cincinnati, and when people from Silverton are asked where they live, they say Cincinnati. It's just easier. (What's that, Max? Middle America? Perfect. Oh, great.)

They made him an only child, which is as it should be. No sibling rivalry around this special person. No stealing his thunder. No, sir.

OK, now we'll bring him carefully through his childhood, give him the best possible education, teach him the right way and the wrong way, the straight and narrow. Hey, something a little different. Let's get him to be a pianist, too. Well, sort of a pianist. "My mother made me practice, wanted me to learn, but I never wanted any of it," he remembered. "It reached a peak when I was 11. I had a recital at a music hall. They made me wear a tuxedo, the whole thing, and then, when I sat down to play the 'William Tell Overture,' I just flat-out forgot it. But I had to do something, so I just began pounding on the keys, and every once in a while I'd remember a few bars so I'd play them. It was just terrible, and when I was done I looked up and all the parents in the audience were laughing. That ended my musical career. In a hurry."

(Great idea, Max. A little pathos. perfect. Make the kid fail at something, it's humbling. Max, it's gonna be a hit. You'll get a raise.)

Things got better after that (as you and Max knew they would). Roger Staubach became a star at quarterback and halfback for Purcell High School in Cincinnati. People began to call him Roger the Dodger (perfect, no?). He met his future wife, Marianne, when he was a star eighth-grader and she was a cheerleader (oh, be still, my heart).

And now it's off to college. More than 40 universities were showering Roger the Dodger with offers to accept their scholarships. He was 6-1, weighed 190, had a rifle arm, could run like the wind, was tough and loyal and faithful and courageous and the only thing he knew about drugs was that aspirin was one so he wouldn't take it.

Where else could a young star like this choose to matriculate but Notre Dame? Right? It's perfect. He was a Catholic from Cincinnati, he knew all about the Golden Dome and the Gipper. So he would go to Notre Dame, become one of the 90 or so Fighting Irish quarterbacks to win the Heisman Trophy and go on to wealth and fame forever.

Right?

"Notre Dame never called," said Staubach. "There were a bunch of good players at Purcell, and at some of the other high schools in Cincinnati, and Notre Dame never contacted any of us. I had kind of decided to go to Purdue, but Ohio State had come close, a few of the other Big Ten schools. But it was Purdue. I signed a tender (agreement to attend, but not yet binding), yet when I graduated in June I started to think maybe I hadn't made the right decision. Maybe Purdue was too big, and I didn't want a big campus. That was one of the reasons I turned down Ohio State and Michigan. I just didn't want to get lost on a big campus.

"All the while, a guy had been recruiting me for the Naval Academy. His name was Rick Forzano (who would later become the head coach there), and he finally convinced me to go there, to Annapolis, and visit. I was very impressed, especially when the midshipmen who were assigned to take me around talked about education and the value of it and not about strip joints and beer. I made up my mind to accept the Naval Academy offer, and then I took my SATs (Scholastic Aptitude Tests) and realized I couldn't have been accepted. My math score was very high, but my English score was very low. Rick told me about a junior college the Naval Academy recommended, the New Mexico Military Institute, said that I could go there for a year, work my English score up and reapply. I had decided to do that, and I told Purdue I wasn't going to accept their scholarship.

"Then I played in the Ohio High School All-Star game and had a pretty good day. I played defensive back, halfback, a little quarterback, made 11 tackles as a safety . . . and after the game even Notre Dame scouts were after me. They offered me the full four-year scholarship, told me I was good enough to be their next great quarterback.

"But I had made a commitment to Rick Forzano and the Naval Academy. It was too bad that Notre Dame hadn't thought to contact me a few months earlier. But once I had given my word, there just wasn't any way in the world I would go back on it."

The Heisman Trophy for quarterbacks moved from what was then its accustomed spot and took up residence at the Naval Academy five years later, because Roger Staubach, soon to be Lt. j.g. Roger Staubach, became the best damned quarterback in the United States. He was a passer with a strong and accurate arm, a scrambling runner with a long and powerful stride, a reader of defenses par excellence, far beyond what would normally be expected from a college player whose opponents included Rutgers, Colgate, Columbia and Temple.

He was Superhero, the kid with the flashing smile and the neat hair, the wide, white-toothed grin and the disturbing quality of calling everyone "sir" and "ma'am" and speaking out on those qualities in which he believed.

"I guess I was a square in those days," he said, making the assumption he is no longer a square today. "I mean, things like God, the American flag, apple pie and patriotism weren't just words to me. I believe in them. I worked to make them become a part of my life. I remember I got in a little trouble one year, much later on, in Dallas, when a sportswriter asked me what my main goal really was. I said it wasn't in this life, that my goal was to be a good enough person to be able to go to heaven. Then I added that 'all passes are completions in heaven' and the guy asked me why, and I said, 'There aren't any defensive backs in heaven, that's why.' I didn't mean it to come out the way it sounded, but a lot of defensive backs got pretty angry at me."

Graduation from the Naval Academy meant the beginning of another career, the four-year service obligation, and for the young Staubach that included a year in Vietnam and three more in Pensacola, Fla. But in 1964, when he did graduate, the same year the Dallas Cowboys spent their first-round draft choice on quarterback Craig Morton, they also took a risk and, in the 10th round, drafted Roger Staubach. If at any time in the future he wanted to play professional football, his rights to do so would be controlled by the Cowboys.

In retrospect, that may have been the best bargain the Dallas Cowboys ever struck.

"Sure, I had thought about pro football, and while it was a nice thing to think about, I really didn't see any chance for it to come true for me. I was going to miss four, maybe five years right after graduation . . . the years most athletes are at their absolute peak . . . and to try to master the quarterback position in the National Football League, I knew I'd have to devote every minute to studying and practicing. Missing those years, I figured, just about ended any hope I ever had of being a professional football player."

But the Cowboys were patient. "I'd go to summer training camp for two weeks every summer," Staubach said. "I'd work with the coaches, with the players. I'd get playbooks to study, I'd keep in touch with the team, do everything I could to learn something, anything, while I was still in the Navy. And when I finally got my discharge (it was July 5, 1969, the same day Don Meredith announced his premature retirement), I was 27 years old. I was probably the oldest rookie the team ever had."

"My first impression of Coach Landry, my initial perception of him, was that of a top commanding officer. He had a presence, an aura, and people just naturally listened to him, watched him, took their lead from him. It was a feeling of . . . I don't know, exactly . . . of someone you just knew had a handle on everything, who was very knowledgeable about everything he did, who knew a lot about everything you wanted to learn. I felt I could learn from him, learn about football in all its details.

"I had already learned how important Coach Landry thought preparation was, and I learned that he was a great psychologist, too. He knew how to handle all kinds of personalities, how to make players want to do better, how to motivate them to give even more than they thought they had to give. I was very impressed with his sense of competition, because he was . . . and is . . . a highly competitive man, in everything.

"You know, he had true leadership qualities. He had been in the service (a pilot during World War II), and it seems to me that he probably would have retired as a general if he stayed in. He had the knack of getting people to follow him, to listen to him, to want to do things for him. He was not a rah-rah guy, didn't lead us in fight songs or cheers. That wears thin after a short while unless there is substance behind the chatter, and I think that's Tom, a man of substance."

But Staubach did not perceive a perfect man when he looked at and began to know Tom Landry.

"There were people in fear of him, and I think he had a way of expressing to them that they had reason to fear him. Remember, he knew how to motivate people, and if it was their fear of him that kept them motivated, on the right track, then I don't think he minded using it. They were also afraid of his sudden unexpected move, of something he'd say that nobody expected, and that triggered a response in many people to keep learning, keep anticipating what he might want, might say, might do. It was a great learning experience to just watch him, to observe him, and when I began to work closely with him, I started to see more sides, more facets, than perhaps anybody had ever seen.

"For instance, he personally analyzed each game himself, and when you worked with him as one of the quarterbacks, that was something only we saw . . . something none of the other players saw all week. He always wanted to be a quarterback, I think, and he took great delight in calling the plays, being right, anticipating what defense the other team would be in. He never tolerated less than 100 percent effort from anybody, including himself, and if you gave him a great effort, even if you lost, or didn't get the job fully accomplished, that was OK. He respected the effort. He might not have thought you were going to be a superstar player for him . . . and he might have decided that eventually you would have to be replaced . . . but he always respected desire and determination, and he truly believed that all you could do was your best, that no man could do any more than that.

"Once he saw that you were going to do that, every time, in practices and games and film meetings, then he gave as much of himself as a coach has to give. He worked overtime with you, he studied with you, he encouraged and explained and did everything you'd ever want from a coach. But better, and more of it, and in much more detail.

"But, you see, he had a problem . . . he had a hard time . . . with the human side of relationships. He just couldn't let himself get too close, or wouldn't let that happen. And in the end, I think maybe that was part of the reason for his demise. He was not able to deal with major decisions, with cutting players who deserved to be cut, with trading players other teams wanted who just weren't going to help the Cowboys. He hated to give up on a player, and he wouldn't go against the people who had worked

for him for a long time, either, and I think maybe that was a failing, a weakness of sorts, because when things started to change,
when the Dallas Cowboys just weren't making the magic happen
the way they had done for so long, he didn't quite know how to
deal with it. I love that man, I respect him, I admire him and I
will do anything I can for him, but he just didn't give enough of
what a lot of the players needed, which was a pat on the back
sometime, just that, some recognition of a good job, some small
way of complimenting a good game, a big play. I didn't need it.
I was an only child and I learned early to work for everything
I wanted, not to rely on anybody else to do it for me, and to know
when I did something right, when I did a good job. I was able
to tell when I deserved the pat on the back, but I didn't need it.
I knew I had done well, and I had enough self-confidence not to
need confirmation from Coach Landry. But others did. And they
never got it from him. He should have done more of it, I agree
with that, but he just didn't know how. He really didn't know how
to get close to the players without somehow affecting his position,
somehow giving up some of the authority he had worked so hard
to build."

Staubach pauses, and for a man with so much going on inside,
with so much character and compassion for this man he calls
friend, he started to think, clearly, that he was being less than
kind. He did not intend that nor, to the interviewer, did it take
on any of that meaning.

"Now, and then, too . . . for as long as I've known him, and
before that, from talking to other players, there was always this
about Tom Landry: If you needed him for something, he was there
for you. If you needed help, advice, anything, he was ready to do
whatever needed to be done, all the time. He has a great compassion about him, he cares about everybody he meets, and that's another part of him that only those who have spent a lot of time
getting to know him have found out.

"It's not that he's the kind of guy you go out to have a beer
with. I don't think I've played golf with him more than twice in
my life. You don't just call him to make small talk. But there's
something about him that makes you sure he'll be there when you

need him, like he's steady as a rock and he'll be happy to help you over the rough spots. He is a shy person, smart, well read. Did you know he graduated from college (the University of Texas) as an industrial engineer? He did, and it shows.

"Tom is a very goal-oriented person, and he knows how to establish believable, achievable goals. That's how he coached, really, and I guess you could put a label on it: Management by Objective.

"It's what industrial engineers try to accomplish, and he did it with the Cowboys. He set up goals for himself, goals for the players, and then implemented the effort necessary to reach those goals. I have always admired the way he worked, the pace he was able to keep, the understanding he had of his job. And it was no secret to any of us that he loved it all . . . football, the players, the challenges, the games. He really loved it and I think that's what kept him going, and successful, for as long as he was the Cowboys' head coach. Hey, he won more than anybody, and more consistently than anybody, and you just don't do that if you aren't totally dedicated and in love with your job."

The firing, the day Jerry Jones decided to bring this legend crashing down, was a tough one for Roger Staubach. He remembers, and yet he tries to view a silver lining, a bright side. He almost makes it.

"I'd rather call it the day Tom announced his retirement," he began, "or had it announced for him. See, it was one of those scenarios that we all knew was possible, but it was tremendously disappointing in how it was handled. There had to be another way, some other way of telling him it was finished, not just firing him, replacing him the same day and conducting business as if nothing had happened. I mean, something vitally important had happened. Tom Landry was no longer head coach of the Dallas Cowboys, and there were lots of people who automatically associated him with the team. . . . You know, you'd think about the Dallas Cowboys and you'd picture him, standing there on the sidelines, wearing a suit, tie, that hat, maybe the play list under his arm or in his hand. I really think that happened, that he became almost synonymous with the team, the symbol of the Cowboys.

"I think he'd still be an effective coach today, and I'm not going

to get involved with whether he would have had that 1-15 record
or not. Maybe. Maybe it was just meant to be. But the bright side
is that I know he'll relax a little more now, start enjoying life a
little more frequently. He worked long enough and hard enough
to earn a little rest and relaxation now, and I think he'll find
enough things to keep him busy. He's writing a book, he's still
making commercials, speeches, appearances. I think, in a way, it
ended properly, all things considered.

"See, that side tells me that it allowed all the people to express
themselves, their outrage or their emotions, because it was so sudden and unexpected that it caught them by surprise, and when
people get caught like that they start talking about it, their feelings. It also allowed his entire career to be kept in its proper perspective, because if nothing had happened, if the team hadn't been
sold, Tom would have coached another season, probably, and if
it had been a poor one, he would have been more remembered
for the losing years at the end. People would have shown a tendency, I think, to forget all the championships, all the winning, all
the drama and excitement his teams generated.

"But because they felt poorly about how he was treated . . .
maybe because the firing made a martyr out of him . . . they
weren't happy and it didn't sit well with the fans and now, well,
he is being looked at for all the good things he accomplished,
which is human nature. The firing brought out the emotion in people, and if he had coached in 1989 and then retired, it wouldn't
have been nearly as emotional. The whole mystique of Tom Landry would have been diminished."

In truth, there was no reason for many of sports' most storied
men to continue careers after they had logically ended. Casey
Stengel, the man who managed the New York Yankees to 14
World Series championships, including a major league record five
straight, came out of retirement to manage the bumbling New
York Mets, an expansion team with virtually no major league talent, and he is best remembered now, at least by a younger generation, as the clown who managed the clowns.

Landry will never coach again. His reputation will remain un-
sullied, a bright and shining testament to hard work, all-

consuming dedication and sharp intelligence. He will not become Casey Stengel, nor will he be like many older players, certain Hall of Famers, who for the money or the refusal to quit allowed the world to see them stripped of those special, unique talents that made them different.

The toughest thing, coaches say, is for a superstar to know when he's finished. And with Tom Landry, the toughest thing for him to do was to break that news to those who had played for him for so long and had done so well, contributed so much to the overall success and glory of the Cowboys.

"You know," Staubach continued, "he coached the Cowboys for 29 years, and almost none of the losses can be blamed on him. I don't think a decision of his, pure and simple, ever cost the Cowboys a game. I really don't. And that's amazing, that is really amazing. I credit most of it, most of the success and the winning, to his preparation. Nobody was better prepared for a game than Tom Landry.

"But the game changed, requirements changed, and maybe those around him didn't change with them. Take their drafts, for instance. Dallas just seemed to get stale, to get trapped in its own creation of computer printouts and statistics and specialized skills that a player had to display before the Cowboys would draft him. I mean, Tom would listen to them, and he'd understand everything they said, but maybe he, too, fell victim to the successes of the past. I mean, they kept trying to fit players into patterns, into mathematical formulas, and it doesn't work. It's difficult, if not impossible, to correlate a great athlete to the height of his vertical leap, for instance, but the Cowboys got all caught up in a guy's vertical leap, as if it was some magic equation that would translate into Pro Bowl talent. As a result, I think the Cowboys made some terrible mistakes in their more recent drafts, and I'm not going to try to find who was at fault, who should take the blame. But not Tom, either. He was the head coach and for years people had provided him with enough information to make a logical decision on drafted players. He counted on those people, depended on them, and if the requirements changed, if the players of today exhibited more of one thing than the kind of thing the Cowboys wanted . . . well, I'm afraid they passed up a lot of talent because they were victimized by their own science of drafting, of gambling, sometimes, in the draft.

"For one thing, I think coaches should be out there scouting just as soon as the season ends, and I don't think many of the Cowboy coaches ever did that. There was a scouting department, and those men provided the information for Tom to make his decisions. But you need to see more of the intangibles, too, more of the kid's heart and drive and potential for overachieving. If you rely too much on those athletic criteria, you can get in trouble. There is a definite need to find more of the intangibles and then take a chance.

"Look at that linebacker in Chicago, Mike Singletary of Baylor. He's too short. He's barely 6 feet tall. He could never have fit into the Cowboys' scouting parameters, and they never even thought about drafting him, even though he played nearby (in Waco), and even though everybody raved at what great football instincts and intensity he had. So the Bears took him, and he's an annual Pro Bowl middle linebacker. Nobody is more intense, more willing to give his body, to sacrifice his body. But he wasn't quite tall enough for the Dallas system, so he was ignored.

"It just doesn't make sense. It's just not possible to draft without looking at the intangibles, and if you don't, if you just allow players who fit the mold that you established a long time ago to be considered, then you are going to miss a lot of kids who could be of great help. It's shortsighted."

In all the 30 years of Dallas Cowboy history, there have only been a handful of quarterbacks who counted. At the beginning there was Eddie LeBaron. He was followed by Don Meredith, who in turn was followed by Craig Morton. Then Staubach replaced him and finally Danny White replaced Staubach, who had to retire in 1980 because his doctors were growing increasingly concerned at his predeliction for collecting concussions.

In each case, the passing of the quarterback's torch was a painful incident. LeBaron and Meredith were pitted against each other, but it wasn't for long and it was never vicious. LeBaron was a veteran when he joined the Cowboys, and it was time for him to retire.

But the Meredith-Morton transition was psychologically damaging to the team, as well as to the players, as was the Morton-Staubach sweepstakes, which lasted five full seasons after Staubach joined the team fresh from naval duty in 1969.

"Tom just hated to let go of a veteran," Staubach remembered. "But it was getting to be bad between me and Craig, and we are good friends. I think he was a marvelous quarterback, and I think he had some of the best pure talents I have ever seen in a quarterback. But he couldn't sit on the bench, and I sure didn't want to do it, and I have told people for years now that if something didn't happen, I would have had to insist on being traded. I was not about to spend my career sitting on the bench, being a backup quarterback to anybody, even a good friend.

"Craig felt the same way, and he had a similar experience earlier, when Meredith announced his retirement. If that hadn't happened, Craig was going to have to make a hard decision about being traded. He was going to have to demand to be sent elsewhere, because as good as Meredith was—and personally, I think he was absolutely sensational—Craig was talented enough to expect to be a starter.

"I know the stories about how Landry picked Meredith to be the only player he ever criticized in public, and how Don couldn't handle the pressure from the fans and the media, and I suppose I understand it all. I still think Don retired way too early. I still think he could have played for seven or eight years after he retired (he was 31 when he left), and frankly, if Tom Landry had treated Meredith better, you wouldn't be talking to me now. I might have had to go elsewhere, or maybe the Cowboys would never have drafted Craig.

"See, Don left in 1969, before the season started. That put the job directly in Craig's hands, and when I got there that same summer, it was his job and it stayed his job for a while. But if Meredith had been there, Craig probably would have gotten very unhappy, because Don would have continued to start, and he (Morton) would have had no choice but to be the second-string quarterback or demand to be traded.

"Now, if the Cowboys decided they didn't want to trade him, there was no way I could have stayed. They probably wouldn't even have expected it. I know there were teams willing to trade for me and I guess they would have had to make the best deal they could. Don Meredith was a great, great quarterback, and whatever the real story was (about his retirement) only he knows. I wish he hadn't done it, though. I would have loved to see him continue to improve."

Given that Meredith played only nine seasons, and not nine full ones, and that they were the first nine years of the Cowboys' existence, the fact that he ranks second or third in almost all of the team's career passing records is a tribute to his abilities and toughness.

"See, Craig would have had to make a decision as to where he wanted his career to go, and how he wanted to spend it. I wouldn't have had much choice until I saw what he did. If he left, I would have stayed and worked behind Meredith. If he stayed, I certainly wouldn't have chosen to remain as the third-string quarterback, or one day hope to replace him as the first backup. No, sir. I had to start somewhere."

A man named Bob Shaw was Staubach's coach at New Mexico Military Institute, and the junior college mentor soon left for the NFL when New Orleans was added to the league by way of expansion. He became an assistant coach under Tom Fears, and when he got there, he made Fears think he had just hired a crazy person.

In the book, *Staubach: First Down, Lifetime To Go,* (Waco: Word Inc., 1974), Shaw is quoted by the authors thusly:

"After I left New Mexico Military I coached in Canada for a while, and then I joined Tom Fears in New Orleans in 1967. I told Tom he ought to give Dallas a call and offer a No. 1 draft choice for Roger Staubach. I told him if the Cowboys wouldn't take that, to offer them two No. 1 choices, and if that wasn't enough, offer them three No. 1s. I knew Roger could play. No matter if he did miss those four years I knew he was such a great athlete and competitor that he could play."

Staubach smiled at the anecdote, and admitted that the three years he spent at Pensacola were highlighted by his two weeks of summer camp each year with the Cowboys. "I'd get my work finished by late afternoon and then I'd run and run and run," he said of his duties at Pensacola. "And I'd throw a ball to anybody who would catch for me. If there was nobody around, I'd throw to a spot and then run after the ball. I had to write to Gil Brandt (the Dallas pro personnel director) a few times for replacement footballs. The ground I had to work out on was rough, and the ball used to get chewed up after a while."

Bob Hayes, who was there for the first six years of Staubach's career, laughed. "I think what happened is that Roger used up about a hundred footballs while he was in the Navy, but he only threw them the last two minutes of the day, you know?"

In 1971, Staubach finally got to play regularly. But the following year he lost the job to Morton, only to recapture it—this time for good—in 1973. The next year Craig was traded to the New York Giants and the reign began.

"When I first got the job, I mean really got the job, it was a great feeling. I had accomplished something I had set out to do, something that required hard work and dedication and a single-mindedness of purpose. I was used to that. I had always been that way, all my life, and I was only concerned that I would be treated fairly, given an equal chance to compete, and then leave it up to performance. For both of us.

"I began to know Tom Landry more after I became the starting quarterback, and I had a great feeling about him. I really started to like him, and I think there was a chemistry between us that forged a bond. But I also had to make things right with the team. I didn't want to be perceived as 'Tom Landry's boy,' you know? So I didn't spend all my time with him . . . I didn't always take his side in locker room discussions. I went out with the boys, became one of the guys, and I didn't mind that. I never minded being part of that kind of atmosphere, but to a point. I had to get close to the players, so that they would accept me as me, rather than as somebody appointed by Tom to be the new leader.

"I even downplayed my role in the Fellowship of Christian Athletes, in which I believe very strongly, because Tom was one of the leading proponents of the FCA and, again, I didn't want anybody to think I was playing up to him by becoming more and more active. After a while, of course, it was all right. I was the team's leader and it didn't matter what I did with Tom or without him. The players knew I was for them, and they knew that as long as we were winning I'd be able to keep Landry away from them, a little.

"An example of that. I had always wished Tom would have given me more freedom—I called the plays once, for almost the entire 1973 season—but Tom took that back. Anyway, the one area I did have more freedom was to utilize the receivers any way I thought would be best. They'd come in with the play, and say it was a Sixteen-Cut, which called for a deep route down the left sideline. I'd change it at the line of scrimmage . . . audible the play . . . and maybe the only change would be to make it a post pattern (down the center of the field) instead of the sideline route.

"The next day, watching the films, Tom might say something to one of the receivers, you know, 'Drew, you're not supposed to run the Sixteen-Cut that way, what happened?' and Drew would start to say, 'Coach, Roger said . . . ' and then Tom would stop him. 'OK, I understand,' he'd say, and we'd just go on with the film session.

"But I really had no problem dealing with Coach Landry. You see, we had our differences. We even argued. But we had an equal drive, to win. We both wanted that very much, but we disagreed a lot as to how we would go about trying to win. See, I liked to run with the ball. I was a scrambler. Tom didn't really want me to run much, he preferred his quarterbacks to stay in the pocket, to wait for the open receiver, not to risk getting hurt or even disrupting the play that had been called. But if I could get a first down, a long gain, even a touchdown by running, I was going to run. It was instinctive, anyway. I'd just tuck the ball away and run if things got sticky, if I saw everything falling apart.

"You also see a man through his actions, you know, and that's what set Tom apart from most men I have known. He was loyal to his faith and to his beliefs, and he spent all of his life living his value system. We had a strong mutual bond that could not be broken. I just wish he would have given me more freedom to call the plays, to be my own quarterback a little more.

"As I said, I called the plays for most of 1973 and enjoyed it very much, but with the season mostly over, we had a Thanksgiving Day game in Texas Stadium against the Miami Dolphins, an important game for both teams and for both coaches, too. I think Tom and Don Shula, two of the very best coaches in history, had this rivalry thing between them, a matter of pride. Anyway, Miami was winning but late in the game we're driving downfield and we get really close to their end zone when I audibled one of his plays into a goal-line call, even though we were in short-yardage and not in goal-line situation. And that play just didn't work. We lost the ball, or didn't make the first down, something like that. Anyway, the next day Tom told me he was taking back the play calling, but he used another reason to make it easier for me, he thought.

"You see, my mother was dying of cancer that year, during that football season, and my thoughts were constantly with her. It was a very bad time, a sorry time in my life and for my family. Tom called me in and told me I had too much on my mind, that he would take back the play-calling responsibility because it wasn't fair to put so much more on my shoulders.

"That wasn't the reason, I don't think. I always felt he just wanted to take back the plays because he loved to call them. I called all my plays at the Academy, and I do believe there is something to being in the game, on the field, and getting a feel for what will work and what won't, although that, too, can be a bit overdone. But Tom used my personal crisis as an excuse.

"There were three games left, and we won them all, won the division and lost to Minnesota in the conference championship game. My mother died, and by the time the next season rolled around, there was no more talk of who would call the plays. It just never came up. It was his job, he did it, and that was that.

"The problem, you see . . . and I understand that all coaches call their own plays these days . . . I understand that, and I guess I agree with it . . . but the problem is that if I called a play it was one I believed in, and when you believe in something like that you seem to do better, execute better. If the play comes in from the bench and I don't like it . . . or don't agree with it being called at that particular time, I feel worse about it, like I'm being forced to use it, to call it, and if it doesn't work there's a tendency to say, you know, 'I told you so, I told you it wouldn't work.' But the coach is in charge. He gets to make the decisions. That's what he's paid to do."

Staubach's perception of the quarterback, on any team, is that of the leader. Perhaps it's his military training, or his own strength of conviction, but he seems to identify the quarterback almost on the same level as the head coach.

"People need somebody they can look up to," he says. "On football teams, that is almost always the quarterback. And after I had to retire, I think Tom made the only major mistake of his entire career with the Cowboys. He conducted a quarterback sweepstakes between Danny White and Gary Hogeboom, and he allowed team sentiment to influence him for the first time I can ever remember. See, Danny was probably the most underrated player Dallas ever had. He was a great quarterback, with skills I never had, with skills Morton and Meredith never had. But for some reason I still don't understand, the team seemed to turn on him. When Tom honored that, and gave the job to Hogeboom instead of Danny, it was a critical error. The team never recovered from it, either. Nor did Danny ever get over it, and I think when he finally stopped playing he was a little bitter and a little broken because of it.

"He was courageous and brilliant and tough as nails, and Gary Hogeboom has yet to get the ball into the end zone on any consistent basis. I don't know why Tom did it . . . hey, it never lasted even a full season . . . but that terrible display of a lack of confidence just ruined him, and believe me, he could have been the best Cowboy quarterback ever. I don't know what happened, who he listened to, whose opinion was so valuable that he would allow himself to be persuaded, but it was a terrible, terrible mistake.

Now, looking at the hapless Cowboys of 1989, Staubach sees nothing but the bright lights.

"Troy Aikman is going to be a franchise player. He was just a rookie in 1989 and he absolutely startled people with his talents. Danny could have helped him, too, and I don't think it's true that he was let go because he couldn't be a backup quarterback. I don't believe that. He could have been a great asset to Aikman. I guess the players thought that a change would be best when they convinced Tom, or lobbied, to give the job to Hogeboom, you know? That had to have had an influence on him. But do you know what I would have done? I would have gone right into the locker room and called a meeting and taken it right to the players . . . what's the problem? are you guys nuts? I'm the quarterback around here and you damned well better get used to it. I would have done that. I really would have. And I think it would have worked, too. Danny was a great quarterback. Hogeboom was a great practice player."

Staubach next turned to his reputation as being the best two-minute offense quarterback in the history of the game, and he laughed at it.

"You need the players to make it work, and even before that you need the defense to get you the ball. How can anybody move his team downfield and make one of those miracle finishes happen if he doesn't have the ball, if he's sitting on the bench watching the other team kill the clock?

"I have a theory about why two-minute offenses work so frequently, too. You see, at the beginning of a game, all the players aren't on the same page yet. They're still getting the feel of the game, you have to do that, play and feel the ebb and flow, before you can really feel the pulse of it, and before you can get everything working in unison.

"Also, you have to be in the game. I mean, even if you're losing, you have to be close enough so that a dramatic two-minute offense that turns into a touchdown will also turn into a victory, you know? It's nice to cut a big deficit to one a little smaller, but losing is still losing, and it stinks. The really good teams believe they are going to win, are sometimes absolutely convinced of it. The weaker teams, even good teams that don't believe in themselves yet, they're just waiting to see what's going to happen, how they are going to miss a play, drop a ball, give the other team the chance it needs to pull it out. We had to believe in ourselves, and I think something like a two-minute miracle feeds on itself. You know, you do it once and the players are excited. Do it again and they start to think you have something going. Do it a third time, and a fourth, and they'll follow you anywhere, pick up their level of performance without ever realizing it. If they start to believe in you as the quarterback who can make it happen, then I was able to get a higher level of performance from them, and that made me play better, too. It's all tied together, it's all impossible to explain.

"The bottom line, I think, is that if you don't believe it will work, then it won't. And if you do believe in it, then you'll surprise everybody else who looks at your situation and calls it impossible."

Perhaps the best-known of all those final, frantic two-minute offensive victories came in a playoff game in 1975 in Minnesota. The Vikings were winning, 14-10, and there was virtually no time left on the clock. The Cowboys were on their own 9-yard line, 91 yards away from the end zone, and a field goal wouldn't have made anybody happy, or changed the result one iota.

"It had to be a touchdown, and I frankly didn't think we could pull it off," Staubach remembers. "I mean, how can you go deep on a team that knows you have to go deep? That's about as tough an assignment as there is in offensive football.

"Well, we moved to the 50 by throwing passes to Drew Pearson, and then it's all down to one more play. The fans are on their feet, cheering this great Viking victory, see, and we are really down to one play because there isn't enough time to try two or three passes, certainly no time to run the ball. So we kind of make up a play in the huddle. We had no time-outs left, and they knew we were going to go deep. I figure they knew I was going to Drew, too, because he was not only our best receiver but the guy who had made all the clutch catches in other come-from-behind dramas.

"I knew I had to get the safety (Paul Krause) off him, so I told Drew to run a sideline pattern, wait for me to pump-fake Krause, and then turn it on and get even with the cornerback (Nate Wright). I figured if he was side by side with Wright, and if I could keep Krause off him, then Drew could catch the ball.

"Well, I pumped so hard I almost lost the ball, and as it turned out—see what happens when you have everything working on your side?—that was the best thing of all, because it forced me to underthrow the ball a little. I just couldn't get all the steam I wanted behind the throw, and it's a lucky thing I didn't because I would have overthrown Drew. But Krause is coming over two steps late—out of the play, really—and Drew draws even with Wright, and I underthrow it a little and Drew cuts across him and catches the ball, and steps into the end zone. And I don't believe I heard any more cheering from the fans. It was dead quiet. It's still the one memory that will stay in my mind forever, about my career. It shouldn't have happened. We were more than just lucky.

"Anyway, the 'Hail Mary' game set us up for a few years after that. We got to the Super Bowl that year and made it to two more the next three years. I believe the dramatic come-from-behind victory in that game just propelled us from then on. It was like we couldn't lose, would always be able to find a way to pull out lost causes. . . . And as I said before, when you think you can, you're a long way toward doing it."

Staubach is a permanent, and popular, fixture in Dallas these days. It is home, and strangely, he says it is the only home he and Marianne and the children have ever had. "I never had a home after I went to college, and our kids were born all over the country. When we got to Dallas, it was the first time we ever bought a house, and it was the first city we were living in permanently since we had been married.

"I love Dallas, but it is not a city without its own significant problems. They are everywhere, and I guess the main issue is racism, prejudice. It's in people's bones, and we have to take it out of them, out of their bones, before it can be put away forever. Dallas still has its unfair housing problems, really a pathetic situation, and I admire the hell out of those guys I played with for putting up with it. But Dallas, while it is much more cosmopolitan now, still needs to be cleaned up. As a team, we came through it, because we all got along well, because the black players were insulated, in a way. I think the Cowboys helped all the blacks in Dallas. Maybe we made people look around and say, 'Hey, this black human being is the same as me, and there are good people, bad people, of all colors.' I hope so, I hope that's true. I can't believe people feel so strongly negative about other people just because of their skin color. It's amazing. We always brought our girls up to have black dolls and white dolls, so they'd see there was no difference, and we told them if they ever heard any bigoted remarks in school to tell us about them, so we could clear it up, explain, show why other people were wrong.

"I love Dallas, and because I do, it bothers me so much more when I hear about problems. My God, we're in the last decade of this century, and we're still dealing with race as a viable issue. It isn't. It's terrible, it should never have happened in the first place, and I hope it goes away because good people are getting hurt.

"There was a rookie in camp one year . . . he didn't make the team, but he was really smart, and friendly, and we used to talk at night about books and philosophy and history. And one night he said to me . . . he was black, you see . . . he said, 'Roger, you're a good guy, a nice man. I enjoy talking with you, being with you. But when all the blacks are given guns, I am going to have no choice but to shoot you.' That is so sad, so sad. I hope I live long enough to see it stopped, to see prejudice disappear."

Roger Staubach, these days, is building a multimillion-dollar conglomerate of commercial and residential real estate holdings.

Roger Staubach Inc. has offices not only in Dallas but in Los Angeles, Houston and Washington, D.C. RSI has employed several former Cowboy teammates, including Bob Hayes and Robert Shaw, a former first-round draft pick offensive lineman.

"I'm still friendly with a lot of my former teammates," he says, "and I do have some social contact with Coach Landry. But I see Drew a lot . . . Cliff Harris and I play basketball . . . I talk to Lee Roy Jordan and Chuck Howley and Bobby Hayes. Bob Bruenig and Billy Joe Dupree . . . Jethro Pugh . . . a few others . . .

we still play touch football. I loved being a Cowboy and I loved working with Coach Landry.

"He took a chance with me, because when he drafted me I still had all that time to serve in the Navy. He told me not to worry about it, to throw the ball, to stay in shape, to think about my duty first and that the Cowboys would be here, and be ready for me, when I was discharged.

"I would get leave each summer and work out with the team, and each time I left he always told me I'd be back, that he was counting on me, that I had a good chance to be the Dallas Cowboy quarterback. I think Tom Landry has had the greatest effect on my life of anyone I ever met in football. Maybe the most important thing I learned from him, the thing that will stay with me forever, is that it makes no sense to panic, to lose your poise and composure. That never helps, and on the other hand, there is always a solution, always some positive action you can take. I consider myself a lucky, lucky man to have known him and worked with him."

And maybe of all the 'Boys who ever played for Tom Landry, this one, this Perfect American, stands as his finest product.

CHAPTER 8

DOUG TODD

THE PUBLICIST

He was the state sports editor for the Associated Press bureau in Oklahoma City, Okla.

He was a sportswriter, mainly specializing in high school sports, for The Daily Oklahoman, also in Oklahoma City.

But a friend and former colleague on the newspaper, Curt Mosher, called him one day and asked whether he'd be interested in joining the Dallas Cowboys' publicity department.

"First I thought he was joking," says Doug Todd. "Then he convinced me he was serious, so I accepted the obvious initiation fee. I asked him who I was supposed to kill . . . and how soon?"

And so, in 1971, just in time for the Cowboys to appear in—and win—Super Bowl VI, Doug Todd joined the organization. He stayed until the spring of 1989, when he became part of the sweeping changes wrought by Jerry Jones, the man who bought the Cowboys, fired head coach Tom Landry, forced president Tex Schramm to resign and then began mowing down the head of every department in the corporate structure.

"They're not hungry any more," he said, "and we need hungry, driven people."

Well, of course, that was nonsense, and Todd views it the way it should be viewed—with cynical, gallows humor. "The man said I wasn't hungry? Hey, since I had to stop drinking, I was nothing but hungry."

For the purpose of this series of interviews, Doug Todd provides a unique overview. He was there for most of the dynasty. He felt the pulse of the city, the state and the nation as the players never could. He knew just how intense was the demand for, as he says, "anything that had to do with the Dallas Cowboys." He explains that players could have spent entire days completing 15-minute interviews for newspapers and radio stations all around the country, that when he showed up in the city of the next road game, to "advance" the game, he was besieged not for statistics and medical reports but photographs, telephone numbers and personal insights into "almost any one of the players."

For the 19 seasons he served the organization, the final 14 of them as head of the public relations department, Todd established himself as perhaps the best in that most demanding and seldom appreciated business. His many innovations have been turned into mandatory press box protocol by the National Football League, such as the dispensing of sheets of player and coach comments immediately after the game, for those journalists whose deadlines preclude an unhurried stroll through the postgame locker room, and whose newspapers did not have the budget to staff a road game with more than one reporter.

But overall, perhaps the most significant contribution Doug Todd made to the Dallas Cowboys and to the league—was the coining of the magic nickname:

America's Team.

"We were up in Mount Laurel, in New Jersey, editing the 1978 highlight film," Todd remembered. "This was at the peak of our popularity, I guess. We had been in five Super Bowls . . . always seemed to be in the playoffs, in the championship games . . . had all those players who became household names . . . and as we're going over the films of each game, Bob Ryan of NFL Films and myself, we kept seeing crowds in other stadiums, whole blocks of seats occupied by people waving Cowboy banners and wearing Cowboy items and cheering for the Cowboys. I mean, it was like that in Philadelphia and New York and Miami and Green Bay, of all places. And the phrase just popped up.

"We're like 'America's Team,' I said to Ryan, and it sounded perfect for the title of the highlight film. And truthfully, that's how it started."

Todd was supposed to have started with the Cowboys early in the 1971 season, when Mosher finally convinced Schramm that he was overworked and needed to hire an assistant. So an appointment was made for Todd to come down from Oklahoma City, meet with Schramm and start working in a week or two.

"My appointment was for a Tuesday morning," he said, "and Monday night the Cowboys took what had to be the worst beating in their history, losing a Monday night game in St. Louis, getting shut out (38-0), falling to a 5-4 record, three games behind the Cardinals. I mean, it was awful. So I show up anyway, and Tex just wasn't interested. He looked like he had just been dragged through a knothole, you know? He shook hands, said thanks for coming, and wandered away.

"That game was the watershed of the 1970 season. The Cowboys looked out of it . . . and then they didn't lose another game until the Super Bowl, the Cardinals managed to come apart and self-destruct and early in January Mosher calls me again. I was to start immediately, so I showed up in Miami and worked the Super Bowl. We lost to Baltimore (16-13) on a last-second field goal, but that was really the start of a glorious decade. You know, at one point NFL Properties told us that 40 percent of all merchandise ordered was for the Cowboys. Just the other day I read that it's down to 1.3 percent now. That's sad."

But when the wave crested, according to Todd, "the people involved experienced something that we all knew, even when it was happening, we'd never feel again, never go through again. It was just one of those rare moments when all the chemistry was right, when all the pieces fit together, and they just won't be able to be that right again. It was like it was written, somewhere.

"I mean, Clint (Murchison) was the perfect owner. He let the football people do their job, left them alone, didn't interfere, paid all the bills and said yes every time Schramm or Coach Landry said something had to be purchased, or some player had to be signed. He was perfect.

"When the team hadn't won anything, and the fans and the

newspapers were screaming for his job, for him to get fired, he
asked Tex what to do, should Tom be fired. Tex said no, he didn't
think that was necessary, but the constant pressure was getting
to the coach. So Clint did the only thing he felt was reasonable.
He signed Landry to a new 10-year contract, and felt that would
get everybody off Tom's back. It did, too.

"For his part, Tex kept the whip out . . . everywhere, not just
with the players. He never let anybody relax. I think his greatest
enemy, or how he perceived it, anyway, was complacency. If we
got to thinking about how great things were working, how we
were winning, how all the problems had gone away, I think he
was afraid it would be like jinxing everything. So he never let anybody ease off. It was always hustle, hustle, hustle. Don't take anything for granted.

"Tex was a great marketing man, a genius. Everything he
touched turned out right. He knew what to do, how to do it, when
to do something. Like the cheerleaders. I mean, sure, they were
nice girls, beautiful and all, but he marketed them, he packaged
the thing, the whole concept of the Dallas Cowboys Cheerleaders.
See, they never were the Cowgirls, because that would have been
tacky, commercial. They were the Dallas Cowboys Cheerleaders,
and they wore the silver and blue, just like the players, and since
we were on television so often, they were, too. They caught on.
Everybody in the country wanted to see the cheerleaders. It just
added to our image.

"And Tom was always the same. He always got through the
crises with more calm and poise than anybody I have ever known.
He was a tremendous competitor, and he had great confidence in
his ability to prepare the team. You know, it was unusual in that
when we were playing a top team, with first place or even a division championship riding on the outcome, he'd be OK all week,
loose, even kid around with us.

"But if we were playing a dog, then he'd be grouchy and mean
that whole week, and we learned to stay away from him,
because . . . see? . . . a lousy team scared him, because they'd do
something by mistake and mess everything up, all the plans. It's
like when you're not expecting a guy to do something because it

just doesn't make sense, and he does it, you don't quite know how to react. And he just loved to go to New York, because he had friends there, he had played and coached there, and it was his favorite arena. It was the center of things, and he loved to win there. I think the one thing I'll always remember about Tom Landry is that he never changed, he was always the same, you could depend on him.

"Tom never made impulsive decisions. I mean, there were guys, even on his staff, who would nag him to cut so-and-so, he isn't playing, he can't help us, he keeps making mistakes, dropping the ball, something. Usually, though, Tom wouldn't do anything, and after a while the noise would go away, and then a month later, a season later, the guy would do something spectacular and win a game, or he'd suddenly understand what the coaches had been saying and turn into a star. He had great patience, legendary patience with his players, and I know he loved them. He absolutely loved his players because he knew what they went through, how critical everything was. He had been there, and he understood.

"It just killed him to cut people, especially veterans, and I know he'd keep some guys around a year or two longer than another coach might have, but somehow it always worked out. Maybe the players knew how far out on a limb he had gone for them, and they found a way to perform, if only for one more critical moment in one more game."

In Todd's job, the most important product is a cooperative head coach, and Doug insists that Landry was "World Champ." There never was a disappointed newspaperman somewhere in the country who had asked for 10 minutes with The Coach.

But Todd also had to resort to base trickery at times, too.

"See, Tom was a creature of habit. He had a schedule and he hated to do anything else. He wasn't wild about returning calls, either, but he thought it was part of the overall routine. Why? Because I told him it was, that's why. You know, I'd have a guy who wanted to talk to him and he never had done it before, so I knew it would be a problem, that Tom wouldn't want to take time away from his day to do something that hadn't been scheduled.

"So I learned to approach him quietly, no long explanations, tell him that it was time to call the guy we always call at such and such a time during the week, or the month, or the year, and he'd just look up and say, 'Oh, OK, let's get it done.'

"I'm really blowin' it now, you know? I hope he doesn't get angry when he reads this. But the funniest thing was once summer out at Thousand Oaks, we had this promotional deal set up with the California Forestry Service. The thing was, this guy was dressed in a Smokey the Bear suit and he had a baseball hat, you know, with a big Smokey the Bear face on the front of it, and he had to get Tom to pose with him, wearing that damned hat, the guy wearin' his goofy suit, with people watching.

"Now come on, you know how silly that looked? But I promised, and it was important in community involvement, too, so I just interrupted him during the afternoon one day, before practice, and told him, 'Oh, Coach, you know that Forestry Service thing we do each year . . . three, four years now?' He looked up and said yes, he remembered. 'Well,' I said, 'they're here, it time to take those pictures again, we have to go get the pictures now because they can't come back and they can't wait.' So he just got up, smiled at the people, shook hands, put on the silly hat and posed with the guy in the goofy Smokey the Bear suit until they had enough.

"I mean, the man was my hero. He made my job so easy."

Todd indicates that things learned from just observing Landry have helped him in his daily life, and for a man who seemed to take a pure delight in laughter and partying, such seriousness was difficult to accept.

But it was no less real, and no less true.

"Tom Landry had his priorities right, he knew what was important and what was just a waste of time, and if you look at things carefully in your own life, it's not hard to make the same decisions. That's one thing I learned from him . . . where to put the worry, where to put the importance.

"Also, he taught me that you should never second-guess yourself, that once you make a decision don't worry about things you can't control. He surprised people who thought he was always so organized, so much under control, by sometimes just making an important decision by the seat of his pants, so to speak. And once he made that decision, he never once went back to worry about it. And he always tried to teach his players, and the other people around him, that you can't be something you're not, that what one man can do easily another can't do at all."

Todd arrived in Dallas after quarterback Don Meredith had retired, which was, officially, July 5, 1969. The accepted story is that Meredith was tired of the public abuse from the fans and the press, as well as the private (and sometimes public) chastising by Landry. Still, there are those who question whether Meredith really wanted the on-field pressure, because he had lived with the off-field aggravation long enough to let it run off his back.

"From what I was able to determine," said Todd, "Tom never understood Don Meredith, probably never approved of his lifestyle and, in the end, used the problems they had to act differently when faced with similar difficulties later. He learned how to deal with players who weren't the kind of people he was used to, he loosened up, sort of, and tried to be more lenient, more understanding. For instance, when Duane Thomas created all the troubles, Tom really operated on a double standard—what was good for the rest of the team, what applied to the rest of the team, didn't necessarily apply to Duane."

As Curt Mosher's assistant, and later the head of the publicity department of the Cowboys, Todd had to deal, in his way, with the obvious racial problems in Dallas.

"I can remember a few times when local business people or organizations would call and ask us to send a player to them on a personal appearance, that they'd pay, and what was the fee. But these people said to make sure it was a white player, and I used to tell them that the Dallas Cowboys didn't do business that way and that we would not choose to do business with them in the future. Ever. And I made sure to take their names, so that if they called again, a year or two later, they were told we *still* wouldn't do business with them. Those kind of people . . . they just make my skin crawl."

The local civil rights issues in Dallas, according to Todd, "never really found their way into the newspapers in the early 1970s . . . you just wouldn't read anything about it, from either side. But I do have to say that by the end of the 1970s most of the black players had moved to north Dallas, where there hadn't been a single black homeowner or family renting a house before. I mean not ever, and quietly things just got better in Dallas. Truthfully, too, we lived in an insular atmosphere. You know, we worked for the Dallas Cowboys, the players were heroes—black or white—and we just didn't hear many of the stories or see overt examples of prejudice. But I'd never deny it was there, because it was and everybody knew it. But, see, the city seems to have solved its own problems without a lot of outside interference, and I think that's good, too.

"A great many of the black players who experienced prejudice chose to live in Dallas anyway, and some of them have been here for nearly 30 years. That says something for the town, too."

Through his years with the team, Todd says he tried never to socialize with the players or get too close. "I didn't want to be a victim of cloudy vision," he explained. "It was out of self-defense, too, because players are subject to suddenly waking up as members of a different team in another part of the country, and I just didn't want to lose friends because they'd been cut or traded. I also didn't want to get angry at Tex or Tom, because they had a job to do and the last thing I wanted was to sulk for a month because a good friend got moved to Oakland or Philadelphia, you know?

"Besides, I got paid to be nice, but I didn't necessarily want to do it on my own time. When I did want to socialize, it was with people who I didn't see every day."

Working so closely with the players, day after day, year after year, often convincing them to do things they did not want to do—public appearances for no money, long telephone conversations with "foreign" newspapermen—Todd says he developed, in the last few years, a new respect for players.

"You know, I really started to empathize with them . . . with professional athletes . . . as a breed. I finally figured out what makes them tick. It's fear. I mean, look at it. They absolutely have to perform at their peak level every day, practice or game, and if they don't manage to do that absolutely all the time, they get fired. Who could accept a job like that outside sports? I know, I know, air traffic controllers, but they don't get to practice, right?

"Seriously, they can get injured and find themselves fired. Another guy can walk in off the street, do the job better and take a veteran's place. Just like that. Thanks for the time, but please have your locker cleaned out by 5:00, OK? I think players are constantly motivated by fear, because in almost every case, they are making more money as an athlete than they will ever make after their careers are over—and most of those careers are over before they're 30 years old. You know, they're not prepared for anything else, they've never learned to do anything else, and football is all they've got.

"So the guy who hears the same stupid question for the hundredth time—you know, do you prefer a left-handed or right-handed quarterback throwing you the ball?—is either going to snap something rude at the dope or come tell me that he isn't going to talk to the press any more. And you know what? I understand. It's just that my job is to make him cooperate. Or was."

The players in this book, every one of them, chose to live in Dallas when their careers were over, with the exception of Bob Lilly, and he resides two hours south of Dallas in Graham. And every one of the players became friendly with Doug Todd. So what does he remember about them, in a highly personal sense? How can he apply the brush of humanity to these legends?

Bob Lilly: "I only met him toward the end of his career, but he was still at his peak when I first showed up in 1971. I remember a game in 1972 at Texas Stadium against the Philadelphia Eagles, when I just happened to be watching him. You know, there were only two defensive linemen I ever singled out to watch during a game—Lilly and Randy White, because they were such exceptional players they could turn entire games by what they did on one or two plays.

"Anyway, I'm watching Bob, and the Eagles called a sweep to his side. He beat his initial blocker and then . . . and I swear to God this happened . . . he picked up the pulling guard, literally picked him up, and threw him at the ball carrier, who got knocked back and into the quarterback, and they all fell in a pile, all three of them, with Lilly standing over them, looking down, almost as if he was daring them to get up.

"I remember Bob always had very sensitive skin, he'd sunburn easily, so every year when we went to training camp in California he wouldn't be able to wear shorts on the practice field, he'd have to wear sweatpants. But it was very hot, too, so to get some ventilation, one year he cut these diamond-shaped holes all up and down his legs—and that night in the cafeteria he was walking around, in shorts, with these hideous-looking diamond-shaped sunburn patches all over his legs.

"Lilly was very careful with his body, so much so that he never let the trainers or the doctors tape him up before a practice or a game. He'd wrap himself, from ankle to hip, with Ace bandages, in his own special style that he insisted prevented him from getting hurt. It must have worked, because he never got hurt. But one of the doctors once told me something that seemed a lot more reasonable—that Bob had extraordinarily 'loose' knees, which is why he never got hurt there, anyway. They'd rock and roll on their own and could take a lot more stress and pressure.

"The most impressive thing I ever heard anybody say about Bob Lilly came from Coach Landry, who said, at practice one day: 'Gentlemen, you are observing a man who will become a legend.' And he did, too. Players who saw him at work, who were teammates or opponents, still talk about him in almost reverent tones.

"Bob was very nice to me right from the first, and I appreciated it immensely. It was my first big-league experience, I was just a kid from Oklahoma and he was a big help to me when the other players saw him accept me, because then they did, too. I think Bob Lilly was maybe the best player we ever had in the history of the Dallas Cowboys in terms of all-around excellence and performance."

Bob Hayes: "He was a sweet guy, a genuinely nice man who seemed like he would do anything for anybody just so they'd like him. He's the same now as when he played, too. Just a pleasure to be with. Everybody liked him, and even when he had the trouble, when he was in jail for 10 months under the most suspicious of circumstances—and nobody who ever knew him ever thought he did anything like they said he did—the state penal system board got him a weekend pass so he could take part in the team's 20th anniversary celebration and be photographed on the field at Texas Stadium as part of the 20th anniversary all-star team. I remember that weekend he smiled and shook hands with everybody and never once complained about a raw deal or a setup or anything.

"Maybe the one thing that always left an impression on me was just how damned fast he was. Even in 1971, he was clearly the fastest man in pro football. But you know something? He never would agree to be timed again, not after the Olympics. I guess being the World's Fastest Human was special to him, and he never wanted to know if his speed had slipped any. All I know is that every year in training camp, if anybody wanted to run against him, he'd agree, smile and make a game out of it, a joke, and then run away from all the challengers. He beat everybody, but he never did get timed again in his life."

Lee Roy Jordan: "I remember checking into the hotel the day before I started to work for the team, a hotel outside Miami that the team basically took over, and the first player I saw was Lee Roy. Hey, he was tough looking, a craggy-faced guy with bruises and knuckles and muscle knots all over, and he just looked like a pro football player, the prototype player. He was the leader of the team, absolutely, and he wasn't a very pleasant guy. He just wanted to win and he wouldn't put up with anything that stood in the way of that, nor did he have much time for things that didn't help him get better and make the team better.

"But I remember when I was in the hospital in 1983, in Memphis, where I almost died, the first call I got from a non–family member was from Lee Roy. It really surprised me, because we were never that close, and it was a real thrill. I have always appreciated that. Afterwards, I got calls from Roger Staubach, Tom Landry, Charlie Waters . . . a bunch of other players, lots of newspaper friends around the country . . . and I appreciated them all, but getting the call from Lee Roy just surprised the hell out of me."

Drew Pearson: "He was one of my favorites, and after he stopped playing football he became one of my closest friends. I really hold him in high regard, because of the courage he showed his rookie year in training camp. I mean, he never had a chance. He was a free agent, a skinny little kid, couldn't have weighed more than 155, 160. But he worked his ass off, did everything they asked, took a fearful pounding and somehow managed to stick.

"I know he worked the entire months of May and June with Staubach. He just moved to Dallas and worked out with Roger every day. That helped him a lot, and it impressed Roger, too.

"I guess the thing most people remember about him—me, too—was that he was so dependable in the games. If a big play was needed, you knew he'd make it. Even when the other teams knew Roger was going to have to throw the ball to him, Drew would somehow get clear and make the catch. I don't think anybody in the history of this game has made as many game-winning catches as Drew Pearson. In big games, too.

"Oh, and he always threw up in the huddles. I mean, the other players didn't want to stand next to him, you know?"

Randy White: "I remember it was a day in 1988 when we had just been beaten by the Bears in Chicago, and we were on the bus to the airport and I was sitting next to Randy. I almost always found myself sitting next to him, by the way. We just hit it off. He started talking to me about his career ending soon, and he said he was looking at that with mixed emotions. 'You know,' he said, 'I think I'm looking forward to the day when I don't have to be the meanest s.o.b. in the valley any more.' I always thought that was a pretty deep statement, because everything pictured Randy as this tough, mean guy and really he wasn't that way at all.

"Randy made the single most unbelievable play I ever saw. It was in Texas Stadium against the Eagles, and he was rushing the passer when the quarterback, I think it was Ron Jaworski, completed a pass in the medium flat, off to the side. Randy had penetrated and he was past the line of scrimmage when the pass was caught, and by a pretty fast wide receiver.

"So he turns around and starts chasing him, and caught the guy from behind about 40 yards downfield. It was just impossible. A guy that big and strong couldn't possibly have been that fast, too.

"He was also the most intimidating defensive lineman I ever saw. I mean, he'd just club people, drive them into the ground, and it didn't matter if he was playing against a rookie or an All-Pro offensive lineman."

Tony Dorsett: "He was one of my favorite guys, even though he suffered from Dorsett Disease. What was that? He'd say something and then apologize later. Everybody saw that side of him, but he did a lot that people never knew about. Charity stuff, community service, favors to fans, things like that.

"Cocky? Of course he was cocky. He was the best damned running back on the planet for almost 15 years, why shouldn't he be cocky? And he was tougher, a lot tougher, than most people knew. I remember a game in Philadelphia when a safety named Ray Ellis knocked him out, cold-conked him, right near halftime. I mean, nobody thought he'd come back. But he played in the second half and gained over a hundred yards.

"And yes, he did alienate people because of his mouth. He was a little guy, and he felt he was getting picked on all the time. He was also impulsive, and that never hurt him more than the oil-options tax shelters he invested in. He put all his money in the deal, took money out of his annuity and deferred payment structure with the team, and lost $600,000. You know, those annuities would have paid him $300,000 a year for the next 20 years, starting the day he retired? That was a real shame."

Doug Todd is now in the promotions and public relations business in Dallas, with projects reaching out to both coasts. He has recently remarried and his life is perfectly fine, thank you.

But does he miss the Cowboys? "Not the way they are currently constituted," he says. "Those years were special. I don't think they'd be able to be duplicated ever again."

CHAPTER 9

FRANK AND BLACKIE
THE CHRONICLERS

They are the two most popular, important and influential sports columnists in Dallas—William Forrest "Blackie" Sherrod of the Morning News and Frank Luska of the Times Herald.

Blackie is the one drinking vodka.

Frank is drinking scotch.

Blackie is older. Considerably. He just became 70; Frank is 55. If anybody looks exactly like a Texan should look, it's Blackie Sherrod. His square face is leathered, weathered and lined. He speaks his mind and, more crucially, he writes his mind. It has been a long time now since anyone in local or national sports has decided to criticize him in public. He hails from Belton, Texas—and don't you forget it, heah?

Frank Luksa looks exactly like a Texan should look, too, except different from Blackie, who also looks exactly like a Texan should look. Frank is long and lean, rawhide and rawbone, speaks softly, has a dry sense of humor—somewhat more dry than Blackie's, but no less pointed—and like the Quiet Man everywhere he will defer to Blackie, a man he truly idolizes. He grew up in Georgetown, Texas. Right, you've never heard of it. Why should you have?

Years ago . . . so many, too many, years ago . . . Blackie and Frank both worked in Fort Worth, Blackie for the defunct Press, Frank for the Star-Telegram. Then they both "moved up" to Dallas, taking jobs on the Times Herald, though not at the same time.

Blackie made the move in 1958. Frank came to Dallas 14 years later. The Cowboys came to Dallas in 1960. Blackie later moved— to the fanfare of great public celebration—to the Dallas Morning News in the mid-'80s, the prized plum that capped a bitter two-paper war.

It should be noted that when Blackie was the sports editor of the Fort Worth Press, he put together a staff of writers that included Dan Jenkins, Bud Shrake and Gary Cartwright. As the commercial goes, it doesn't get any better than that.

Blackie was in Miami Beach when the National Football League held its winter meetings in January of 1960, and one of the items on the agenda was the awarding of two franchises, expansion franchises. There were several cities bidding for this honor, and frankly Dallas wasn't originally thought to be in the top two. But then the American Football League placed a franchise in Dallas, and as Sherrod remembers, "Pete Rozelle took up the challenge like a gunfighter."

Pete Rozelle, then in the first of what would turn out to be a 30-season career as the commissioner of the National Football League (a time exactly spanning that of the head coaching career of Tom Landry and, in the minds of many, the life of the Cowboys' franchise as well), was ready for a showdown. He convinced the owners, who had already agreed on Minneapolis and were debating the merits of Atlanta and Miami as the other new city, to strap on the iron and ride hard into Dallas.

So Blackie Sherrod, who had been dispatched by the Times Herald for what was expected to be a two-day stay, wound up working 11 consecutive days in the Miami Beach sun before, as he says, "I came home with a team in the NFL and a suitcase full of dirty laundry. We didn't get much in the way of expenses in those days."

And now we are sitting at the bar of the elegant Stoneleigh Hotel in an older, more fashionable, more residential, "kinder and gentler" section of Dallas. Ironically, this is the hotel the New York Giants chose to occupy in 1961, when they made their first road trips to Dallas to play the Cowboys, because it was one of the few in town in those days—at a time when there were far fewer hotels at all—that would accept black players as well as white.

Now, three decades later, following extensive renovation, the Stoneleigh is one of the more tasteful older hotels in Cowtown. At the risk of being provincial, it would fit right in with any watering hole in Manhattan.

It is where Frank and Blackie choose to drink, where the two close friends, who between them have much to say about creating the opinions carried by hundreds of thousands of Texas sports fans, meet. "Not often enough," says lanky Frank, his white hair and white mustache looking somehow out of place as he drives the visitor to the meeting not in his car but in his daughter's sleek white Probe. "Six hundred bucks for a damn fuel pump or some such nonsense," he grouses. "Damn."

Blackie has been waiting for us. For hours. But he is as two-fisted a drinker as there is in these days of Diet Coke and Diet Pepsi and pink Seven-Up, of all things, and no one could possibly know that the vodka in the squat, fat pony glasses has been flowing for three hours already. "Blackie drinks to get sociable, not to get drunk," says one of his friends. "Oh, if he wanted to, he'd get drunk. But he doesn't want to."

He has had cause to celebrate that day. One of his few "really good friends" in the business, columnist Jim Murray of the Los Angeles Times, had been awarded a Pulitzer that day. "About damned time, too," he says. "How many sports columnists have gotten the Pulitzer, three?"

Right. Three. Arthur Daley of the New York Times. Red Smith of the New York Herald Tribune and later of the New York Times. Dave Anderson of the New York Times. The shame is that such as Jimmy Cannon and Grantland Rice and Damon Runyan—and Blackie Sherrod—have not been so honored. On the other hand, they did not, or do not, work for the New York Times. You may feel free to draw your own conclusions, political or otherwise. Suffice to say that Jim Murray's inclusion was an overdue breath of fresh air.

"I tried calling Murray but his telephone was busy for two

hours and then I had to come here," Blackie said. "What took you so long, anyway?"

Luksa explained that he had been driving, had to pick up the visitor at the hotel and, besides, that he had family matters to clear up first, not the least of which was to convince his daughter to part with her car. Blackie didn't want to hear any of it. So he ordered another round, looked a bit perplexed when the visitor ordered beer but smiled happily when Luksa said, "Scotch, rocks, straight." For the visitor, he simply wore a look of disdain. Beer might be acceptable with dinner, or even in the early morning as a wake-me-up, but in the evening, at a gentlemen's bar . . . well, there is just no accounting for Easterners.

He looked equally askance at the visitor's tape recorder. "Put it on or put it away," he said. "No, put it away. Decide what you want to use and the rest of it will be off the record, all right?"

You, the reader, must understand something here. Both these men, I am proud to say, are my friends. I have known them for almost 30 years, and sometimes they suffer my "back-East" ways, but they nevertheless, and mysteriously, choose to put up with me anyway. We share that tragic bond of having lost many other close friends through those years, too, like Steve Perkins and Dick Young, Red Smith and Jack Griffin, Jimmy Cannon and Wells Twombley, Jack Murphy and John Hollis. And, dammit, too many others. I am somewhat younger than they are, and just as it felt when they first were met, it is with no small amount of secret pride that I savor the fact that I am allowed to hang out with them. They are, absolutely and positively, part of the upper echelon of this sportswriting business.

I still have a frayed, blurred copy of a recipe for chili, sent to me by Blackie several years ago, after I had remarked that I had attempted, several times, to duplicate what I had tasted, and really, truly liked, on early trips to Dallas.

"Where did you find this chili?" he once asked.

I mentioned the name of a restaurant. He shuddered.

"Only guys from New York," he said. Then he asked for an address, said he would send a chili recipe, and that if I gave it to anyone else he'd have me killed. It was entitled "J. Blackstone

Sherrod's Perfect Chili," and among its instructions are, by way
of introduction, " . . . never use ground beef, only shredded, and
shred it yourself," and later, " . . . never, ever use beans, because
chili isn't made with beans," and, near the end, " . . . tie a bandana
around your forehead because this is so hot you'll sweat like a hog
and start pourin' the mix down your neck."

It is great, magnificent chili. It is also made with beer—"put
half the can in the pot and the other half in your stomach." Blackie said he got it from an old cowboy (not Cowboy) named Shang-
hai Jim. And no, you cannot have a copy. Blackie Sherrod is part
Indian—Comanche, don't you know—and he said never to give
a copy of this particular recipe to anybody, and I believe that Indi-
ans never make a promise they don't intend to keep.

So here we sat, stompin' at the Stoneleigh, surrounded by fellow
drinkers who stopped by, periodically, to say hello to Blackie and
Frank, who were known to them only by their work in the two
rival newspapers, to talk for a moment or two about the sad state
of the Cowboys; the apparent hopelessness of the baseball Rangers, who play just down the highway in Arlington; the confusing
situation involving the basketball Mavericks and their troubled
star, Roy Tarpley; the down-years at U.T. and the slow rebirth
of SMU's Mustangs after that NCAA-imposed "death penalty"
and the general mess in which Dallas sports finds itself these days.

"You really need to understand that when the Cowboys first
started playing here, nobody really cared worth a damn about
them, or about pro football at all," Blackie was saying. "I mean,
Tom Landry was more well known in New York (where he had
played and then served as an assistant coach for the Giants) than
he was here in Dallas. So he went to the University of Texas. So
what? So he made All-America, or maybe he didn't, as a football
player. So what? He never coached here. He never stayed here.
He went to the war (the one before Korea; look it up) and then
he played in New York. Big deal. Bobby Layne was the big football name down here. Kyle Rote. Doak Walker. Buddy Parker.
And we did have the other team (the AFL Texans) come in at
the same time, you know? So the Cowboys weren't really much.

Sure, we covered their games. Had to. It was our city, our area. But there just wasn't much interest."

Quickly, though, a few developments began to unfold. First of all, even though the Texans were owned by one of the world's richest men, Lamar Hunt, it just wasn't going to happen. Lamar was one of the sons of H.L. Hunt, the oil billionaire, and a few years into his son's grand experiment with professional football, a friend of H.L.'s came to chat.

"H.L.," he said, "that boy of yours is really screwin' up the football team, you know? Why, he's losin' a million dollars a year."

H.L. Hunt nodded sadly. "Why, hell," he said, just the trace of a mischievous smile playing on his lips, "that means he's goin' to be flat broke in just 350 years."

It was amusing to Luksa, and he said so, that two of the richest men in Dallas, and therefore the country, were Lamar Hunt and Clint Murchison, that Clint owned the NFL franchise—and that the two never met. "Not before the football teams either," he said. "Imagine, both of them lived in Dallas, must have been invited to the same inner circle, high-power parties and such, and the two of them never met. Not once. They were both kind of reclusive and shy, but that was ridiculous. And then, all of a sudden, they found themselves with the two pro football teams in town and neither one was doing that great. But the Cowboys had to win, because they had the other NFL teams, the ones with all the well-known players, coming into town."

Both teams played in the Cotton Bowl, which has long since reverted to being the exclusive home field of the SMU football team, and both teams tried all manner of promotions and ticket giveaways to fill the seats. One year, a visiting observer noted that the Cowboy-Giant game that day was the beneficiary of a "Father-Son" promotion during which an adult male need only buy a ticket for himself and then he would be permitted to bring with him—for free, mind you—his children. And certainly if an enterprising father brought not only his two kids but seven more from the neighborhood, so what? Better kids in the stadium than thousands of fans disguised as empty seats, right?

It took three full seasons before Hunt and the Texans moved

to Kansas City in 1963 to become the Chiefs. Even then, the locals chose to continue to mostly ignore the Cowboys. For the seven home games of the 1963 season, the average attendance was less than 23,000. By way of comparison, just two years later the Cowboys drew more fans in their first three home games than they had all during that 1963 season—when they didn't have the Texans to worry about.

"This was college football country," Blackie was saying, "and it still is, too. People didn't mind drivin' a hundred miles for a good college game on a Saturday, but they wouldn't go across town for the Cowboys on Sunday. Not until they started to win, anyway."

But for Frank and Blackie, the Cowboys quickly became a way of their lives. So, too, did the characters who were peripheral contributors to the growing, budding legend.

"One of Clint's friends," Luksa said, "was a guy named Bedford Wynne. When the franchise was awarded, it was said that the NFL gave it to Murchison and Wynne, so everybody just assumed that Bedford was a 50-percent partner. But that never was true. I think he owned less than 5 percent, and it was because he and Clint were friends."

Blackie interrupted. "You know why Bedford was around? Because he was smooth, social, he could meet people and charm them and he genuinely liked the spotlight. Clint was painfully shy and embarrassed . . . uncomfortable . . . with being in public. You might say that Bedford was Clint's alter ego, the guy he appointed to meet people for him."

Back to Luksa.

"So Bedford would make all the road trips, you see, and he'd be the guy in charge of the fun, dinner and drinks, a hospitality suite. He'd do everything that had to be done, everything he thought should be done, to make people aware of the team.

"One time we're in Chicago . . . you know, I think it was the first year . . . and Bedford decides to do something in keeping with the team we were going to play. So he rents a bear. Right, a great big old black bear, from a circus or something, and he brings the bear to the hospitality suite. Well, near early evening everybody starts showin' up, and we all took a turn at feeding the bear beer and peanuts, see, and the bear gets drunk and breaks up some of the furniture, rips wallpaper off the walls, just makes a general all-around fool out of himself.

"Now they get the bear muzzled and they decide to take him downstairs and back to his handler . . . or wait, I think the handler was there, but he got drunk . . . anyway, the bear and about three guys are in the elevator, and the bear is drunk and makin' a horrible racket, and they get to the ground floor, the elevator doors open, and there is a group of maybe 10, 12 nuns, and the first thing they see is this great big black bear standing up about seven feet tall, and the next thing is he makes this horrible screaming noise and starts out of the car, and the guys who were there said they never saw nuns run so fast."

Bedford Wynne did that.

Bedford Wynne was also responsible for the Great Pigeon Caper in Washington, too, but that was mild compared to the Beered-Up Bear Incident (which cost, Luksa thinks, roughly $5,000 once the hotel finally stopped figuring out the damage. Fortunately, the nuns never sued).

"The Cowboys were in Washington," Luksa remembered, "and the Redskins were planning this monster halftime show, with thousands of birds and pigeons to be released from these great covered containers as the finale to some musical extravaganza. So Bedford hired some kid to sneak down onto the field during the first half, open all the containers and release the birds. It worked. They left the stadium, the Redskin people were really pissed, and Bedford thought it was a great joy."

But through it all, and through all the losing, both Sherrod and Luksa admitted they felt a certain provincial love affair take root.

"Damned right," Blackie said. "I mean, it was a terrible team, but it was *our* terrible team, you see? We could make fun of them, be critical, that was OK. But let some other city's sportswriters start doin' the same thing, and that just wasn't right. Of course they were bad. We knew that. And because they got so much ridicule, we started to take it personally. You know, it just started to piss us off that people were havin' such a good time makin' fun of the Cowboys. Now, if they were the *Houston* Cowboys, or the *Oklahoma* Cowboys, that would be all right. Why would anybody in Dallas give a shit? But they were ours, and I guess like with a problem child, you can yell at him but you sure wouldn't let the neighbor do it, you know? So we started to . . . I don't know, maybe it doesn't sound right, but we started to make excuses for them when they lost. And damn, they did lose most of their games. Hey, once Lamar left to go to Kansas City with his outfit, the only pro football team we had was Clint's Cowboys, for better or for worse, so we protected them a little bit.

"Provincial? Damned right it was provincial. So what?"

Frank and Blackie were there when Don Meredith came to town, when Bob Lilly and Lee Roy Jordan showed up, when Chuck Howley and Mel Renfro and Don Perkins began to do their part to pull this team up from the garbage dumps.

"Is Meredith in this book?" Blackie asked. "Did he sit down for an interview session."

I explained that Meredith was invited to participate, but that he refused, graciously and charmingly, saying that "the time I spent with the Cowboys wasn't much fun, and my relationship with Coach Landry wasn't particularly good, and I wouldn't want to say bad things about anybody or any place but I don't want to be a hypocrite and say good things that I don't mean, so I think I'd just rather not do this, Dave."

I repeated that to Blackie. He nodded his head.

"I didn't think he'd do it," he said, "but I hope you got in what he said, why he decided not to talk about it."

I assured him I had. And I just did.

"You know, when Landry first started to coach here, and when the team did nothing but lose, there was a major cry for him to be fired," Luksa was saying. "He wasn't a legend then, he was just another coach who couldn't win games, who couldn't find the right players and who had this mysterious theory about defense that just didn't work . . . or that's what people thought. Remember, what we do as reporters (and later as columnists) is reflect what the readers want to see. If they're interested in soccer, we give 'em soccer. If it's baseball, that's where you'll find us. But the Cowboys, even then, I think, were different. They were our team and we were in the NFL. I mean all of us, the fans and the city, we were all in the NFL, and that was important.

"I remember writing stories about Tom's job bein' in danger, about how another coach might find a way to win a few games so we'd stop bein' embarrassed like we were, and instead of listening to the people . . . to us sportswriters . . . Murchison called Tex (Schramm, the team's general manager) and asked how the pulse was, and Tex said something had to be done about Landry, because the press and the public were all over him.

"So Clint said to give him a 10-year extension of his contract. That was . . . let's see, like just after the 1963 season, and now that the Landry thing was settled, everybody could sit back and wait for him to deliver. Damned if he didn't."

Blackie remembers the players on those early Cowboy teams as being "some of the best people I've ever had the chance to work with . . . guys like Lilly and Jordan, especially, and Meredith. And Eddie LeBaron. And Tom was always available for us, not that he would always say something great, not that he'd always give you a terrific story, but he was always there, head up, takin' most of the crap from people.

"I don't agree that he helped drive Meredith out of the game. I don't agree that Meredith would have played another five, six, seven years if Tom wasn't the coach, or if he was with another team in another part of the country. I just don't believe that. Meredith didn't get lousy treatment from the media, or from Tom. Remember, this was pro football. Not college. People were allowed to be publicly critical of the team and the players. I just think Meredith didn't like it, didn't like the criticism. And people say he wasn't the kind who would do all the work, all the studying, that Landry's system required. But what the hell? We never drove him out of football. He made that decision all by himself."

Both men, when drawn deeper into the subject of the early years of the Dallas Cowboys, grew more animated. This was more than mere memory, more than casual, random remembrances. This was the birth of America's Team, the dynasty that gave Dallas a mystique, a glory and an allure that surely nothing else in sports ever had . . . or ever will.

In another sense, no less real and valid, and even though both will deny it, those early years, coupled with the painful birthing into magnificence, may well have composed the best years of their professional lives. It was great and good fun to be assigned to the Dallas Cowboys in those times, those years. It was a joy to see the excitement build and turn, in turn, into genuine electricity. The glamor was taken in, as if by osmosis, by those who were part of it, those who described the theatrics to the anxious, feverish fans back home . . . those who went with the jangling-spurs warriors into the badlands of Chicago and New York, Philadelphia and Washington, and came out bloody and bruised and battered, but victorious.

Even the mythical defeats, the pair of league championship losses to Green Bay, followed by the pair of conference championship disappointments to Cleveland . . . even those bitter disappointments bound and tied the chroniclers to the team, the sportswriters to the athletes. It was not something planned, nor was it capable of being duplicated. It happened. It was a chemistry, it was a series of freakish happenings, it wasn't there to be turned on like a faucet, to be plugged in like an electrical wire.

It lasted for nearly 20 years, two decades, and in that time Frank and Blackie and all the rest of us went from young to old, from a time when it was all new and shiny to now, when much of it has become tiresome.

But those old Dallas Cowboy days? Aah, the stuff to make an evening's drinking worthwhile.

"After a while," Luksa said, "it got to be that we'd expect them to win every game. I mean it, every game. You know, in the six seasons between 1968 and 1973, the Cowboys had a record of 64-19-1, they lost their first Super Bowl, then won their first Super bowl, they played in 11 playoff games. And through it all such a parade of characters, players, personalities that made it all exciting. It was a great time, it really was that.

"And almost every one of them, of the stars, was just a nice kid, a nice kid who happened to have God-given athletic abilities and then we'd see the kids turned into men, mature and grow, and they stayed nice. Real people. I don't think there were more than a handful who were difficult, who I wouldn't want to be friends with, and I don't know that I can say as much about all the non–football players I've met in my life.

"Take Bob Hayes. There just wasn't anybody nicer than Bobby. Yep, he went to jail, and it sounded like some trumped-up charge involving drugs. But I know . . . I swear, I know to this day and I'll bet on it . . . that he wouldn't have even gotten close to that kind of trouble if he wasn't so damned anxious for people to like him. I mean, he would do anything, I mean anything, to get somebody to like him. Maybe it had something to do with his childhood, which was just a terrible experience. I don't know for sure. But he was the nicest, sweetest guy I ever met, and he would, literally, do anything he could for you. For anybody."

Both Sherrod and Luksa were there, of course, when the city caught fire, when the people forced the Cowboys into national prominence by the intensity of their loyalty.

Dallas, of course, has not been up there on anybody's list of best places to be. President John Fitzgerald Kennedy died in Dallas, victim of a crazed, mentally disturbed Dallas citizen's hatred. And rifle. (Personally, your correspondent doesn't believe a word of the theory of conspiracy. Lee Harvey Oswald did what he did because he was a sick, unbalanced piece of flotsam, a barnacle on the scrotum of society, and if there was a fault to pin on the city of Dallas, it may be that nobody realized what he was and took steps to remedy his problems.)

Dallas never had a great record in terms of racial justice and equal rights, either. The problems experienced by the black players of the 1960s and early 1970s have been well documented in their interview chapters elsewhere in this book. Even in sports, the infrequent success of the earlier SMU teams hardly seemed enough to make up for all the mediocrity and relative obscurity of the rest of its sporting endeavors.

But then came the Cowboys, sparkling and shining and silver-and-blue, with the peachcake cheerleaders and the dour old coach and the impossibly heroic players. Few teams at the peak of their greatness ever elicited such pure hero worship as the Dallas Cowboys did when they lost those dramatic, heartbreaking games. It was the new kids on the block, if the phrase still means what it did, against the establishment; it was glamor and glitz against boring, old establishment grays and browns.

It was Meredith and Morton, Staubach and Lilly, Lee Roy and Dorsett, Jethro and Rayfield and Renfro and Cornell. And Landry. Always, looming above the rest, was Landry.

And there was the most famous failure, Tom Landry's failure. Duane Thomas.

"Look, let's clear up something quick about Duane Thomas," Blackie snapped, suddenly annoyed, his deep brown eyes beginning to flash and sparkle just enough to warn his listeners to . . . well, to listen. "People say that Landry tried to 'save' Duane, tried to bring him back out of the drug problems, the emotional problems. They say Tom tried to affect the rest of Duane's life, not just his football career. I say that is nonsense.

"He kept Duane . . . because Duane was a marvelous running back, without whom the Dallas Cowboys would never have gotten to those first two Super Bowls. If Duane had been a third-string back, or a third-string defensive tackle, there is just no way he would have stayed, no way Tom would have put up with all that distraction. Sure, he said he did it because he wanted to help the kid, and he said he decided to do it because he had a veteran team that could put up with it and not be affected, and maybe that part was true. You know, the players didn't much care what Duane went through, what he did or said . . . or didn't say, since he spent most of 1971 not talking to anybody . . . but they all knew why Tom was holding on to him. So that he could get them into a Super Bowl, and he did that, twice, two times in his two years. And then he was gone because he had done what they wanted him to do and the trouble he created had just gotten too heavy.

"Listen, Tom Landry is a great man and he had a sensational record and I know he's going into the Hall of Fame this summer (1990), and that's how it should be. But he was a coach, just a coach, and when he saw a back with Duane's talent, he was going to do everything possible to make it pay off."

Luksa, too, had a reflection on troubled Duane.

"When they were holding that draft (in the spring of 1970), Tom had just come off the second straight loss to Cleveland for the conference championship, a real ass-kicking it was, too (38-14), and he knew what he needed. The Cowboys had to have a great running back, a game-breaker. The kind of player who takes the handoff on third-and-six and goes 50, 60 yards.

"Well, Duane was that kind of back, but he was troubled. He had a 'record' at West Texas State, a history of attitude problems, but he was such a great running back. I mean, he was a big man (6-1, 220) and he ran with a fluidity and a grace that made him look like a little scatback. But when you tried to tackle him he could break out of your grasp with a pent-up fury. I mean, he was just ferocious, and he was a Dallas kid and he had watched the team practice when he was in high school and I guess Tom figured that if any team had a chance with him, if any team could get out of him everything he had to give, it was the Cowboys.

"Anyway, the Cowboys were drafting in the 23rd position in that first round, and when it started Tom looked over at Red Hickey, who had scouted Duane, and said, 'Hey, Red, what about this kid Thomas?' And Hickey told him, oh, something like, 'Tom, he can play the game, but he's going to be some trouble.'

"Well, the round moved along and Duane is still there and now it's about halfway down to the Cowboys and again Tom looks over at Hickey. 'Hey, Red, tell me about this Thomas boy again.' And again, Hickey says, you know, 'Tom, he's big and he's fast and he is going to be a player, but I don't know about his attitude.' OK, now the teams keep picking and finally it's the Cowboys' turn and Duane is still there.

"Landry looks up. 'Red, now listen, what's all this about the Thomas kid? Come on, tell me now.' And Red finally gets fed up and says: 'Tom, dammit, he's better than any running back on your team and he is going to be a star but he's trouble. But take him, because we need a running back and he's the best damned one in the draft.'

"So Landry just nodded, turned to Gil Brandt, who ran the

draft, and said: 'Thomas. Take the Thomas kid.' They did, and for a while he was the steal of the draft."

Both men, in turn, were asked their opinion of the greatest single Cowboy in the history of the franchise.

Blackie responded first. "You mean in terms of what he produced or how he treated the newspaper guys? I mean, how he treated us is what really counts, right?"

Based on that premise, Blackie immediately picked not one but three former players—"Bob Lilly, Lee Roy Jordan and Benny Barnes."

Lilly and Jordan were well documented. Superstars, heroes of the past and future. But Benny Barnes? A cornerback from Stanford who played for the Cowboys for 11 years, from 1972 through 1982? He never made the Pro Bowl. He didn't always start. His only entry into the team's record book is for the 72-yard fumble recovery returned for a touchdown against San Francisco in 1981.

So why Benny Barnes?

"Because he always answered questions, always smiled when you spoke to him and always said he read my column," Blackie said. "Hey, what's important, anyway?"

Luksa picked Roger Staubach, on the more widespread conclusion that he was the single most dramatic, heroic and productive player in team history—as well as being cooperative and friendly, at least most of the time. And, he hastened to add, "Meredith was the most fascinating character of them all."

Both men think Landry was a great coach with flaws, a man with warts for those close enough to look for them.

"You know, I think he learned a great lesson with Don Meredith," Blackie said. "I think what happened with Meredith taught Tom that he just couldn't bad-mouth a player in public, especially a quarterback. See, Meredith was a great athlete, a great quarterback, but he was a fun guy. And Tom didn't believe there was room for fun in football, not pro football. I know, I know . . . when he coached as an assistant with the Giants, some of the players said they remember him being a lot easier to deal with, a guy who would go out and have a beer with the guys. Hey, if that's true, if he really did just go out to slop up some beer with the other players, I want to know the date—because it's probably the only time it ever happened.

"Tom Landry was one of a kind, all right. But he was just a coach, too. A great coach? Absolutely. But just a coach, a guy who made mistakes, who did the wrong thing sometimes . . . but probably a lot less than I have . . . and a man I was proud to know."

The Cowboys, once they became the team that always made the playoffs, the team that was always on the verge of winning the Super Bowl, began to be perceived around the country as something special, unlike the way any other team had ever been viewed before. Frank Luksa and Blackie Sherrod, because they traveled wherever the Cowboys did, saw it all, chronicled it, and now have recollections of how the myth achieved stature.

"See, Dallas wasn't quite a major city back in 1960," Luksa said. "It was just what people called it, a cowtown that started to grow. And because it was kind of centrally located, some large corporations decided to set up headquarters, home offices, like that. But the thing is, this was Texas. You know, every Texan is proud of his state, proud of his heritage, everything is bigger, better. There was oil money here, cattle money. It was the Old West, except it was today, modern. They just expected any team from Dallas to be better, and when the Cowboys first started and weren't better, the people didn't know how to handle it. So they resorted to ridicule, but it hurt, you know, even when they did it, and just as soon as the team started to win, why, then out came all that Texas pride, which was just sitting there, waiting, hoping, getting ready to come out and brag.

"Remember the motto of the true Texan: 'It ain't braggin' if you can do it.' "

Luksa and Sherrod, as with all the rest of the Dallas and Fort Worth reporters and columnists who became part of the greater Cowboy retinue, felt the legend grow. "I remember being somewhere, maybe Philadelphia," Luksa said, "and I seem to remember it was the night before an important game. I was just sitting in the hotel lobby and Staubach came in from somewhere, and almost instantly a crowd collected around him. So he was signing autographs, smiling, posing for pictures, when some guy with a big voice said: 'Hey, Staubach, no way you win tomorrow.' Roger turned, real quiet, looked the guy down and said: 'I'm sorry, sir, but you're wrong.'

"I mean, Roger Staubach never said anything like that, to anybody. He always made sure to praise the other team, to downplay himself. And he wasn't being critical of the Eagles that time, either. It was just that he believed so strongly in the Cowboys, in their ability to win, that the thought of losing a major game to them, whether it was in Texas Stadium or up there in Philadelphia, just never occurred to him as being possible."

So the guys with the cowboy boots wandered around the country, winning most of their games, making converts wherever they roamed, breaking hearts and records and setting the league on fire. There were better teams, in some of those years. The Pittsburgh Steelers, the Miami Dolphins, sometimes the Minnesota Vikings, occasionally a one- or two-season wonder.

But the Cowboys remained static. They were always in the playoffs. They almost never self-destructed. When you won, when you beat them, it was a day to remember, a game to cherish. When you lost . . . well, it was Dallas, you know, and next week you'd get to play a team you could beat. So forget it. Shrug it off.

"We were provincial, and we knew it," said Blackie, "but we were honest, too. We argued with Tex Schramm and we argued with Tom Landry and we said things about the players that they didn't like. But it was never vicious, never spiteful or mean. Later, maybe, some of the younger writers showed up, and they thought it was fashionable to knock everything. Tex used to get damned near apoplectic at some of the stories. But the older guys, 'the regulars,' knew what it was all about and what it took and we didn't go around looking to make either enemies or fools of ourselves."

Luksa referred to a young reporter's story that he blames for directly contributing to ending the career of quarterback Danny White.

"It was my paper, and we had this young guy from out of state who just made something out of nothing," he remembered. "He asked a bunch of the players whether they thought Danny White or Gary Hogeboom had been more effective, something like that, and so they answered him. But in the paper, when he printed the results of his 'survey,' the question he used, the one he said he had asked, was: 'Which quarterback would you like to see start for the Cowboys?' and that was a lot different from what he had asked the players.

"A lot of them got really angry, but it was done. It was over. And if it was unethical, whatever you want to call it, the damage was done. And you know, he painted us all with the same brush. It was very damaging to the relationship between the players and the press."

Blackie simply snorted. He neither understands the unethical journalist nor intends to waste his time talking about one. "Hey, bartender, if I tip my glass I can see bottom. Where you been?"

Both men blame Bum Bright, the man who sold the Cowboys to Jerry Jones, for the ungainly, humiliating firing of Landry. "Hey, he was working with the guy for a month," Luksa said. "At any time during that period he could have gotten in touch with Landry, told him what was happening. But he didn't. And he obscured facts, made up stories . . . did the whole thing kind of embarrassingly badly. It was his fault, but in the end, you know, he did Landry a favor. He let him leave as a martyr, remembered only for the successes, the Super Bowls and the championships and the two decades of playoffs.

"In point of fact, why wouldn't he have been remembered as a coach who lost his job because his last season was 3-13, because the season before was 7-8, because the season before that was 7-9, you know? But the way it was done, the way it came down, made the old guy an object of sympathy. He was workin' at his desk, left after dark, had papers under his arm because he was getting ready for a minicamp . . . and a reporter chases after him, tells him he has just been fired. I mean, that's terrible, right?

"It was time for him to retire, I think. The people were getting restless anyway, the team had been losing, things just weren't magic any more. And then Bum Bright creates the situation for Jones to fire him, and everything breaks loose."

Blackie, one more time: "It was lousy, but people get fired in sports every day. Everybody gets fired. Whether you stay in a job for a long time or a short time, if you're in sports you get fired. What do you think it is when a player is put on waivers? He's fired. When a player is told that the coach thinks it's time for him to retire, what do you think that is? Just idle conversation? He's being fired.

"A lot of the players who were the stars on the Cowboy teams that built the legend have stayed in Dallas, you know. They liked it here, they became part of the city, they found people who would help them set up businesses, get them good jobs. It's a nice feeling to know that the town turned into a city and that the kids on the team turned into men and that all of us passed a few years together and had some fun and made some memories."

And for the most part, the players who stayed in Dallas have done well, especially those who set up their own businesses. Like Roger Staubach. Drew Pearson. Bob Lilly.

Lee Roy Jordan?

"Hey, if Lee Roy is doing so well, how come he wanted to be athletic director at Alabama?" Blackie asked.

Some things never change. And some never should.

CHAPTER 10

TOM LANDRY

THE COACH

The house is hidden from the street, nestled among a carefully designed complex of private roads and exclusive homes. The mini-estates are probably maxi-expensive, but maybe not as high in Dallas as they might be if transplanted to Bel Air or Atherton, Short Hills or Scarsdale.

It's raining, and that made the long drive from Bob Lilly's home in Graham, Texas, more difficult, turning the network of unfamiliar connecting highways and feeder roads slick and treacherous. Besides, who ever heard of a highway called North West Highway? Do young men and women near Dallas tell their folks they're goin' out to cruise up and down old N.W.?

Anyway, this is where Tom Landry lives, off old N.W., which is also called Loop 12 . . . don't ask . . . which requires moving from old N.W. or Loop 12 to Inwood Road, thence to Rock Cliff Place, "and remember to park on the curve and walk in, because you can't see the house from the street."

One also has trouble seeing the house in the dark, and in the rain. It's perfect. If Tom Landry had been in this house, hard by old N.W. and Loop 12, Jerry Jones would never have found him, he'd still be coaching the Dallas Cowboys and there is no reason to believe they would have come even close to a record of 1-15 in the 1989 season under the man Jones named to replace him, Jimmy Johnson.

For the longest time, it seemed as though T.L. had misdirected the visitor from the East. "Just get on Loop 12," he said, "and keep going until you see Inwood Road on the right." Clearly, that is easier to say than to do, because Loop 12, or North West Highway, is really a wide street clustered with businesses of every description, including something called Cowboy Chicken—a fast-food enterprise, not a commentary on the 1989 team.

And it's raining, remember? And it's been a long day, what with seeing Lee Roy Jordan in the morning, Bob Lilly in the afternoon and then fighting the rain and the dark and the highways and the concept of Graham, Texas, in order to arrive at this juncture shortly after 6:00 in the evening, Central Standard Time.

And as the fast-food businesses and the dry cleaners and the hardware stores and the feed-and-grain buildings and the gasoline stations began to blur and waver, the visitor gave up on ever finding Inwood Road. Finally, desperate, he pulled into an Exxon oasis, asked the man in charge how to get to Inwood Road and drew a blank Texas stare.

Then . . . a light! "Oh, Inwood. Right. Well, sir, you need to get onto Highway 35 just up yonder after that overpass and take it six exits and make a right off the highway. That's Inwood."

That's Inwood? Tom Landry said nothing about another highway, or about six exits off anything, and you're late now and if you believe this fellow you are going to be a lot later if he's wrong and the coach sounded like he had plans for the evening and . . . well, it's a choice. Believe the man or stop at the Cowboy Chicken and make a telephone call to reschedule. Imagine, keeping Tom Landry waiting.

Then, unexpectedly, salvation. A storefront sign, barely discernable in the gloomy dark, proclaims "Inwood Florist." Now, if the Inwood Florist shop is right here, here on old N.W. . . . er, Loop 12 . . . can Inwood Road be far behind? Or ahead? Go for it, keep driving. In a matter of minutes . . . maybe two or three miles . . . the road becomes a highway again and the clot of businesses disappears and suddenly, on the right, just the way Tom Landry said it would be, is Inwood Road. And the first left is, in fact, Rock Cliff Place. And the house is, just as billed, invisible